Jonestown: "Don't Drink the Kool-Aid"

(The complete story behind Jim Jones & his mysterious exodus to Guyana)

By

Will Savive

Del-Grande Publishing Inc.
New Jersey   Hackensack

Jonestown: "Don't Drink the Kool-Aid"

(The complete story behind **Jim Jones & his mysterious exodus to Guyana**)

Copyright © 2007-2014 by Will Savive

Cover photo courtesy of the *"California Historical Society"*

Del-Grande books may be ordered through most booksellers

www.delgrandepublishing.webs.com

ISBN-13: 978-0615865942
ISBN-10: 0615865941
BISAC: True Crime / Murder / General

Printed in the United States of America
Del-Grande - date: 3/25/14

TABLE OF CONTENTS

Visit Will Savive's blog for continued coverage
of this & other stories:
www.willsavive.blogspot.com

You can also visit the author's website at:
www.willsavive.webs.com

Will Savive can be reached at:
willsavive@live.com

Other books by Will Savive include:

Mentally Ill In Amityville (2ⁿᵈ Edition)
&
The Study Abroad Murder

*If you purchase or have previously purchased a *print-book* by Will
Savive from Amazon you can now get the *Kindle version* for FREE

CHAPTER 1 – KEEPING UP WITH THE JONESES

There is no doubt times were tough in the 1930s in America. The decade was rudely ushered in by the October 29, 1929, stock market crash known as *Black Tuesday*. On that day the *New York Times* index of industrial stocks dropped nearly 40 points; the worst drop in Wall Street history up to that point. The affects were devastating to urban as well as rural America, and it would later come to be known as *The Great Depression*. Many farmers in the mid-west region had a surplus of wheat that held up pretty well through 1931. But the moisture was quickly moving out of that area. The economy stabilized briefly during the early months of 1930. However, it was short lived. Money soon became scarce, the banks failed, and the United States economy subsequently went on a steady decline, reaching a low point by 1933. Heavily industrial-dependant cities were demoralized and farming areas suffered 40 to 60 percent price drops. Many farmers were forced to forfeit their lands to banks and mortgage companies.

In 1931, the sky rocketing global temperatures led to considerably reduced rainfall; and the United States found itself in the midst of a drought. The friable soil composition and the arid conditions in the agricultural heartland led to winds blowing tons and tons of dry dust to the south, as if being sucked away by a vacuum. Visibility was threatened. The air became thick and dry, and the grit from the dry, dusty dirt could be felt in the mouths of the residents of the affected areas. This dust also had a high content of silica, which irritated the lungs and caused many to suffer from dust pneumonia—children were especially susceptible.

By 1934, more than 65 percent of the United States suffered from the drought. The hardest hit area was approximately 97-million acres, located in the mid-west, covering parts of Colorado, Kansas,

New Mexico, Oklahoma, and Texas. This area was unaffectionately known as *The Dust Bowl*. Many were forced to pack up and abandon the area. Those who could withstand the horrendous conditions initially had not seen the worst yet. With the combination of all the events and elements in the dust bowl over a four year period, a horrifying new phenomenon emerged—called *Black Blizzards*— which caused an increasing threat to the inhabitants of the area.

The true devastating effects of the extreme heat, dust, and wind erosion were clearly realized between the years of 1934-1937 within the dust bowl. Huge clouds of thick-black dust standing almost a mile high formed. These odious clouds resembled extreme oil fires, and they stormed the area of the Great Plains in mass. Raging Black-Dusters moved upwards and outwards over the terrain at the average rate of 75 miles-per-hour. They were so powerful that they actually carried large rocks and other debris with them as they rumbled over the landscape. So thick were they that the headlights on cars could not penetrate them. On April 14, 1935 (a.k.a. *Black Sunday*) more than 20 dust-blizzards swept through the Great Plains, from Amarillo, Texas to South Dakota. People froze in awe and shock at the site of this phenomenon, before desperately fleeing for their lives.

When all was said and done, many from the Texas-Oklahoma Panhandle region had become refugees in search of a new homeland. Fifteen-percent of Oklahoma packed up and moved west. Most of them moved to California. Estimates between three-hundred-thousand to one-million *"Okies"* packed up and moved west. By the spring of 1941 the rains came back and the lands slowly stabilized. As a result, the U.S. economy also began recovering.

The Depression touched many lives and caused a ripple-effect throughout the world. Amongst the sea of endless faces that were negatively impacted by the drought and Great Depression were Lynetta and James Thurman Jones, who were expecting a baby boy in the spring of 1931. The Jones' were one of many couples deeply affected by the ill-fated 1930s. For Lynetta [28] and James [44], things were at their bleakest just when they were at a time of joyful expectance.

Lynetta, however, was a fighter. If anyone could make it, it would be her. This skinny—almost sickly looking—woman was determined to bull her way through these sparse times. Born Lynetta

Putnam, she was a very headstrong woman who had early aspirations of perusing a business career. Lynetta attended two different colleges, but dropped out after only two years at each. This independent female at no point considered marriage or children until her mother died of Typhoid fever in 1925. The death of her mother raised her dormant motherly instincts and she decided that she would take a shot at having a family of her own. So resolute was she that even before she had a male suitor she had decided that she would bear one child—a boy—who she'd raise in the image of Lewis Parker: her humanitarian father's foster father, who had raised her after her biological father had passed away. Lynetta admired Parker so much that she aspired to follow in his image, but she was stifled by a world that didn't take women seriously as thinkers or leaders. However, Lynetta was forced to wear the pants in the family and bring home the bacon.

James Thurman Jones was born to a family of Quakers who also happened to be natives of Indiana. James was a road-construction foreman until he flew off to France to fight in World War I. There, James suffered scarred lungs from the most lethal of all the poisonous chemicals used during the war: *mustard gas*. James suffered the devastating effects of the chemical and was never the same. Upon his return home, he was in very poor health and nearly crippled. With a less than adequate education and in bad health, he met a stubborn, fiery Lynetta and the two married in the late 1920s.

This was a huge compromise for Lynetta and she knew that she would have to set her dreams aside and be the breadwinner of the family. Lynetta never fooled herself; she knew what she was getting into. She knew that this marriage could never be greater than her abilities. Her stubborn personality had her believe that nothing was impossible, and all her ambition was channeled towards the hopes and dreams that she had for her son to be. Considering the time period and her gender, Lynetta's hope was remarkable. The Jones' were certainly an anomaly in the fact that the female was the main source of income. However, Lynetta knew it was the only way. Despite his poor health, James still managed to work menial jobs in construction and on the railroads. Lynetta and James also found work on a small farm after the depression forced them to sell their farm, and the couple found a small home in Crete, Indiana.

Little Jimmy

On May 13, 1931, the couple rushed to a Crete hospital where Lynetta gave birth to a healthy baby boy that they named James Warren Jones. Jimmy, as they referred to him, was a dark skinned boy with an olive complexion and brown, slanted eyes. The boy of Welsh-European persuasion had a big round face, straight jet-black hair, and looked as if he was an amalgamation of an Eskimo and an Indian. When Jimmy was just three-years-old the family's finances were in dire-straights. Their financial situation became so bad, in fact, that in 1934, they packed-up and moved to a gray, two-story home several miles west—to *Lynn, Indiana*. Times were made even tougher because of prohibition, and the poor could not even rely on a drink to temporarily escape their troubles. The intrinsic law of *supply and demand* did, however, force many to drive some eighty-miles over the Ohio line to commandeer some booze. Dancing was even seen as immoral in rural "footloose" Indiana at the time. Many had the "end of days" mentality, and it was a rough time to bring a child into the world.

By Lynn's rigid social standards, the Jones' were seen as odd. They did not attend church, and Lynetta assumed the male role in the relationship. Their relationship was categorized as passionless; the two did not even share a bed. During the day Lynetta went to work and James senior was left home to tend to little Jimmy. The cantankerous James senior was not very attentive to his young son, and Jimmy was often seen by neighbors running around on his own, unattended to. Though not the conventional family, Lynetta loved her son very much and was determined to make him a success. She did not want Jimmy to be a slave to the rich; she wanted him to be a leader. She worked very hard to provide for the family and saved a penny here and there for young Jimmy's college fund. The Jones' made their marriage work for their son's sake.

As time went on James became even more of a recluse. If he wasn't plopped on a chair in front of his radio listening to a Cincinnati Red's baseball game; he was down at the local pool hall or making a trip to the Veterans Administration Hospital for personal care. While Lynetta was off working and James was absent, a neighbor of the family's, Mrs. Myrtle Kennedy, became his surrogate mother and spiritual advisor. One day Jimmy was playing too close to the railroad tracks and was nearly run over by a train that steam-rolled past him, missing him by only inches. Mrs. Kennedy witnessed the incident and decided to take Jimmy under her wing. She began taking care of him during the day until Lynetta returned home from work. Mrs. Kennedy's home on Grant Street became Jimmy's second home.

When Jimmy was old enough to comprehend "the word," Mrs. Kennedy would spend hours teaching him about God. On Sundays Jimmy would attend the *Nazarene Church* with Mr. and Mrs. Kennedy and Myrtle made sure that he attended Sunday school and revival meetings. Lynetta was happy to have Myrtle looking after Jimmy and the two were friends in passing, mostly due to their mutual relationship with Jimmy. Myrtle, however, did not approve of Lynetta's non-church-going lifestyle, and Lynetta would sometimes curse in Myrtle's presence just to get a rise out of her.

At four-years-old Jimmy met a boy of the same age by the name of Donald Freedman. The Freedman's lived across the street from the Jones' and the boys soon became best friends. When they were old enough, the two would walk to school together. By the time Jimmy was in fourth grade he was already at an eighth grade reading level. He was an exceptionally smart child who was fascinated by books. Needless to say, he was a very good student. Jimmy spent most of his spare time at the school library, where he lugged home several books at once. Unlike his earlier child hood days, when Jimmy became socially conscious he kept himself very well groomed.

The first sign that Jimmy was different from other boys came when he refused to take part in physical activities with his classmates. The children found it odd that Jimmy would stand and watch as they played baseball or basketball. Some boys would pick on him, but Jimmy's loud and witty mouth stumped most of the bullies, making their jobs unsatisfying. Sensing that his father was not going to be an effective guide, Jimmy began morphing into a self-sufficient thinker, developing into his own ideals, many of which purposely counteracted the "norms" of society. As his home life grew more unsatisfying, his rebellious nature grew, mostly in isolated instances at first. Seeking approval from others became the primary focus for Jimmy. He began to develop the skills to be a different person with different people by mirroring them in order to fit-in and gain acceptance. In other words he took on a uniquely different personality approach with each person or group he encountered. At the ripe old age of ten, young Jimmy Jones became enamored with religion. Jimmy was way ahead of his time right from the beginning. He began to experiment with every church in the surrounding area before deciding on one that suited him. It was an effort to try and seek out a place that would truly accept him. He was captivated by religion, but his search for the right one was fueled by his need to be accepted. He felt as though he was an outcast in all social, and even religious, circles.

Jimmy and his father never had a good relationship. He saw his father as a very bitter, cynical person. The lack of proper nurturing and the lack of a traditional family—in an area where not having a stable family base was uncommon and looked down upon—made Jimmy more rebellious. That coupled with his already intrinsically rebellious nature made him act out against the conformities of the community. Jimmy never felt accepted anywhere, even in the churches that he had attended; but all that was about to change.

The Young Preacher Child

One day Jimmy and his buddy Don traveled to the west end of town, down Highway 36, to the *Gospel Tabernacle Church*. Many of the local townspeople looked upon this religion with contempt. Moreover, the established churches looked-down-on these Pentecostal churches as "holy rollers." Many saw this *Pentecostal church* as a radical, delusional form of religion that was known as cultish before the word cult was ever coined. Though located on the edge of Indiana many of the church members were hillbillies from Kentucky & Tennessee. The scene was intimidating and overly theatrical, especially in the eyes of two young boys. As they stood outside they heard a commotion coming from inside that sounded more like people in pain rather than people celebrating. The boys looked through the window and were exposed to a whole new world. Inside the walls of this intense Pentecostal experience, the atmosphere was electric. People publicly testified and danced around to music as if possessed by a magical spirit. Heads were thumbed with anointing oil, and people were so overcome by the spirit that they collapsed and were caught by other members. The place was alive and everyone felt it!

Jimmy noticed immediately that this extreme Pentecostal church was filled with the outcasts and the rejects of the community. Jimmy was accepted by them right away. They were delighted to have a new enthusiastic walk-in, especially one as young and vulnerable as Jimmy. The love that Jimmy was shown in this church seemed purely genuine to him, according to his own interpretation:

> "I joined a Pentecostal Church, the most *extreme* Pentecostal Church, the oneness, because they were the most despised. They were the rejects of the community. I uh, found immediate acceptance, and I must say, in all honesty, about as much love as I could interpret love" (Q134 – Jim Jones).

At his young age, Jimmy's persona and self-image as an outcast had already been deeply ingrained into his psyche and mental imagery. It wasn't as much about the beliefs of Pentecostalism as it was about finding a genuine acceptance for himself. After a few visits the fanatical female minister took a particular liking to Jimmy and began preparing the young child-prodigy for greatness. This minister recognized the child's verbal maturity and sensed his mental superiority. She believed that he was destined for a higher purpose. When Mrs. Kennedy heard about Jimmy's new found interest in the "holy rollers" she was aghast. She prayed that the members would not corrupt him. Lynetta was mostly indifferent about it until she heard that this female minister placed Jimmy in the pulpit and had him address the congregation. Lynetta believed that her son was being taken advantage of and used by the church, and this enraged her.

Jimmy began spending more and more time with the female minister. She even invited him to her farm in the country, where they discussed religion. When Jimmy began having nightmares of a horrifying serpent and experiencing spells of insomnia, Lynetta took action. During a visit to the Jones' home Lynetta had it out with the female minister. Lynetta blamed the minister for her son's nightmares, and accused her of exploiting her son. Lynetta threw the woman out in a fury and forbid Jimmy from returning to the church.

This pattern of nightmares and insomnia would shape Jimmy's mind throughout the course of his life and would later lead him to vicious paranoid delusions.

Jimmy's first experience in the pulpit was life changing. There he had an epiphany. The attention that he commanded and the rush that he received was life altering, indeed, and one he would seek out and hold onto for the rest of his life. In his mind he had finally found the one thing that could fill the void inside. This gift that he would soon nurture made him feel like he was finally worth something.

> "But after some time, intellectually, I outgrew Pentecostalism; but still a rebel; still not a part of the society; never accepted; born as it were on the wrong side of the tracks" (Q134 – Jim Jones).

Jimmy began inviting children back to his home where he had a small barn in the back. He would light candles and preach the word to the children of the town. The young prodigy learned quickly how to keep people's attention, all while molding his verbal skills at the same time. Lynetta found it amusing and believed that it was harmless. "Better a leader than a servant," she thought. She had seen the exploitation of the poor in her lifetime and had been a victim of it herself. She was determined not to have her son be on the receiving end of such exploitation. Jimmy began attracting more and more children. He sometimes preached to upwards of twelve kids, all boys. He would sometimes speak for more than two hours at a time. At twelve-years-old Jimmy was a better public speaker than most adults. The boy was well read for his age—not only about the Bible, but about many of the social issues of the day. What's more is he possessed an inherent charisma and his presence—both verbally and non-verbally—made him an irresistible public speaker.

The Burgeoning of a Madman

Jimmy's behavior became more bizarre and erratic as he neared his teens. He had alienated himself from many of the people in town as well as his friends. In the small town of Lynn everyone knew everyone else's business, and they looked upon him with contempt for practicing a dissident religion. Not participating in physical activities with the other boys didn't help either. Random acts of aggression followed that were sure warning signs that he needed help that never came.

At twelve-years-old, James senior gave Jimmy a gift: a BB gun. Jimmy rarely touched the rifle; but one day he and Don were playing around on his porch. Out of nowhere Jimmy took aim at Don and shot him point blank in the stomach, lodging the BB (bullet) into Don's skin. Another incident took place when Don persuaded Jimmy to go rabbit hunting with him. Don gave Jimmy a .22 caliber rifle and Don carried a .410 gauge shotgun. Halfway into the woods Jimmy turned the gun on Don and shot him in the foot. The bullet went through Don's shoe, barely missing his toe.

On another occasion, Jimmy invited Don and another boy over to his house to help him in his loft. Once they were there, Jimmy informed them that he had forgotten something downstairs and he'd be right back. As Jimmy exited and closed the door the boys heard a metal latch slam into place. The boys paused for a moment, in shock, wondering if they had just been bamboozled. They rushed toward the window and saw a young Jimmy Jones with an evil grin on his face. The more the children screamed and banged on the door the more Jimmy smiled. After quenching his desire for human suffering, Jimmy went inside, leaving the boys locked in the loft, incommunicado, for the better part of the night. Jimmy's glaring smile at the boys before going into the house shows the true sadistic characteristic that had by then developed.

Jimmy could have run in the house without looking at the boys and later claim that he merely forgot that he left the boys inside. However, Jimmy's narcissistic personality was developing quickly. He wanted the boys to know that he had outsmarted them and that he was in control. It was a very dangerous time for young Jimmy. With no one to hold him accountable for his actions or explain to him what he had done wrong, Jimmy felt satisfied with his actions. Don had never told anyone about the other two instances, but he told his parents about this one, and they warned him to stay away from Jimmy after that. Throughout the course of Jimmy's life he would always push the boundaries of control. With little parental guidance, these warning signs that could have been corrected early on had become a part of his personality.

High School

Jimmy entered high school in 1945, and continued to accept the role of outcast. While the other boys became even more amassed in sports; Jimmy was more concerned with spirituality and the Bible. Jimmy's newest obsession, however, was with current worldly events and social figures. He began seeing his ideal-self in the images of Joseph Stalin, Adolph Hitler, Mahatma Gandhi, and Karl Marx. These were powerful figures and it was no secret that Jimmy was in awe of their domineering characters. He poured over their words daily, which gave him a different way of looking at the world. He did not stand for everything that each of these men stood for, but he admired the despotic characteristic in each of them.

Jimmy once again was at the top of his class as a student, holding an IQ of 118. He was as well read as some of his teachers and had developed a far wittier tongue than he had as a child. Jimmy had also grown very concerned with his appearance. He knew that his jet-black hair was his best feature and he was frequently seen running a comb through it. This newly acquired consciousness was due in most part to his growing attraction to the opposite sex. There were a few females that caught his eye and he made his boyish attempts at them. Mostly innocent of course, taking into consideration the time period and location in which this occurred. Jimmy strolled around town with a girl or two, fine tuning his oratory skills with the females. His charm with the ladies and their parents was clearly evident early on.

By Jimmy's sophomore year he and Don had grown apart and ran in completely different circles. These onetime best friends were now merely peers in passing, and their past relationship was by then old hat. One day Jimmy saw Don and his friends playing basketball. Jimmy approached them and insisted that they stop their game and read the Bible with him. The boys laughed in ridicule and continued playing. Agitated with their insolence, Jimmy stood on the court and began reading the Bible. Don's fuse with Jimmy was understandably short by then. Don walked over to him and took a swing at Jimmy, hitting him in the face and knocking him to the ground. The incident drove the two even further apart. Although Jimmy would continue these tactics of persuasion for a time, he soon learned to play on people's fears and ambitions with precision. He became a master at it. Within these lessons he seemed to learn that manipulation and deception worked much better than insistence; although, he would later learn to seamlessly combine the two.

During his sophomore and junior years Jimmy regularly put on an evangelical robe and hit the main street in Lynn to preach to passing pedestrians. Armed with only a big black Bible, he offered the residents salvation. Most people who passed by knew of Jimmy and his family and were far from impressed. Most just ignored him and continued walking passed him as he preached. Jejune to most, this only fueled young Jimmy. He was determined with an inner strength almost unequaled. Instead of becoming more flaccid because of his failures, Jimmy became more vocal and combative. He was often seen screaming at people who ignored him, "You're all going to hell!" he would yell. He also had a particular distain for locals that hung out at the pool hall where his father frequented. Jimmy would sometimes stand outside—sometimes enter—the pool hall and scream, "You're all going to hell if you stay here!" Even Jimmy's father would casually ignore him. "I'll be home soon Jimmy," he would respond. At times Jimmy would covertly gather up all the rat poison laid out at the pool hall so the rats would continue to infest the place.

Though Jimmy was vengeful and not big on compromise, he was intelligent enough to realize that his insolent outbursts were hurting his cause. He soon dropped the robe and preached in street clothes. The town of Lynn, however, was still not receptive. Jimmy had taken a part-time job at *Reid Memorial Hospital* in Richmond, Indiana and had been scouting other areas to do his Bible-bidding. When he believed that his preaching days in Lynn had run their course, he began hitchhiking to Richmond to preach by the railroad tracks. It was there that Jimmy began to tweak his message, speaking more about racial equality. He did this because the area that he chose was a poor, predominantly Black neighborhood. He had also learned that the best way to get people to listen was to appeal to their interests—a valuable lesson that would take him very far in his later years. Jimmy—sixteen at the time—was undeterred by the drunks who strolled out of the corner bar and mocked him. However, Jimmy weathered the storm and began to have much more success in Richmond than he did in Lynn. His sermons on the streets of Richmond kept his mission going. Sometimes he would preach to upwards of thirty people, most were Black and few were White. Jimmy was learning quickly that the subject of race could draw crowds, especially coming from a White person who was taking the side of Blacks.

During Jimmy's preaching days in Richmond he met Dan Mitrione, a Richmond police officer at the time. Although Mitrione was a few years older than Jimmy, it's alleged that he took a liking to young Jimmy. Some say that Mitrione was the only reason that Jones did not get arrested and run out of town. Not much is known about their mysterious relationship. Mitrione soon became the chief of the Richmond PD and he later entered the International Police Academy, allegedly a Central Intelligence Agency (CIA) front for training in counterinsurgency and torture techniques. Mitrione would soon become a central character in the secret life of Jim Jones (see pgs. 38, 39, & 40).

At the same time that Jimmy was having success in Richmond, Jimmy's parents were having serious marital problems at home. No longer could the fiery Lynetta carry her vapid husband, and the two would soon separate. With some persuasion from Jimmy, he and Lynetta decided to move to Richmond where they would regroup. Though embarrassed about his parent's separation, Jimmy was glad that his mother had rid herself of his father, and he was happy to be moving to Richmond. He would finish out his senior year of high school at Richmond High, which had a superior curriculum compared to his school in Lynn. Richmond was also a better overall fit for his unorthodox character. Although his mother and father had decided to "split," nothing had changed much initially. The Jones' still lived in the same home for some time and Lynetta and James still did not sleep in the same bed. With the future plans set in motion, Lynetta became more dissident and James Sr. more cantankerous.

Frenemy

With the news of his impending move to Richmond, Jimmy took the opportunity to invite his old friend Don Freedman over to his home for a farewell dinner. Ever since the basketball court altercation the two boys had not spoken. Don still felt bad about socking Jimmy and had wanted to bury the hatchet. For Don, this was the perfect opportunity to do so. No peer had been closer to Jimmy growing up than Donald Freedman. Although Jimmy had done some bad things to Don over the years, he still seemed to be angry and vengeful about their last encounter. It was either that or once Jimmy got control over an individual, he did not want to relinquish it.

Don accepted the invitation and the two sat down in Jones' kitchen. Lynetta served the boys sandwiches and left them to get reacquainted; while James senior sat indifferently in the living room. The boys ate and filled each other in on what they had been up to since their falling-out. After a lengthy stay, Don told Jimmy that he had to get going and wished him luck. Jimmy, however, was not ready for Don to leave and asked him to stay a bit longer. Don reiterated that he had to go, but Jimmy would not take "no" for an answer. Don felt a little uncomfortable, but decided to stay a little longer. After more time went by, Don again announced that he had to leave, but this time Jimmy became more insistent on Don staying. Again, Don compromised and stayed a bit longer. Finally, after more time had passed Don firmly announced that he would be leaving then got up and began walking towards the door. Jimmy followed closely, insisting that Don stay longer. Don continued through the front door in haste, while informing Jimmy that he had to go.

Jimmy made a quick stop behind the chair where his father was seated and wasn't paying the boys any mind. Jimmy quickly grabbed his father's gun from behind the chair and continued unabated outside. Jimmy opened the door and walked out onto the porch. Don was making his way down the walkway toward the sidewalk. "I really don't want you to go," Jimmy shouted in a desperate tone. Unaware that Jimmy was armed with his father's pistol, Don continued walking away from the house, overwhelmed by the bizarre scene that has just taken place. Jimmy was stationed on the porch waiting for Don to respond, but Don didn't; he just continued walking, and had reached the sidewalk by this time. "Just stop or I'll shoot ya," Jimmy shouted firmly. Puzzled, but recalling the BB-gun incident, Don picked up the pace with urgency and made a left and continued on. "I'm going home," Don screeched. Some fifty-feet from the porch, Don heard a blast! Simultaneously, Don noticed a chunk of tree—that he had just walked passed—go flying by his head. Jimmy had fired a shot! Don quickly ducked for cover to regroup and assess the situation. After a few seconds, Don peeked out to see where Jimmy was. He looked up at the porch and there he saw a glaring Jimmy Jones standing with the gun at his side. Mortified, Don took off running all the way home, never looking back. As he raced home, Don thought to himself that he was done with Jimmy for good this time—or so he thought.

Jim kept his part time job as an orderly at the hospital and his preaching separate. Already he was leading separate lives and had learned how to con people. He had the gift of appealing to what people wanted and he was learning that you can catch more bees with honey than with vinegar. He portrayed a benign disposition to those that he hated the most and jeered at them behind their backs. It was those he was closest to that he would abuse and be his true self with. At the hospital Jimmy had shortened his name to Jim, which gave him a more distinguished and older appeal. Jim was known by most as a well-mannered, bright youngster who fashioned himself as a potential future doctor or hospital administrator. Jim learned all the medical terminology and wore a sparkling clean white doctor's coat. He was truly intrigued with the medical profession. Unlike high school, Jim was very popular with the patients, the nurses, and even the doctors. Jim earned about $30 a week in salary at the hospital and enjoyed working in a place that cured people.

As his humanitarian interests grew, so did his liking for the efforts of the hospital and the work they did. Jim's awareness of each situation and his surroundings progressed rapidly, and with that a sadistic need for total control was developing. Every move that he made became calculated; yet, seemed so effortless. His true intent was well hidden under his boyish charm. Already Jim was a loner at school, popular at the hospital, and a renegade preacher on the streets. The multifaceted Jones was coming of age and was learning how to master the territory at an alarming rate.

Jim had been working at the hospital for two years by the summer of 1948. One day during work Jim had been doing his rounds, when he ran into his old pal Donald Freedman. The two had not seen each other since the shooting incident at Jim's place. The two cordially got reacquainted, and Jim was once again brainstorming ideas to get his sidekick back. One of the perks of working at the hospital was the young student nurses, who were more sophisticated than most of the young women in the area. Jim persuaded Don to apply to the hospital as an orderly. He did so by explaining to him that there were a lot of beautiful nurses that worker there. Don had surely made up his mind after the shooting incident to steer clear of Jim, but money and pretty nurses helped him overlook Jim's earlier transgressions. After getting the job, Don's trainer was Jim, and Jim rode him hard during training! After training ended, Jim continued a senior role over Don, making him perform all the hard labor under his instruction and strict supervision. Don quickly realized that he had once again naively fallen into the same trap and pattern with Jim Jones. Don was not happy with Jim's domineering ways and would not have signed on if he had thought Jim was going to be his superior. Don did find some comfort, however, as he dated a few of the female nurses.

Jim felt most comfortable at the hospital—a stark contrast to his poor home life and being an outcast at school. On the other hand, Don enjoyed a more normal home life: he was popular in school; he was a Hoosier basketball player; and he did well with the ladies. Jim enjoyed the power that he had over Don at the hospital—a power that he did not have in school. Jim frequently asked Don to clean the dark hallway during their over-night shifts. Though this did not sound like a horrifying task, it was for Don. Jim had lent his ear to Don once, and he confessed to Jim that he was afraid of the dark. He also informed Jim that he did not really have the stomach for some of the more grotesque duties required in hospital work. Perhaps this was the first instance where Jim listened intently as a friend confessed their fears, only to turn around and use those very fears against them. This is something that Jim would master and later rely on heavily with his congregation. As Don swept the dark hallway, Jim would run pranks on him. Jim would sneak up on him and throw a severed arm at him, or secretly plant a severed head for him to stumble upon.

Don's patience with Jim and his antics were wearing very thin. The final straw for Don came when Jim had ordered him to take a freshly severed leg wrapped in newspaper to the incinerator and burn it. When Don had finished Jim ordered him to clean up every bit of blood and flesh while Jim blocked the door until Don finished. This had to remind Don of the time when Jim had locked him in the barn some years back. Don had been belittled and humiliated by Jim for the last time. He left the hospital that night and never returned.

After Don quit he stayed as far away from Jim as possible. Their relationship had come to an abrupt end. This was a significant relationship for Jim that shows early warning signs of things to come. The two boys had grown up together since the age of four. Don had certainly been Jim's best friend, on and off, for several years, if not his only friend during that time. It was the first bridge that Jim would burn, but definitely not the last. With that, Don became the first survivor of Jim Jones. The next person that he became close to, however, would not be so lucky.

CHAPTER 2 – BECOMING A MAN

Jim Meets Marceline

One day at the hospital a pregnant woman died of trichinosis. Jim was on call and ordered to prepare the body for the undertaker. He was aided by a nurse in her last year of training by the name of Marceline Baldwin. Marceline witnessed Jim genuinely saddened by the events of the woman's death. Jim showed particular concern for the woman's grieving family. Marceline had already thought he was handsome, but this show of emotion and caring from Jim drew her over the edge. She was now fully attracted to a boy nearly four years younger than she was. When Marceline returned to her dorm she immediately told her roommate, Evelyn Eadler, about her new found attraction. The young nurses had known of Jim and had crossed paths with him several times. It was this incident, however, that really opened Marceline's tender heart to him. Jim was more mature than most boys his age and smarter than most boys Marceline's age. Jim played it cool. He seemed humble, respectful, compassionate, honest, and ambitious. By now he had fully cultivated the skills needed in order to become a more persuasive individual. He had developed an uncanny knack for knowing what each person wanted and showing himself as a reflection of their desires.

Headed into his senior year of high school, Jim began dating Marceline. In only a few short months their relationship had gotten serious, and Marceline wanted her parents to meet her new love interest. In March of 1948, Marceline finished nursing school and chose her graduation party as the time to introduce Jim to her parents, Walter and Charlotte Baldwin. The Baldwin's were not overjoyed with the age difference, but Jim's cunning, charm, and longing for a stable family won them over almost immediately. Jim was soon treated as a member of the family; the type of family he never had. As if their courtship had not moved quickly enough already, Jim made an announcement that put an ultimatum on the relationship. One day Marceline approached her roommate Evelyn to discuss her relationship with Jim. She told Evelyn that Jim had announced he was graduating from Richmond High School early—

in the fall—to attend Indiana University at mid-term. The fact that Marceline was four years Jim's senior concerned her, and she knew the time had come for her to make the decision whether to break it off or commit. The two young ladies wrestled with the idea for hours. Jim worked his last day at Reid Memorial Hospital in November and graduated with honors in the winter of 1948-49.

The Baldwin's were an upper-middle-class, conservative, Republican family and Marceline was the oldest of three daughters. They were a close-knit family that pretty much did everything together. They were regulars at the nearby Methodist church in Richmond. The girls were very well behaved and would regularly spend Saturday nights with the family rather than attending at social gatherings with others their age. Marceline was the most trusted and most mature—being twelve years older than her youngest sister—and she was sometimes like another parent to her sister, Sharon. The family had taught the girls to be strong, speak their minds, and stay grounded. They were also firm believers in equality and treating others the way they want to be treated. Marceline worked hard in school; and rather than attend a University, she decided to go to nursing school through a federally funded WWII program. She knew at a young age that nursing was her calling, and it worked out because it was easier on her parents financially.

Marceline decided that Jim might be the one for her, despite his age, and her parents trusted her judgment. Before Jim left for college he and Marceline began making wedding plans. In January of 1949, sixteen-year-old Jim Jones left his mother's second-story apartment on Main Street in Richmond and arrived at the *Bloomington Campus at Indiana University* (approximately 98-miles from Richmond). The campus was filled with young GI's in their twenties and upperclassmen from wealthy families. Jim was once again playing the familiar role of "outsider." Campus clicks were solid by the time Jim had arrived. There weren't any kids Jim's age, and entering the campus in mid-term didn't help his social standing.

Jim found a way to press-on and eventually overcome all of these obstacles. He stayed focused on Marceline, his school work, and the Bible. Jim practiced his rhetoric with the others and was frequently challenged for his radical ideas. One of those boys was a boy named Lemmons; who was raised as a member of the *Dispels of Christ denomination.* Jim seemed out of his league in many of his discussions with Lemmons. Although Jim was a very intelligent boy, he was from a small town of old-fashioned thinkers. That coupled with his age made his arguments sound more like hollow-rhetoric. Although the youngest kid on campus, Jim did not look for acceptance through drinking or drugs. Instead, he saw the sinful-party-ways of many of the older students as immature. This and other things made Jim again a loner, and he made a concerted effort to steer clear of others. Jim stayed focused on, and remained faithful to, Marceline. He took the bus to visit her on weekends and they shared many intimate phone conversations during the week. The two were planning to be married in June of 1949.

On Sunday, June 12, 1949, both families gathered at *Trinity United Methodist Church* in Richmond. Clearly this was bigger for the Baldwin family, as they would see-off two daughters in a double wedding ceremony. In a fabulous ceremony, Marceline married Jim and Eloise Baldwin [19] married Dale Klingman. The church was filled to capacity with family, friends, and some of Walter Baldwin's city council member co-workers. Even the Mayor attended this gala spectacle.

There was literally no honeymoon for Jim and Marceline. After the wedding they moved to their first apartment in Bloomington. Their new one-room home was located across the street from the hospital where Marceline worked. It was also close enough to the Indiana University campus where Jim was attending. The two struggled to eke out a living, like many newlyweds. Jim attended school and took on a part-time job, while Marceline worked as a nurse and continued her education. Most of the bills were taken care of by Marceline, which included Jim's school tuition. Marceline's parents often contributed as well from time to time. Marceline held family very dear to her heart. The couple made the trip to Richmond to see the Baldwin's whenever they could. Marceline felt confident that Jim would be a success. Yet, Jim did not exactly have a plan for the future; he was going through a lot of mental changes and the direction of his life was very much uncertain. Things were happening too fast for young Jim. Within a few short months, he had gone from high school senior, to college student, and now married.

Soon after their marriage Jim began to speak more and more about his belief in *communism*. Jim's social ideologies were taking major shape in his life, which included more about the injustices endured by Blacks in America. During this time schools and churches were still totally segregated. There were a plethora of *"Whites only"* establishments, and Blacks rarely stepped foot into White neighborhoods. Moreover, the occasional cross was still burned on a Black family's property, compliments of the Klan. One day, as Jim struggled to find his way, the most unlikely of circumstances began to unfold. Jim Jones, the once Bible thumping youngster, became an atheist! In his mind one religion was not comprehensive enough to sum up the complexities of the human condition or answer the question: Why are we here? While Jim tried to make sense of his lack of faith and his inherent spirituality, he denied the presence of God in the biblical sense all together.

One night when Marceline had knelt down to pray, Jim became irritated and erratic. He believed that what Marceline was doing was ridiculous. "There is no God!" he shouted. The two fought for hours and Jim would not back down. He did not want his wife being a religious robot for what he perceived was a canard. Marceline was a devout Methodist and Jim's tirades hurt her deeply. One day Marceline was doing the dishes and Jim walked into the kitchen. Tensions were high, because the two had recently been arguing over religious issues. The great antagonist that Jim was becoming did not help their situation. When he tried to bring the sore subject up crassly, Marceline said, "I love you Jim, but don't say another word about the Lord!" Jim snapped, "Fuck the Lord!" he said in a rage. A full-fledged fight ensued that became so heated that Marceline threw a glass that she had just washed at Jim.

Jim and Marceline both worked exhausting hours. This made them grow apart even further. Their financial situation became so severe that they were forced to move into a trailer-home outside of Bloomington. Jim jumped from job to job desperately trying to uphold his financial end of the relationship. He was also attending *Butler University*. Marceline was growing more impatient by the day. She wanted a traditional family of her own and she didn't want to play second fiddle in the marriage, especially when she was the breadwinner. This also manifested thoughts in Jim's own mind of similarities between him and his father. In his head he could remember his mother saying, "Don't be a nothing like your father." Jim's self-perceived inadequacies were never far behind. His fear of failure was so strong that it compromised his decision making significantly throughout his life. Everything was a test to Jim Jones. His constant testing of his surroundings and of others showed his insecurity, his vulnerability, his paranoid lack of trust, and his evil intent all wrapped in one.

In 1950, Marceline got word that her ten-year-old cousin, Ronnie Baldwin, had been hospitalized for severe stomach pains. Jim and Marceline rushed to the hospital to see him. Ronnie's plight stemmed from the fact that his father had died prematurely and his mother was incapable of caring for him. Because if this he was put it a foster home. In the summer of 1951, Jim and Marceline decided to take the boy into their home. They treated Ronnie just like he was their son; he even called them mom and dad. Jim was still unsure what he wanted to do with his life. After more thought, Jim decided to attend *Indiana Universities' Law School program*. The I.U. campus was in Indianapolis, so the family packed up again and moved to an apartment there. However, the family was evicted for having too many pets, which included the recent acquisition of a chimpanzee. The chimp mysteriously died of strychnine poisoning soon after, which Jim blamed on a neighbor. Looking back, this was perhaps Jim's first experimentation with using poison to manipulate. It was very possible that from this experimentation Jim learned that it didn't take much of a dose of poison for life to expire. Judging from future events (that will be discussed in later chapters) Jim was likely not trying to kill the animal. After purchasing a small home on the north-side of town, Jim replaced the chimp with a monkey. The new home put an even bigger financial burden on the family and Jim was forced to work longer hours for supplemental income, which made his grades suffer.

Jim and Marceline held Ronnie to high standards and good grades were a prerequisite. Jim was particularly hard on Ronnie, assuming a fatherly role right from the beginning. Marceline acted more like a big sister to him. Jim was becoming more bombastic than ever about his passions for communism and supporting Blacks. Jim trained his new pet monkey to attack on command and would sometimes sic the animal on Ronnie for a laugh. Marceline rarely intervened on Jim's sick little games, but when she did it was more passive than anything. Mostly she was content to sit back and wait for Jim's episodes to pass rather than stir him up even more than he already was. More restless than ever, Jim was fixated on finding a solid career path. This overachiever was killing himself on low paying jobs and working extra hours. His current situation did not feed his hunger to lead and blaze new trails. The Jones' marriage continued to teeter on the brink of destruction, but Jim would always do something to bring Marceline back from the edge at the last moment. Jim needed Marceline at this time in his life more than he ever would later. He continued to treat those closest to him much as he treated Don years earlier; one minute Jim was a saint the next, Satan.

Jim's Epiphany

On the edge again, Jim had an epiphany and would make an announcement that would change his life and every life around him forever. In 1952, the *Somerset Methodist Church* released a five-page creed, documenting their goals as an organization. The list included abatement of poverty, a form of security for the aged, and most importantly, for *the rights of racial groups*. Jim believed the creed was in line with his social ideology and—though still an atheist—the perfect vehicle for him. In April of 1952, Jim made the announcement to the Baldwin family that he would peruse a career as a Methodist minister. The family was stunned, but excited. Once again Jim had bought himself more time with Marceline. Being Methodist, this was also in line with the future that Marceline had dreamed of and had brought her one step closer to her own goals.

Less than two months after his decision, Jim became associate pastor at the poor White church in Indianapolis that issued the creed. Yet again, the family packed up and moved to a small bungalow near the church. Later that same year, Jim and Marceline wanted to make Ronnie a permanent part of their family. They met with a social worker and received the necessary adoption papers. Ronnie, on the other hand, was opposed to this because he feared Jim. One of Jim's manipulative tactics was telling Ronnie that his mother didn't love him. The effort—to persuade the child to stay based on false pretenses—backfired when Ronnie met up with his mother at his brother's wedding soon after. Ronnie's suspicions of Jim were confirmed, and for the first time Jim was exposed as a blatant liar. Ronnie saw right through Jim's threats and lies, and the two had it out on Ronnie's final night. Jim tried every verbal trick in the book on that sleepless night. His aim was to make Ronnie stay, but even a young boy's undeveloped mind can at times sense when things are wrong. Marceline had learned to stand by Jim as he went on his mendacious, pernicious rampages; but she was not happy with the tactics Jim used that night. The following morning Ronnie boarded a plan for Richmond to live with his mother, and made it a point never to see Jim Jones again.

Jim Jones never thought like a traditional clergyman, nor did he ever plan to be one; although, he continued peddling that disguise. Right from the start Jim's epiphany was self-serving and his purpose was to become a minister on his own terms. His goal was to take the Methodist Creed—which met his social goals—and mix it with the uninhibited Pentecostal style of preaching. A big part of his goal included contrived healings. Jim realized quickly that the Methodist Creed was one thing on paper and another thing in practice. Blacks were still not welcome in White Methodist churches—a hypocrisy that Jim planned to expose and use as a self-serving vehicle that would launch him into a unique category of leaders.

Much as he did as a child, Jim began scouting many different churches. He did so in an effort to pick up on some of the techniques of an eclectic group of ministers. Jim knew that if he could adopt the unrestrained preaching style of Pentecostalism he could draw bigger crowds, and he believed that the Black preacher's had cornered the market on this charismatic style of delivery. Perhaps no one was more shocked to learn how gifted of a speaker Jim was than his own wife. Jim created an instant buzz with his unique style of preaching. Jim's "If they could do it, I can do it" attitude led him to his nerve-racking pulpit debut at a *Church Convention in Columbus, Indiana*. Despite his pre-sermon jitters, Jim managed to *woo* the crowd and affirmed that he was not just another proletarian breaking onto the scene.

His true debut onto the big stage, however, came in 1953, at the *Bethesda Missionary Temple in Detroit* at the *Interdenominational Missionary Seminar*. Hundreds of Protestant Ministers gathered for this spectacular event. Although Jones was not scheduled to speak, a female organizer gave him the opportunity that he had been waiting for. Jim relied heavily on deception: calling out names, prophesying, and healing illnesses. He captivated the crowd with his charismatic character and managed to steal the show, which upset many of the seasoned clergymen in attendance. Jones was an immediate hit, but had managed to gain many skeptics amidst the men of the cloth. Many of them felt that Jones' unorthodox style was a sideshow and an embarrassment more than the word of God. However, there were a few high-ranking evangelists who were moved by the newcomers' undeniable personal appeal.

Among them was Rev. Edwin Wilson from Elmwood Temple in Cincinnati, and the two formed an immediate friendship. Others closer to home also approached Jones with words of encouragement, such as authorities from the *Laurel Street Tabernacle* in Indianapolis. Jim had kept his special healings a secret from everyone up to that point, including Marceline. Jim would gather-up information beforehand about the subjects that he would later call on to prophesize about. In doing so, Jones knew about their illnesses and issues prior to claiming to heal or solve them. Jim continued to preach two days per week while working various jobs. Mysteriously, Jim's tie to South America—whether mere coincidence or not—stemmed back to this time period, as he had somehow managed to import monkeys from the region that he would sell from door to door for $29.00 each. Much as Jim gathered stray animals as a child, he began doing the same with people.

In 1954, the Jones' took in several strays:

- Ester Mueller (a middle-aged religious woman)
- Goldie (an eighteen-year-old blonde female)
- Ozzie (a live-in-housekeeper)

Jim knew that Somerset was never going to live up to its creed or accept Blacks into their congregation as fast as he wanted. Moreover, his ultimate need for control had led him to explore other options. Mysteriously, Jim somehow managed to save enough money to leave Somerset Methodist and start his own church. Jim rented a small building on Hoyt and Randolph streets he termed, "*Community Unity*," located in a racially mixed area. Word was spreading fast about the young preacher and he lined the aisles of his church with recruits that he had picked up from the convention, the seminar, and his previous Somerset gig. Jim now had a forum all his own where he began to introduce his personal social messages. However, as enticing as his social messages were, people came to be healed and to witness the healings.

Jim was becoming commonly known for his healings and prophesies; and though it angered him as well as wore him out, his success was rapidly increasing because of it. Jim had become more like a rock star than a man of the cloth. Women had become like groupies of this young, handsome preacher whose ministerial strength was seducing the masses by fraudulent, clandestine tactics. And like some rock stars, Jim's image became as, or more important than, his work. As Jim's reputation grew his healings became more dramatic. Soon he began elevating his game, instituting miracles as a way to keep his followers in awe. One day, officials from the Laurel Street Tabernacle elected to send associate pastor, Rev. Russell Winberg to visit Jones' church to get a closer look at this new phenomenon. Winberg and about 150 of his members were on hand to witness Jones's sermon. During the session, Jones managed to get everyone to believe that they'd just witnessed him turn tap water into wine, including Winberg.

Soon after, Jones was invited to the Tabernacle as a guest preacher at the recommendation of Rev. Winberg. Jones arrived along with several members of his own congregation. It was the first time that Jones had employed this new approach of traveling deep with his followers—a staple that Jones would expand upon and use most effectively later in his life. He would go nowhere without bringing a busload of his own supporters, and later true fanatics, to cheer him on. Jones steamrolled the crowd and continued his streak of gaining immediate favor as a public speaker amongst unfamiliar crowds. Jones performed so well that he was invited back numerous times. Jim drew such big crowds at the Tabernacle that rumors began surfacing that he might be the one to succeed the retiring head minister. However, Jones outraged many church officials when he brought several Black members onto the stage of the church. This incident enraged the church board so much so that they voted down the proposal to elect Jones as head pastor. Jim made out, though, in the end, taking about half of the Laurel Street congregation with him when he left.

With Jim's new acquisitions and word still spreading, he continued to establish himself as a noticeable force in the local religious community. Jim continued banking money and growing his congregation. By 1956, his church had become overcrowded with followers and Jones put a down payment on a bigger church in another racially mixed area of Indianapolis. Jim was embarking on a new beginning in his life and he wanted this to reflect in all aspects. One way that he did this was by changing the name of his church from Community Unity to *Wings of Deliverance*. The twenty-five-year-old preacher had become a success beyond what he had dreamed and many saw even bigger things on the horizon for him. The nucleus of Jim's group was his Laurel Street defectors. Rev. Russell Winberg—knowing that he, himself, was not going to take over the Tabernacle after the head minister's retirement—along with his wife, Wilma, also joined Jones' church, both as associate pastors, further legitimizing Jim's authenticity.

Along with Jim's Laurel Street recruits was a young pharmaceutical company maintenance man named Jack Beam. Jones and Beam hit it off immediately during Jim's guest speaking days at the Tabernacle. Jim noticed that Jack was a vital resource in their congregation and envisioned him as an elite member of his own church one day. Beam had been a loyal Laurel Street member who was smart, pleasant to be around, and one who dedicated his time fanatically. Jones and Beam became fast friends. Beam was in awe of Jones and became one of Jones' most loyal followers. Jones knew that in order to win over potential members, as well as keep his current ones, he would have to continue the healings. Crowds flocked to see Jones' miraculous gift and he was forced to cultivate new ways and different forms of deception in order to continue to shock and amaze people.

Peoples Temple

Before his first year at Fifteenth and New Jersey had commenced, Jim had decided to change the name of his church to, *Peoples Temple Full Gospel Church* (more commonly referred to as (*Peoples Temple*). Before long Jim's expanding ministry again outgrew the location, and he uprooted his church and moved to a former synagogue on *Tenth and Delaware* to help accommodate his rapidly-growing congregation. Far past the days of healing sick chickens in his barn, Jim had honed his skills and developed into a world-class speaker who could draw tremendous crowds on word of mouth alone. Jim knew that the more people he could recruit the more exposure and money he could bring in. The key to all of this was his healings and prophesies, which continued to receive praise and draw many hard-core spiritualists. Edith Parks was one of those spiritualists who would become one of Jones' biggest supporters, and later convince her whole family to dedicate their lives to the church as well.

Jim believed that it was very important to expand his operation and he worked tirelessly to do so. He came to the conclusion that the best way to do this was to go to religious gatherings where ready-made crowds were on hand looking for something new. Aiding to Jones' recruiting efforts was his willingness to participate in religious conventions featuring big-name ministers with well established congregations. Jim saw the benefits in attending these conventions and was soon confident enough to stage one of his own. His plan was to seduce a highly exalted minister to headline a five-day-event that he had planned. He couldn't have found a better headliner than Rev. William Branham, who agreed to team up with Jones in 1956. The convention would take place over a five day period, from June 11th through June 15th.

Branham was a highly revered healing evangelist and author whose experience and skills strongly exceeded Jones'. The two packed a mean punch and made a brilliant combination. They established themselves immediately as an undeniable force, opening the first day to nearly eleven-thousand faithful. Though Branham was better known than Jones, he was not as popular among Blacks, which only consisted of about a fifth of those in attendance. Jones' flamboyant and animated style coupled with his social stance made him a hit with Blacks immediately, but Blacks were still skeptical whether this White preacher genuinely believed in their social struggles.

This one event single handedly propelled Jones into a new stratosphere and introduced him as a major player in the ministerial arena. The exhibition also introduced Jones to many future allies. Perhaps the greatest ally Jones gained from the event was former pastor Archie Ijames. Born to a poor Black family of seven in 1913, this North Carolina native was only sixteen-years-old when his father died. Ijames dropped out of high school and became a bit of a recluse. After turning to religion, Archie became pastor of a church affiliated with the Church of God, Body of Christ. He decided to leave after years of realization that the church did not care about the civil rights of Blacks. Among their other commonalities, the contradiction of the church in this regard bonded Jones and Ijames and they both were passionate about it. After this realization, Ijames had dropped the pretenses of religion and referred to himself as a free thinker and Universalist. Jones saw this forty-five year old Black man as his key to attaining credence with Blacks and Ijames was in just the vulnerable position to give Jones a chance. Ijames realized that there was a racial imbalance in leadership in the church, in general, and he saw this as his big opportunity to work with a man who had the ability to change things.

After Ijames decided to join the Temple, the inner core was, for now, complete. The team of Jones, Winberg, Ijames, and Beam became an instant force, blowing the doors of the game wide open. By 1959, the Temple had more than 2000 members. By 1960, Jones had received a great deal of good-press and the reputation of the church was seen as positive. However, their reputation was not as large as their resolve or work ethic. The group pressed on furiously in their social quest, putting countless hours into the church. No more was this evident than when they opened up a soup kitchen in February of 1960. Ijames committed to running the free restaurant with his wife, Rosie. Jack Beam's tall, attractive wife, Rheaviana, held chief cook honors, though she was known more for her temper tantrums among restaurant workers. Jim grew more driven to succeed and expand with each passing day. True success to Jones—unbeknownst to anyone at the time—meant control by any means necessary. His idea for the future had not yet fully flourished in his own mind, but he would soon meet a man who would bequeath him with control in practice.

CHAPTER 3 – NOTICEABLE CHANGES

Father Divine

Towards the end of the 1950s Jim had begun reading about a spiritual leader that had notoriously gained national prominence. Father Divine, as he was called, was the founder and leader of the *International Peace Mission Movement* and was seen by his followers as the Dean of the Universe, and even God himself. Father Divine was a mysterious character who is often seen by social scientists as the first cult leader. Apart from being born George Baker in Georgia and believed to be the son of freed slaves, not much is known about Divine before 1914. Estimates say that he was born in 1880, but other sources and legal documents declare that his first marriage took place in 1882. Reverend Major Jealous Divine (a.k.a. Father Divine) himself recognized in 1932, that he was age 52, but he also said that he had "spiritually and mentally no record." Divine refused to give any sort of autobiographical information before 1914, which only added to his mystique.

What is known about Father Divine is that his movement proved very successful and estimates number his international following, at its height, at close to 2 million followers. Divine became widely known around 1919 in Brooklyn, NY, but it wasn't until the 1930s that he gained true prominence and notoriety. Divine had set up his headquarters in Sayville, NY, and had gained a tremendous local following. The house in Sayville was sold to him, because the prior owner wanted to spite a neighbor that he did not get along with by having a Black person live next to him. The ad for the house actually said "...for sale to colored." People would gather at the home of Divine on Sundays to hear him preach or attend the lavish banquets Divine put on at his home. The presence of so many Blacks scared neighbors and many residents of Sayville, because they feared that the town would turn into a Negro haven. On November 21, 1930, the townspeople held a meeting to discuss these very issues and tried to figure out a way to stop Divine.

On November 15, 1931—almost a year after the town meeting—police raided Divine's Sayville home and arrested 80 people, charging them with disturbing the peace. The raid was cited as stemming from "distress calls" from neighbors. Fifty of the eighty people who were arrested pled guilty and paid a $5.00 fine. Divine, however, pled not guilty and refused bail, viewing the incident as racially motivated. Divine was put on trial soon after and was convicted. The jury asked for leniency in the sentencing, but Judge Lewis J. Smith ignored their plea and sentenced Divine to the maximum—a $500 fine and a year in jail. During sentencing, Judge Smith stated, "There may be those of you who believe this defendant is God. There are undoubtedly many who believe he is not God, and those who do not believe he is God are entitled to have their rights protected the same as those who believe he is God." Many of Divine's followers feared the worst for Smith after sentencing "God" to jail.

The irony of the situation became mysterious, tragic, as well as comical all at once when Judge Smith died two-days after the sentencing of what was deemed cardiac problems. When questioned from jail about Smith's death, Divine simply stated, "I hated to do it." After the Judges death, a new trial was ordered, but—yielding to public pressures and protests—nothing ever came of this, and Divine was released after serving only 33 days in jail. It was a big win for Father Divine in many ways, and his membership grew because of the exposure. Even the *NY Times* wrote an article about the trial. The article was published on May 26, 1932, *"Disorder in 'Heaven' Convicts Evangelist."*

Divine's first wife, Peninniah—a portly Black woman decades older than Divine, originally from Macon, Georgia—died in 1943. After Peninniah's death, Divine met Edna Rose Ritchings, who was a slender White woman from Ontario, Canada and only 21-years-old when they married in 1946. Both wives took the name Mother Divine; but it was his second wife, Ritchings, who took a more proactive role in his ministry. Father Divine claimed that Ritchings was the reincarnation of his first wife Peninniah, declaring that her spirit entered Ritchings after her death. Almost twenty-years after his legendary 33-day incarceration, Father Divine had turned his already successful congregation into a world-wide phenomenon, and he sat atop a multi-million dollar empire.

Unknowingly, Father Divine and his massive movement caught the attention of Jim Jones. Before long, Jones planned a trip to meet the iconic preacher. From the mid-west, Jones and Rev. Wilson set out on the road, on their way to Father Divine's home in 1960. Divine had invited Jones and Wilson to drive to his 72-acre estate in Gladwyne, Pennsylvania, located just outside of Philadelphia. *The Woodmont Estate*, as it was called, was a 32-room French Gothic Manor that was given to Divine in 1953, by a wealthy devout follower named John Devoute.

During the visit Jones and Divine spoke of segregation and overpopulation. Jones hoped to soak-up as much about Divine and his mission as he could. Divine revealed to Jones many of his and his followers' beliefs and practices. Divine was seen by his followers as the second coming of Jesus Christ. Divine strongly believed in equality for all; particularly for Blacks, as they were the ones being heavily discriminated against at the time. Divine believed that it was the basic right of all to enjoy life, liberty, and the pursuit of happiness. Divine established a restructuring of living based on the economic and religious reforms of each of his followers. Divine's members lived communally. All possessions and properties were cooperatively owned without compensation. His mission opposed life insurance, social security, and credit. All purchases were made in cash.

Divine had strict rules for his members for which he termed *Father Divine's International Modesty Code*. Under this code there was no drinking, no smoking, no obscenity, no profanity, and no vulgarity. No member was allowed to accept bribes, tips, or gifts. Men and women were restricted from living together and prohibited from having any sexual relations. Divine was a strong believer in the *Constitution of the United States*; and he was particularly adamant about the *Bill of Rights*. Divine and his followers believed that he was fulfilling the scriptural promise of the second coming of Christ, and that he was the personification of God in bodily form. There was even a plaque in his home that read: "Father Divine is the living tree of life, Father, son, and holy ghost. We may take the words of Father Divine's, eat and drink and live forever."

The metaphoric Jones-Divine marriage was a smooth one, indeed. Divine was impressed with the ambition and the beliefs of Jones, and he was no doubt excited to mentor a White preacher such as Jones to help with his own cause. During the visit, Divine requested that Jones deliver a sermon to his followers. Jones once again did what he did best, and delivered a splendid speech. When Jones was finished, people applauded and photos snapped, making it a big PR event for both men. Jones was later featured in Divine's newspaper, *"The New Day."* Yet, this marriage was not accepted by all parties. The first to protest, privately, was Rev. Wilson, who was appalled at Divine's promulgations that he was God. Wilson also believed that Divine's teachings and interpretations of celibacy were completely inaccurate, in biblical terms. Jones on the other hand saw Divine's teachings and interpretations as the perfect model for reforming his own congregation. Jones had witnessed and believed that Divine had found a way to manipulate and control his followers. This was very attractive to Jones from afar, but even more attractive to him when witnessed from within. Although Divine's codes had a more benevolent intent, Jones fit to tweak the model severely, in order to serve his own will and lust for power.

Upon his return home, Jones was so excited that he immediately scheduled another trip. This time, however, he would bring a busload of his most devout Temple members. They would all go along to experience Divine's mentoring first hand. It was Jones getting his "inner-circle" acclimated to a similar model that they were about to merge with their own and would later help reinforce. After returning from the second trip, Jones had a noticeably different disposition. Gene Cordell, a PT member at the time, was just one of the many to have witnessed Jim's immediate transformation.

Gene Cordell and his family began their association with Jones in 1953. At that time Gene's wife, June, had come to find that her pet monkey died and she was looking to purchase another one. On the Saturday before Easter of that year, June's mother-in-law, Edith Cordell, had been looking through the Indianapolis Star and had seen an ad selling monkey's for $29.00 each. She recalled that June wanted both a male and female monkey, so she called the person who had placed the advertisement. Coincidentally, that person happened to be Jim Jones. When Edith went to the Jones' home to purchase the monkey, Jim and Marceline invited her to their church the next day for the Easter service. Excited about her new pastor friend, Edith attended the small service of about twenty-five people along with June, her three children, and Gene's sister, Carol

Ann. Gene was unable to attend, because he worked seven days a week at the time. The family was overwhelmed by Jim's presence—as was just about everyone else—and the entire Cordell family instantly became mainstays at the church.

"When Jimmy came back from seeing Father Divine, he was a changed man," said Gene Cordell. "I saw right away…I sensed the change. After that it was 'My way or the highway.' It was 'I'm in control.' He was not just the pastor in the church. Father Devine convinced him he was The Man—that he was God." Max Knight was a reporter working for the Richmond Palladium in Indianapolis, and was also a childhood acquaintance of Jones back in Lynn, Indiana. Knight also affirms the change in Jones after meeting with Father Divine. "From that moment on, Jim went downhill fast," Knight said. "He got into drugs, he got into sex; you name it. He felt that he was bigger than God himself, and it destroyed him. There is no doubt about it."

Even though many attribute Jones' sudden change as the work of Divine, Jim had always been determined to gain power and control. Moreover, it was Jones that had ulterior motives in his relationship with Divine, not the other way around. Jim knew that Father Divine was getting old and would not be around much longer. At that time Father Divine would regularly play tape recordings of his past sermons, because he was too old to preach on a regular basis. Jones sensed Divine's weakness and would soon make an aggressive attempt to overtake Divine's congregation. Jim had to have seen Divine's congregation as a quick and easy way to pick up boatloads of followers. However, Jim had one big obstacle, someone who also saw through Jones' motives: Mother Divine. Regardless of the close relationship between Jones and her husband, Mother Divine was not very fond of Jones. She sensed evil in him, and she was opposed to her husband's affiliation to him from the beginning. Jones' institution of his new rules—including celibacy amongst his congregation—was not received well by most. Some, however, chose to follow Jones' rigid new rules that mirrored Divine's, in many ways. Others decided that the new-look of the Temple and Jones had gone off the deep end, and they could not continue on with the church. All the better Jones thought, as he was weeding-out the so called weak and building a stronger church base for his future charge for domination.

Reiterman's Chronology

According to Jones' main biographer, Tim Reiterman, in early October of 1961, the Temple leader told his associate pastor, Archie Ijames, that he heard voices from "extraterrestrial beings," and that he had a vision of a nuclear explosion in Chicago of apocalyptic proportions. Because of this vision, Jones announced to his closest confidants that he wanted to move the church to a safe zone to avoid nuclear fallout. This excuse is said to have been the reason for Jones resigning as Director of the Indianapolis Human Rights Commission (a position that he had been appoint to by Indianapolis Mayor Charles Boswell on January 6, 1961), and traveling abroad. However, at first, Jones did not act as if he took his own idea very seriously. One day from the pulpit, Jones shifted the blame for needing to move the church onto others, "while shooting a grin at his two assistants."

Although Tim Reiterman is by far Jones' best, most comprehensive biographer, even he made errors in documenting these mysterious years. Reiterman writes that Jones left for Hawaii by himself in late October of 1961, and later sent for his family. Escaping a nuclear holocaust by going to Hawaii would have been a ridiculous notion, considering the number of military installations there, including Pearl Harbor. It's doubtful that Jones was not well aware of this fact prior to his supposed trip there.

According to Reiterman's chronology, Jones stayed in Hawaii the remainder of 1961 and into 1962. He was there when he read an *Esquire* magazine article about "The nine safest places in the world to escape thermonuclear blasts and fallout." One of the places listed in the article was Belo Horizonte, Brazil. Soon after the article was published, according to Reiterman, Jones stopped over in California, and then told Ijames to meet him in Mexico City to brief him on Temple activities in his absence, before going to Georgetown, Guyana. However, this is not possible. *The Guyana Graphic* newspaper published a page seven article on October 25, 1961, which covers Jones' anti-communist speeches in Georgetown just days earlier.

A more accurate chronology may be seen as this: After traveling to Guyana in late October of 1961, Jones disappeared from public record altogether for about six months. Anthropologist

Kathleen Adams claims that Jones spent time as a missionary in the Northwest District of Guyana at some point. Although Adams does not indicate dates, it's safe to assume that it was during this six-month period for Jones. A close friend of the Jones family, Bonnie Malmin Thielman, claimed to have seen a picture of Jim and Marceline with Fidel Castro, which was allegedly taken during the winter of 1961-62, about six months after Jones' anti-communist speeches in Guyana, on his way to Brazil. The fact that Jones received a Cuban visa and met Fidel Castro after recently giving well-publicized anti-communist speeches raises many questions in and of itself, particularly in light of the Bay of Pigs incident in 1961, in the the U.S. – and more specifically, the CIA – launched an unsuccessful attempt to overthrow the Cuban government.

Passport Confusion?

Jim Jones had passport # 22898751 that was issued to him on June 28, 1960 in Chicago. The passport was still valid when another passport (#0111788) was issued to him on January 30, 1962, in Indianapolis. Why he was issued another passport when he already had a valid one is puzzling. Also, if Jones was already overseas, then who picked up the second passport in Indianapolis? Furthermore, the second passport has a lower number than the first. Researcher Jim Hougan believes that this is because Jim Jones had a double that was used to travel at the same time that he did—for unknown, covert reasons. Hougan believes that this is what caused confusion for Reiterman and others when trying to document these lost years.

Jones' Life of Luxury

According to Brazilian authorities, Jim, his wife Marceline, and their four children arrived at Sao Paulo, Brazil's financial capital on a commercial airliner on April 11, 1962. It's well known that Jim Jones came from a very poor family. It is also well known that Jones and his family lived in virtual squalor up to this point. However, the family initially checked into the expensive Financial Hotel. Later, the family moved into a large house at 203 Maraba Avenue, in the city's well-to-do Santo Antonio section. Reiterman seems to struggle with the affluence that Jones became accustomed to while in Brazil:

"Uncharacteristically, the Jones family wound up living in one of Rio's most prestigious neighborhoods, in a rented seventh-story apartment three blocks from Copacabana Beach." Reiterman explains that Jones maintained this lifestyle of living with the rich by taking on a job as a *"part-time English instructor at a university."*

It was well documented that his church back home was not doing well financially. The congregation that had once drawn nearly two thousand people had dwindled down to fewer than one hundred, and the pastors were having a hard time trying to generate the same interest that Jones had. The congregation as a whole felt abandoned by Jones, and they did not know if he was going to return. Despite Jones' pleas, they could barely support themselves, much less their traveling pastor.

Reiterman claims that Jones supplemented his income by becoming a "gigolo." Jones claimed that he had sex with women in exchange for donations to an orphanage where he worked. One woman allegedly donated a staggering $5,000 for Jones' sexual services, which would equate to an astounding $36,000 by 2008 standards. All this was said to have occurred with the consent of his wife Marceline. This would later appear to be validated when Jones made his many affairs—with both men and women—public, saying that he was doing it for the "cause." Marceline did, however, voice her discontent over Jones' extramarital affairs. This scenario that Reiterman gives for this time period appears to come mainly from Jones' own account of his stay in Brazil. Reiterman may well have been mocking the time period as explained by Jones for lack of more accurate information. There is no evidence that Jones was a gigolo in Brazil, other than the word of him and his wife. Realistically, Marceline had told much bigger lies to cover for her husband over the years. There is evidence of other, even less savory explanations for the source of Jones' wealth.

Brazilian Neighbors

Sebastiaco Carlos Rocha, a man who lived across the street from Jones, said that Jones would leave every morning at 6:00 a.m. with a leather briefcase, and return home around 7:00 p.m. Rocha and his family had many interactions with the Jones family. Rocha said that Jones told him that he was a retired U.S. Naval captain recuperating from the Korean War and that he was receiving monthly checks from the U.S. government for his military service. Several neighbors, including Rocha, said that they often witnessed a U.S. Consulate car in front of Jones' home. Many also said that they witnessed the person in the car regularly delivering groceries to the family. Rocha said that Jones "enjoyed a very expensive lifestyle."

The Rochas' teenage daughter, Maria, said that she spoke to Marceline, who gave a very different story for their stay in Brazil. Marceline told Maria that they were in Brazil because she was suffering from a lung abnormality and her doctor recommended a better climate for her. The Jones' daughter, Suzanne, told other neighbors that they were there to establish a branch of Peoples Temple. But Jones' real job may have been something else. Rocha's wife, Elza, a lawyer in Belo Horizonte who sometimes interpreted for Jones, recalled that her new neighbor told her that he had a job in Belo Horizonte proper, at Eureka Laundries. Sebastian Dias de Magalhaes—head of Industrial Relations for Eureka in 1962—said that Jones was not an employee of Eureka. Furthermore, Dias and two other Eureka employees said that "Jones lied in order to conceal what they believe was his work for the CIA."

Another Brazilian resident, Marco Aurelio, said that he was "absolutely certain that Jones was a spy." At the time, Marco was supposedly dating Joyce Beam, the daughter of Jack Beam, who himself was one of Jones' top lieutenants. Jack and his daughter had reportedly traveled to Brazil with the Joneses. Marco claimed that a detective in the ID-4 section of the local Brazilian PD ordered him to keep an eye on Jones. The detective was certain that Jones was CIA, according to Marco. However, the detective mysteriously died before the investigation could be completed. Jones left the country not long afterwards.

Dan Mitrione

Perhaps the most mysterious and dubious connection that Jim Jones had was his childhood friend, Dan Mitrione. The two met back in Richmond, Indiana, when Jones was a young boy preaching on street corners in a black neighborhood, and Mitrione was a Richmond Police Officer. Although Mitrione was a few years older, he took Jones under his wing. Mitrione later became Chief of the Richmond PD, and some say that he was the only reason that Jones did not get arrested and run out of town. Mitrione was later was recruited into the CIA, under State Department cover, in May of 1960, and was trained in counter-insurgency and torture techniques. Coincidentally, Mitrione had traveled to Brazil as an OPS adviser at the U.S. Consulate not long before Jones had arrived. A CIA file (201) was opened on Jim Jones at about that time. Although Jones later denied having any contact with Mitrione in Brazil, he did admit that he sought him out and actually met with Mitrione's family while there.

Manuel Hevia Conculluela worked for the CIA in Uruguay's police program. In 1970, his duties brought him in contact with Dan Mitrione in Montevideo. In his book, *Passporte 11333: Eight Years With the CIA*, which chronicles his CIA exploitations, Manuel wrote of the many pointers Mitrione gave him on how to torture and interrogate subjects. Former CIA agent John Stockwell wrote a book entitled, *The Praetorian Guard* in which he explained a particular CIA training session for new recruits. After watching various films and teaching various torture techniques, the recruits were sent out on kidnapping missions. Stockwell identifies Dan Mitrione as the teacher of this training session. According to Stockwell, Mitrione gave almost identical advice on how to torture suspects to his students as he gave to Manuel. Not long after Mitrione gave advice to Manuel, he was kidnapped by Tupermaro guerillas in Uruguay, interrogated and murdered. He was found dead in the back seat of a stolen car. Mysteriously, Jones' 201-file was purged by the CIA immediately after Mitrione was kidnapped and murdered in Montevideo, Uruguay. Whether or not Jim Jones was an apprentice of Dan Mitrione is not known, but there is a strong possibility based on the circumstances and their history.

A Bit of History

According to a report by Peter Gribbon, the United States was in a rush to consolidate its new role after WWII as the world's leader. In doing so, the U.S. government's primary focus was to contain certain countries that had begun to pursue an independent course of development during WWII. The U.S. government wanted to control these countries, and if and when change was to occur the U.S. government wanted the change to be ordered and implemented from Washington. In an effort to meet this objective, the establishment of powerful, centralized police forces in Asia, Africa, and especially Latin America became a top priority. In 1957, then U.S. President, Dwight D. Eisenhower, set up the Office of Public Safety (OPS), whose main objective was to train police forces of America's allies.

Among the many functions of the OPS two were allowing the CIA to plant men with the local police in sensitive places around the world; and after careful observation on their home territory, bringing to the United States prime candidates for enrollment as CIA employees. The Eisenhower administration made Byron Engle the director of the OPS and charged him with organizing a task force on international police training. Police-training teams were sent to South Vietnam, Iran, Taiwan, Brazil, Uruguay, and Greece. In the fall of 1961, just as Joao Goulart was taking over the presidency, the U.S. began an expanded incursion of CIA agents and into Brazil. Engle sent Public Safety advisers like Dan Mitrione to Brazil to "improve" the Brazilian police forces. Coincidentally, Jim Jones traveled to Brazil at the exact same time that Dan Mitrione was sent there by the CIA.

Blame it on Rio

It was reported by some that Jones would make frequent visits to the U.S. Consulate in Belo Horizonte. On October 18, 1962, Vice Consul, Jon Lodeesen, wrote a letter to Jones on Foreign Service stationary.

> *Dear Mr. Jones: We received a communication and we believe it's in your interest to come at the consulate at your earliest convenience. Please see me.*

The letter also had a picture attached to it of a man with a mustache, who some say looks strikingly similar to Jim Jones. Jim Hougan suggests that the letter had something to do with a second passport being issued to Jones while the first one was still valid. According to Soviet intelligence officers, Londeesen was a CIA agent who taught at the U.S. intelligence school in Garmisch Partenkirchen, West Germany. Coincidentally, Londeesen was recommended for work with a CIA cover in Hawaii, the "refuge" that Jones was said to have visited. Jones lived in Belo Horizonte for eight months. In mid-December of 1962, Jones moved 250 miles west to Rio de Janeiro, where he and his family resided at #154 Rua Senador Vigueiro in the Flamengo neighborhood. At the same time, Mitrione went to the U.S. on a two month vacation, and then found an apartment in the Botafogo section of Rio de Janeiro. According to Brazilian immigration authorities, Jones left Rio for an unknown country at the end of March of 1963, and never returned.

According to the *Brazil Herald* on December 24-26, 1978, Jones found a job as an investment salesman in Rio for a company called, Invesco, S.A. The company was American owned, and some have speculated, CIA owned. Jones' boss at Invesco, who asked the *Brazil Herald* to remain anonymous, confirmed Jones' employment with the company: "As a salesman with us, he [Jones] didn't make it. He was too shy and I don't remember him selling anything. We hired him on a strictly commission basis and as far as I know, he didn't sell anything in the three months that he worked for us." This is a shocking account of a man who sold monkeys door to door, had people refer to him as God, and supposedly talked more than 900

people into committing suicide. Certainly no one else had ever accused Jones of being diffident!

The Family

Jim and Marceline wanted to a big family. They started by adopting young *Agnes Pauline Jones* in 1954, who was partly of Native American decent. Jim had also encouraged his followers to adopt orphans from war-ravaged Korea. Jim was highly critical of the United States' opposition of North Korea's 1950, invasion of South Korea. Jones called the invasion the "war of liberation," stating that "the south is a living example of all that socialism in the north has overcome."

In accordance with this philosophy, the couple adopted two Korean children in 1958: *Lew Eric Jones* and *Stephanie Jones*. Unfortunately, on May 11, 1959, Stephanie Jones and five other Temple members were killed in car accident. Also in 1959, the couple adopted another Korean child, six-year-old, *Suzanne O. Jones*. And, in June of 1959, the couple bore their only natural born child, whom they named *Stephan Gandhi Jones*. Then, in 1961, Jim and Marceline became the first White couple in Indiana to adopt a Black child, when they adopted 10-month-old, *James Warren Jones Jr*. The couple also adopted, Timothy Glen Tuppe, whose mother was a Temple member, and they changed his name to *Timothy Glen Jones*.

CHAPTER 4 – THE GREAT DEFECTOR

Deborah Layton

As the youngest of four children, Debbie Layton grew up knowing little about her parents' troubled marriage. She felt most comfortable with her father (Dr. Laurence Laird Layton Sr.) who frequently praised her. Her mother (Lisa Philip Layton), however, remained a mystery to her throughout her childhood. Debbie was the product of a very affluent family. They lived in the Berkeley Hills, a range of the Pacific Coast Ranges that overlooks the northeast side of the valley that encompasses the San Francisco Bay. Debbie never seemed to get the necessary attention that she craved, which later led to her becoming a troubled teen. Debbie's Mother Lisa was a Jewish woman who had survived one of Hitler's concentration camps back in Germany several years earlier. However, Debbie grew up not knowing she was Jewish, because her mother did not want her to endure the persecution that she had experienced years earlier. Debbie seemed to be the odd one out of her siblings. The others were scholarly, attentive, and obedient. Meanwhile, Debbie was none of these things. While her siblings went off to college, Debbie became a wild child, displaying her loneliness and anger in destructive activities. Consequently, her parents had a very hard time dealing with her, which led to many alternative ways of supervision. Ironically, this rebellious adolescence would serve her well in the future and ultimately save her life at age twenty-five.

As Debbie became a well-endowed teenager, she grew increasingly argumentative and rebellious. The contrast between Debbie and her siblings became increasingly noticeable in 1968, when her brother Tom passed his Ph.D., qualifying exams at Harvard; her sister Annalisa married a Biochemistry Professor; and her brother Larry had joined Peoples Temple doing humanitarian work. Needless to say, Debbie was feeling like the black sheep of the family. Unwilling to emulate the achievements of her siblings, she became even more unruly and uncontrollable. Formerly the teacher's pet, her grades steadily plummeted. She soon found herself a frequent visitor of detention, where she quickly became friends with the "bad kids." During this time she also began to feel compassion for the less fortunate and the underdogs. The final straw for her parents was when they found a letter she had written to her older boyfriend chronicling her escalating drug usage (Mescaline & speed). Debbie's parents were forced to make a decision about her future. Larry's college sweetheart and new wife, Carolyn Moore Layton, suggested that Debbie go live with her parents in Davis, California where she would also attend high school (tenth grade). Both parents agreed and Debbie was sent packing from her beautiful mansion in the hills.

It was at this point that Debbie became good friends with Carolyn's little sister, Annie Moore, who was a year younger than Debbie. Annie was quiet, sweet, and studious; much the opposite of Debbie. Still, the two became fast friends. However, even with that friendship Debbie was unable to stay out of trouble. After several troubling incidents she was soon headed back home. But this did not last long either; and after she tripped on acid while at school, it was apparent that something dramatic needed to be done with her. After a long decision making process, her parents decided to send her to boarding school in England where she would live with her aunt, Ruth. After two-years in England, she met a popular *bloke* named Mark Blakey. Mark was a good kid and well behaved. The two started dating soon after they met; but even this could not keep Debbie out of trouble. She continued to gravitate towards the outsiders and rejects of the school and began smoking dope. While in boarding school, she did not have access to the same drugs that she was using in the states. Instead of mescaline and speed she drank cough medicine to get high. Her rebelliousness soon caught up with her in England as well, and she found herself constantly quarreling with teachers. It all came to a head when her English Literature schoolmaster accused her of "bastardizing Shakespeare" with her accent and finally expelling her from school for chewing gum. After getting kicked out of boarding school and a brief stint in the hospital for putting her fist through a window, Debbie's parents agreed to let her come home for a six-week break.

Just before returning home, Debbie received a letter from her brother Larry. Little did she know that her destiny was contained within the contents of the letter. In the letter, Larry wrote of a man named Jim Jones and Peoples Temple that he had been involved with. He spoke of Jones as a holy man who knew of her troubles and wanted to meet her. Debbie was skeptical and soon her thoughts wandered to rehabilitating her arm. At about four weeks into her break, she started getting restless and was anxious to see Larry and the man who "knew everything," as Larry had stated in the letter. Her parents were reluctant, however. In the three years since Larry had joined the church, he had visited his parents only once.

Larry and Carolyn

Larry had married his college sweetheart Carolyn Moore in 1967. After they graduated in 1968, Carolyn went on to become a teacher and Larry was seeking a *conscientious objector appeal* to get out of the Vietnam War draft. One day, Carolyn heard a Jim Jones sermon. During that sermon, Jones criticized the war along with other social injustices. Carolyn then brought Larry to hear the flamboyant speaker, and soon after the newlyweds became members. Jones had helped Larry get out of going into the war by helping him write his appeal. Jones took an uncanny liking to Carolyn in particular, as she did for him. Carolyn soon became a "close working comrade" of Jones. No one was aware at the time, but it's easy to see now what Jones' motivation was with the couple. Jones stopped at nothing to get what he wanted and was very cunning about how to do so. During one particular meeting, Jones announced publicly that he had observed a rift between Carolyn and Larry. Larry agreed and announced that Carolyn had grown cold lately; to which Carolyn surprisingly asked for a divorce. Little did Larry know at the time that the reason Carolyn had grown cold was because she was secretly in love with Jim; as was Jim with her.

Larry was in shock, but Jim knew how to cover his tracks. Jones soon introduced Larry to one of his devoted followers. She was a former homecoming queen named Karen. Surely enough they hit it off and started dating. Carolyn and Larry's divorce was final six-months later. The miracle worker had sinisterly struck again! To add to the madness, Larry and Karen married soon after that! Instead of Jones being looked at as the charlatan that he was for steeling Larry's wife, he was looked on as a redeemer, a cupid. No one knew at the time that Jones had a covert relationship with Carolyn. They kept their relationship secret for sometime; though soon many began speculating, as the two were spending a lot of time together.

Jones had an insatiable and salacious appetite for sex and had begun to have sex with men and women. However, his sex drive was not as strong as his need for power. Sex became just another way for him to achieve that power and control. Most of his power trips came out of a lacking of some sort; in his case, insecurity. Yet, Jim and Carolyn had a very special relationship, and Jim would later be quoted as saying that Carolyn is the only woman he ever truly loved. During Jones's long sermons, which lasted for hours, Carolyn would go as far as holding a urinal below the podium so that he could relieve himself while still sermonizing. Jones soon became dependant on Carolyn, who assisted him in many different ways.

Carolyn believed, as many followers did, that Jones was the reincarnation of Jesus. Then they believed he was reincarnated as Ali Muhammad [the Persian Religious leader who founded *Bábism* in the nineteenth century]; and then they believed that he was the reincarnation of Vladimir Lenin [Russian communist revolutionary, politician and political theorist]. Jones had Carolyn under the impression that she was the reincarnation of Inessa Armand [French communist politician and feminist known for allegedly having an affair with Lenin]. Jones also informed everyone that Marceline was often ill and could not keep up with Jim's sexual needs. This basically meant that Carolyn had taken over most of Marceline's duties, including sex.

Debbie meets Jones

Accompanied by her new sister-in-law, Karen, Debbie's first encounter with the church came when she was just a confused 17 year-old-girl. As Jones preached, she felt as though he was speaking directly to her. She was immediately taken in by his soothing voice and striking appearance. Jones spoke of the injustices in the world, such as discrimination and segregation, as if it was a weight that he was himself carrying. After the service she stood on a long line to meet the mysterious Jim Jones. She witnessed the frenzy that accompanied Jones that included the breaking into song and chants of "yes god, thank you Jim."

As she finally stepped up to introduce herself, she was immediately humbled by Jones' intimidating aura. In Jones' grand fashion—as if he'd been waiting for Debbie all his life—he made her feel like she was needed in the church. Using his fortune-telling-trickery, warm caring words, charm, and well spoken manner; he swooned Debbie, making her feel like she was a necessary part of the group. Debbie tried using her parents as an excuse, claiming that they wanted her to return to England for her last year of high school. She emphasized that she would have to talk it over with them. Jones attacked this point in a divide-and-conquer effort. He put down her parents, telling her that they don't appreciate her enough. He assured her that not only would she be appreciated with him and his congregation, but that she would grow and develop under his tutelage and nurturing.

Jones referred to himself as coming from a "higher stage of development" and claimed to "know things that no other man could know." Clearly by this time, Jones was well practiced in the art of manipulation and his megalomania was if full effect. He had also mastered the art of persuasion. Jones could make anyone feel like they were the center of his attention, and it was usually troubled people like Debbie that he made quick work of. More importantly, Jones made people who felt worthless feel like they had a plethora of things to offer the world; and most importantly, that he could help them reach their potential. He made people believe that they did not even know the depths of their own talents and that his vision for the future was deeper than anyone could understand at the time. The effect of this was that it made individuals immediately trust him. It bought him time to suck people in. We are all creatures of habit and Jones preyed on these human traits. "Without your spirit among us, we will not be as effective," Jones said to Debbie. Debbie was still trying to find herself, and it would be an understatement to say that Jones instilled a sense of purpose into those still searching for one.

Not surprisingly, Debbie was buzzing as she left the church and headed home. She decided to return to England and finish her last year of high school. She was also excited to get back and see her boyfriend, Mark Blakey. Debbie just as well figured that Jim Jones would just forget about her anyway. While back in England she told

Mark all about her meeting with Jones and how he appeared so genuinely intrigued with her. Contrary to Debbie's belief, Jones did not forget about her. Instead, he started a relentless letter writing campaign, reinforcing that she was needed at the church and that they were waiting for her. Jones' lure was magnetic and instilled a real sense of purpose into Debbie. She now had the direction that she so desperately had longed for. Jones' relentlessness payed-off and Debbie decided to return to the church the following year.

Mark decided to take the opportunity to spend his summer break with Debbie, and returned with her to California. Mark had no intention on staying in California, but Jim took a particular liking to him. Jones expressed that Mark was "leadership material," and soon gave him additional responsibilities, prepping him for a leadership role. Consequently, Mark's mother was furious when he did not return home after break, and she soon made her way to America to retrieve her son. Upon Mrs. Blakey's arrival, she was immediately catered to by Jones and his staff. Jim was determined to keep Mark with him. Tim and Grace Stoen (two devout Temple members who would later be "responsible" for all hell breaking loose) invited her to stay at their home, and they waited on her hand and foot. Eventually, they wore her down and won her over. They convinced her that Mark was in the right place. She soon returned to Northumberland alone. Jones had successfully thwarted Mrs. Blakey's attempt to take her son, and amazingly she did so willingly. To avoid Mark from being deported, Jones arranged for Debbie and Mark to be married.

Trouble Brewing

By 1972, Jones was holding and running several properties. Their church properties included Christian Science Church building in Los Angeles, San Francisco Peoples Temple, and a Temple in Ukiah with a 41-foot indoor swimming pool. The church also owned a 40-acre children's-home, 3 convalescent centers, and 3 college dormitories. They also ran a heroin rehabilitation center and also boasted that they had their own welfare system.

By this time the Temple had started to outgrow the small church bulletins and Jones began mentioning a need for a church magazine or newspaper. Some of his members overheard the preacher's desire and they hustled to help put together what they could for Jones. They worked late hours, using whatever printing presses that they could get their hands on. Finally, in July of 1972, they had put together the first issue of *The Living World*. Not long after, the Temple purchased its own printing press and set up a corporate venture that they entitled *Valley Enterprises*. Jones used several members that had graduated college to work full-time on the paper. By the fall of 1973, the church launched the *Peoples Forum* newspaper, which didn't take long to grow into a circulation of tens of thousands of readers, all in the San Francisco are.

Yet, amidst all of this success, Jones and his followers were facing a new threat. In September of 1972, Lester Kinsolving, an Episcopal priest and religious editor for the *San FranciscoExaminer,* was the first to give Jones and his church a scathing review. Kinsolving's review was detailed in an eight-part series of articles that documented allegations of physical abuse, financial misdeeds, and suspect theology within Peoples Temple. The first came on the 17th of September and was titled *"The Prophet Who Raises the Dead."* The article centered on a report in the church's news letter that made the bold claim that Jones had raised a Los Angeles man from the dead. Kinsolving also referenced a Temple director's claim that Jones had raised more than 40 persons from the dead. Four articles in total were published and four more were slated for release. Outraged, Temple members wrote letters to the editor of the *Examiner* and picketed the newspaper's office in protest. As a result, the *Examiner* dropped the final four articles. One of the four unpublished articles, entitled *"The People's Temple and Maxine Harpe,"* implied that the Temple was responsible for the death of former Temple member, Maxine Harpe (whose death was ruled a suicide). The other unpublished articles reported that Temple members were punished in group meetings for crimes against the church, noting the example of a young boy being forced to eat his own vomit.

1973 – Rise of the Planning Commission (PC)

By this time, Carolyn had become a very powerful influence in the church. She was literally second in command, next to Jim. The manipulation soon started to escalate, as Jones was informing his members that if they left the church they would be reincarnated as the lowest form of life and that it would take one-hundred-thousand-years to get back to their current form. Sex was also off-limits. This included married couples. Jones believed that temptations of the flesh were selfish and made people weak and unable to focus on their duties. Another controlling technique was to pronounce all men "homosexuals." Jim, of course, would single himself out as the only exception. Just another attempt by Jones to affirm that he was the only real man; hence, bringing all the other males down while lifting himself.

Jones demanded much from his true members. Not only were Jones' recruitment efforts relentless, but his loyal "core" members were as well, which consisted of 400 members. Every other Friday night the group would take eleven buses on a ten-hour drive to L.A. There, the members would spend their twelve-hour days standing on street corners, handing out pamphlets, and requesting donations. In the summer of 1973, the younger members were bused into the ghettos of Chicago, Kansas City, Los Angeles, Vancouver, and Seattle to recruit the less fortunate and announce Jones' impending appearance. Jones was consciously expanding his operation and quickly building a national army of supporters. Spreading the word also consisted of informing people that they were building a new commune in the jungle of South America where all would be housed, fed, clothed, and taken care of.

The true elite members numbered only a few, up until this point. When it came to big decision, Jones counted on votes from Carolyn Moore, Jack Beam, Sharon (Linda) Amos, Timothy Stoen, Marceline, and Mike Cartmell. However, Jones wanted to formalize a board of directors, of sorts, for the church. He wanted a group of his most trusted, which had been expanding slowly, to handle the tough decisions. In doing so he created *The Planning Commission* (PC).

The PC consisted of the most trusted members and was the exclusive governing body of Peoples Temple. Eventually, they numbered about 37 members. Being part of this group meant being part of the Temple's elite. The group discussed and formed decisions regarding every aspect of the church. The PC members had exclusive meetings held on Wednesdays from 8:00 p.m., to 4:00 p.m., and on Saturdays and Sundays from 6:00 p.m., to 2:00 a.m.

Sunday morning at 10:00 a.m., the public service would begin and last until about 4:00p.m. The public meetings were the regular services—the ones where all members could attend. When that service was completed they would all cram into the buses and head back to Ukiah. Many of the members had jobs during the week and would resume their regular schedules on Monday morning. During the week there were two night meetings that members were required to attend: the Monday night socialist meetings and the Wednesday night teach-ins. In 1973, Debbie was appointed to the PC. Mark had been appointed to the PC a year before Debbie.

Perhaps the most important decision that the PC would ever make came on October 8, 1973, when Jim Jones put before them a vote whether or not to establish a branch church and agricultural mission in Guyana, South America. The PC voted unanimously in favor of the mission.

The Toxic Vicar

During one service in 1973 Jim made a bizarre announcement: "I have had a revelation that something strange might happen tonight. No Matter what happens, I don't want anyone to call an ambulance." As the sermon continued, one of the older members, Pinky, collapsed in the rear of the building. Not hearing Jim's earlier announcement, Marceline called 911. As the sirens blared outside the church, the paramedics entered and put Pinky on a stretcher. This was in the back of the building and out of site of those in attendance of the ongoing service. As the paramedics carried Pinky's near lifeless body to the ambulance, Jim heard the sirens and shouted for his guards to go and bring her back inside. The guards ran outside and stopped the men just as they were about to load Pinky into the ambulance. As the altercation got heated, one of the paramedics called the police on his CB radio.

Things only got worse when the police arrived. A fight broke out between police and Temple guards. One of the guards struck one of the police officers and broke his nose. Amidst the chaos, one of the guards managed to grab Pinky off of the stretcher and carry her back into the church. Meanwhile, Marceline had run outside in an effort to stop the fighting. By the time the police were able to regain control of the scene, Marceline and two Temple guards were placed under arrest. No one inside the church knew what was going on outside, and they all sat in wonderment, waiting for Jim to inform them. After the police had left, Jones got back behind the podium and revealed that Pinky was in the back doing fine. Jones claimed that he healed Pinky with his powers. Later, Jim went down to the police station and was also arrested for angering one of the officers. They were all soon released and nothing ever came of the incident. It was obvious to several members that Jones had Pinky poisoned so that he could revive her publicly. Another Jones scam, this time, it almost went horribly wrong. If Pinky had been taken away in the ambulance, it would have surely led to an investigation, after tests would have revealed that she was poisoned.

Jim always appeared to be one step ahead of everyone, even the authorities. But did he have help in this effort? Every member was told over and over that the end justifies the means. Of all the different member accounts, this, among other things, remains consistent. Jones was a fan of Malcolm X and his "by any means necessary" credo. Apparently, so was the CIA. There are many similarities between Jim Jones' methods of "torture" and the CIA's. By 1973, Jones had become increasingly hostile and disciplinary towards the congregation. Several members had begun to get antsy; many began to question Jones' methods, secretly of course, as well as their own involvement with the church.

There are several known instances of Jones drugging people to enforce his control, or what he so eloquently called, "for the cause." Another instance involved a woman who brought her nine year old troubled son, Anthony, to Jim for help. Anthony was in a Los Angeles gang and was known to frequently steel things. At one Saturday night disciplinary session, Jones called Anthony up to the podium. When Jones confronted the child about his steeling, the boy vehemently admitted that he enjoyed steeling and tried to undermine Jim's authority. Jones told the boy that he could strike him dead right there on the spot with his powers, but the boy was not impressed. Jones made a few more attempts to scare Anthony, but he stood his ground and remained unfazed. Jones methodically called one of his henchmen over and quietly whispered in his ear. The man soon returned with a glass of water, which Jones then instructed the boy to drink, as he continued on with the session. As the boy drank the water, Jones warned him several more times that he could strike him dead. Still unimpressed, the boy responded, "Go ahead!"

As the mild poison in the water took effect the boy soon dropped to the ground, unconscious. The next day at a PC meeting the boy was laid out on the floor, where he continued to slip in and out of consciousness. Every time the boy awoke momentarily, the PC members would moan and groan, at Jones' instruction, as if they were suffering. Jones told the boy that he had awoken in hell and that he [Jim] was the devil. Overwhelmed, the boy continued slipping in and out of consciousness, as Jones repeated this dreadful exercise. The next day, fully conscious, Anthony said that he had a strange dream about hell, and he said ardently that he would never steel again. Jones' cunning and "by any means" philosophy was not to be underestimated. Jones would go to great lengths to win over his audience and his test subjects. He would never be made a fool of in front of his congregation. He always had a plan for divergent voices, and it always involved some form of degradation.

During one Sunday service Jim realized that there was not enough food to feed the multitude of followers that were on-hand. It appeared that the last fifty or so people online were not going to get any of the food that was quickly being dispersed. Jones stood up and announced that he was going to bless the food as Jesus did in biblical times and through some "miracle" have more food. Miraculously, minutes later, Eva Pugh (Temple member) came out of the kitchen with a large amount of fried chicken. One member, Chuck Beikman, spoke softly to another member that he had seen Eva driving up moments earlier with buckets of *Kentucky Fried Chicken*. "The person that blessed this chicken was Colonel Sanders," Chuck said facetiously to the other member.

Jones must have either overheard Chuck's comment or been told about it, because later that evening at a Temple meeting Jones made mention of the incident. Pointing at Chuck, Jones said, "He lied to some of the members here, telling them that the chicken had come from a local shop, but the Spirit of Justice has prevailed. Because of his lie Chuck is in the men's room right now wishing that he was dead. He is vomiting and has diarrhea so bad he can't talk!" About an hour later Chuck came out of the bathroom carried by a Temple guard and addressed Jones. "Jim, I apologize for what I said. Please forgive me." Chuck would never question Jones again, at least not out loud. Temple member, Jeannie Mills, would later come to find out and explain in her book, *Six Years With God*, that Jones had given Chuck a piece of cake after putting a mild poison in it.

Sex in Peoples Temple

In 1973, Debbie and Annie were late for one particular Wednesday night meeting. The meeting was already in session when they arrived. They quickly settled in and took a seat on the floor. Jim was in the middle of scolding a member when they entered. When he was done, Jim said, "I want the person who begged me for sex and threatened suicide to stand. You know who you are." As Debbie looked around the room, she wondered what was wrong with these dumb women who couldn't control their desires. Jim began to grow increasingly angry as no one stood up to take their respective punishment, and he continued to call-out the unnamed woman. Suddenly and without warning, young Annie stood up and accepted her plight with a look of devastation. Debbie's jaw dropped and she could not believe that young, innocent Annie (her closest friend) could have done this. Debbie was outraged, as were the others. All the women in the room sneered at her as she announced how good of a lover Jones was and how much he helped her. Debbie and Annie grew apart from that point on. Debbie was disgusted with Annie after that and steered clear of her.

In 1974, the mission to Guyana became the main focus of the church. The PC began to focus all their efforts on planning for their emigration. Each member was given specific things to research about Guyana for purposes of prior planning and consideration. Yet, as Jones planned on expanding his operations, he also began acting more bizarre. The PC meetings in general were becoming more and more bizarre as Jones began to convey his uncontrollable narcissistic behavior and sexually adolescent crux.

During a Monday night PC session, a member named Clifford fell asleep. This was highly frowned upon by Jones, even though no one knew that he was taking uppers and other drugs to stay awake. Clifford's mishap was brought to Jim's attention and an ugly scene ensued. Jones asked Clifford's wife, Clarese, if he acts like that at home. Taking Jim's side, Clarese said that he did. As Jim and Clarese proceeded to publicly berate Clifford, she surprisingly blurted out that he does not like to give oral sex, because he thinks it's vulgar. "He doesn't like pussy," Jones asked. "Well I wonder if he'll like some Black pussy?" Jones then called a shy Black woman named Alice up to the front and told Clifford to give her oral sex on the table in front of all the other PC members.

Alice was frozen stiff and did not know what to do. Jones continued to coax Alice until another Black woman named Tami rescued her from sure persecution. "I'm on my period Jim," Tami said. "I'll give Clifford some bloody Black pussy." Tami jumped up on the table, took her pants down, tampon out, and spread her legs. Clifford denied vehemently as Jones taunted him to do the horrifying deed. Others started chanting "racist, racist, racist...," as Clifford pleaded with Jones not to make him do it. However, Jones was not a merciful man when it came to his orders. You either obeyed, or you were seen as disloyal. Finally defeated and appearing stripped of all his dignity, Clifford went up and angrily began licking Tami's vagina hard. The nightmare was soon over, as Jones ordered him to stop. Clifford was so embarrassed that he ran out of the room. Jones truly seemed to get-off on this type of public display of control.

The public embarrassment and abuse was not restricted just to Jones' orders. His most trusted officials were also exhibiting and picking up traits from their leader. Jones had purchased three apartments in Santa Rosa, California for college students to reside while attending the junior college there. Jim had assigned several counselors to assist the students every Tuesday night, as the problems with the students were becoming too much for Jim to handle. The counseling sessions consisted of all counselors at once confronting one student at a time. During the first counseling session, Jim's assistant minister, Jack Beam, was questioning one of the students as to why her grades were declining. The child claimed that she was not getting much sleep, because her schedule between church and school was beginning to wear her down. Jack quickly caught the girl off guard, changing the conversation to sex. He accused the girl of wanting sex from her sister, claiming that was the reason for the lack of focus on her school work. Confused, the girl denied the ridiculous accusations; but Jack would not let it go. Much like his mentor, Jack was determined to get a confession from her. "Now tell us what you want to do to her breasts," he said. "Do you want to suck on them? Do you want to suck on her vagina?" Jack continued until he forced the girl (unwillingly, and even though it wasn't true) to graphically describe sexual acts that she allegedly wanted to perform with her sister.

Jim had a personal secretary, Patty Cartmell, who acted as a mediator or a go-between for Jim and the other members that wanted to have sex with him. More realistically would be to say that it was truly set up for Jones to pick the women that he wanted to have sex with. During one Wednesday night PC meeting, Jones stood up and began to tell a story about all the sacrifices that he had to make for the cause. He explained that several years earlier he and Marceline had run out of money and didn't know what to do. Jim claimed that several politicians wives' had offered him money to have sex with them. After talking it over with Marceline, they decided it was a good idea. One woman agreed to give Jones $5,000 to spend the night, and Jones went through with it...claiming, "I gave her-her money's worth that night." Incidentally, while he was telling this story, Marceline was sitting nearby. Marceline looked painfully stunned as Jones made this public announcement, and she stood up to make an announcement of her own.

> *"It's true that I have had to share my husband in the past, for the Cause. It was always painful for me because I love him very much, and just like everyone else, it's painful for me to see the person I love with someone else..."*

As her speech continued on, the pain in her eyes was clearly evident. Later in the meeting, Jones insensitively announced that Patty was scheduling make-up sessions with any members that wanted to have sex with him to "learn to relate to the cause." Jokingly he called Patty his "fucking secretary."

By 1974, Jim was going through several noticeable physical changes. He gained weight, dyed his hair black to hide the grays, and even penciled in sideburns to make them look fuller. Jim was certainly aware of these changes and he grew increasingly more self-conscious with time. His true self-image was clashing even more with his superior ideal-self. This began to noticeably affect Jones during the public church services. Jim felt that he needed to re-assure his congregation that he was still the *superior male*. As with any other society or group, for the leader to remain effective, he/she must continue to portray a status quo or position of strength. Any sign of weakness or decline of strength could result in a decline in morale and perception of its leader. Jones was well aware of this. But instead of handling this in a self-assured, mature way, he handled it in an adolescent, destructive manner.

Jones' sexual inadequacies and ugly sexual displays—which were exclusive to the PC meetings at first —were soon introduced to the rest of the church at the public services. By this time Jones' homosexuality was only known by the PC members. During one PC meeting he told the members that he was going to announce it to the rest of the church at the next public service. In doing so, Jim made sure that he was not the one embarrassed in the ordeal. At the following Sunday service, Jones spoke of one of the Temple guards, Randy. Jones claimed that Randy had begged him for sex, something Jones maintained was "completely foreign" to his "natural desires." Jones declared that Randy was not clean when he had anal sex with him and should have at least "taken an enema" before begging him for sex. It was a very big announcement and one that the congregation was not ready for. But in true Jones fashion he found a way to make himself look like he was doing Randy a favor. Jones never made it seem as if he was doing anything for personal pleasure or personal gain. It was all for others and for the cause.

Jones began to incorporate sex more and more into the services. His humble cover was slowly shedding, and revealed was a full-blown mad man. It was at this point that Jones felt as if he could do and say whatever he wanted and his people would accept it. He was now free of hiding behind his most trusted members at the PC meetings. Needless to say, this was only the beginning. Jones had taken his lewd sexual exhibitions from private meetings with his most trusted to the public meetings filled with children and elders. Eventually, this would wear heavily on the congregation; and this, along with the continued physical and mental abuse, would eventually catch up with him.

Jim continually promulgated that "every man wants a dick up his ass and every women wants to eat pussy." He was also known to claim that he had the biggest penis of any man. Few ever challenged Jones and those who did eventually found themselves in the middle of some type of humiliating ritual. He once professed, "If you think you know how to make love, show us. You fuck your wife and I'll fuck mine and we'll see who's able to do it longer and better." No one would ever accept this challenge. Everything always came back to or was in the name of the "cause."

Debbie Layton had the extreme displeasure of having sex with Jones. She described two particular experiences. Debbie confirms that Jones was publicly boasting to over compensate for the fact that he was a less than adequate lover. Debbie's first sexual encounter with Jones occurred while on the infamous number seven-bus; the bus that Jones and his most faithful rode in. As the rest of the passengers were falling asleep, Jones moved into the seat next to Debbie and began whispering of his desire for her. Debbie was stunned as Jones began fondling her breasts and massaging her thighs; just as shocking was the smell of the alcohol on his breath. Paralyzed by fear and shock, Debbie felt "defeated" and wanted to "beg him to stop," but fear of his wrath was overwhelming.

In her head she tried to make sense of this, but things happened so fast and she was in a very compromising position. After further secret fondling, Jones told her that he was going to order everyone off of the bus to exercise at the next rest stop. He told Debbie to stay on the bus as the others exit then sneak into his private compartment and wait for him there. Jones went ahead with his plan and Debbie pretended to be sleeping as the others exited the bus. With her mind racing and thoroughly confused, she snuck into Jim's private quarters.

Jones had a customized, private compartment in the back of the bus that the church mechanics had built for him. It was equip with a soft bed, a refrigerator, a small table with chairs, and a door for privacy. The passengers soon returned and the bus moved onward. Jones soon entered the room and immediately said, "Please unbutton your shirt." Seeing Debbie's reaction after his momentarily insensitive words, Jones tried to console her as he led her to the bed and continued disrobing her. "Please don't be afraid" he murmured. "I am doing this for your own good." Without any kissing, he got on top of her and thrust his penis into her vagina. Numb, traumatized, and wondering how she got into this position, Debbie smelt a "ghastly" smell coming from Jones' body. Just as soon as it began, it was over. Jones cordially got up, put his clothes back on in silence, and covertly snuck Debbie back to her seat. Jones' true persona and sexual prowess was a far cry from his supercilious, ostentatious promulgations.

As Debbie drove home after the episode, her thoughts were racing. She remembered the incident that had occurred over a year before with Annie at the Wednesday night meeting. She began to feel a sense of guilt that she had not been close with Annie since the incident. Things were starting to become clearer. Jim Jones was preying on several women in the church, sexually. After another sexual encounter with Jones in a bathroom, Debbie was promoted and sent back to San Francisco. Her mother, Lisa, had recently joined the church. But when Debbie refused sex with him the next time, Jones was furious and wanted retribution. Soon, it was Debbie's turn to stand up and face the music.

At a meeting soon after her refusal, Jones made the dreaded announcement, calling out another member that begged him for sex. At first, Debbie was not aware that Jones was speaking of her; but soon, that frightening feeling came over her and the knot in her stomach informed her that it was, indeed, her. As Debbie stood up and announced how great Jones was in bed and how many orgasms that she had, she thought of Annie, Sharon, Jan, Teresa, Sandy, Karen, Laura, and all the others who'd made the same pronouncements before. Only at that moment did she truly realize that those women were the prey of Jones and not the pursuers. After the meeting Debbie was thoroughly ashamed of herself. As she embarrassingly walked away, Annie gently kissed her on the forehead and walked away. Annie had felt her pain and she knew that Debbie had just felt hers.

Jones' announcements and "sex-capades" continued. During one PC meeting he spoke of "fucking" a man named Oscar. Jones claimed that Oscar smelled like he hadn't showered in a week and that he gave him some sort of rash. Jones made Oscar strip naked in the meeting, spread his ass cheeks apart, and had other men inspect the area for a rash. Sooner or later Jones made every PC member that he had sex with stand up; which numbered about 20 of the 32 members.

The Peoples Punching Bag

Jim's merciless abuse continued to escalate with time and played out in a public arena for all members to see. One incident took place as college student, Kathy Stahl, was accused of eating too much at the college cafeteria. Jones called Kathy up to the stage and asked her why she thought that she should have more food than others. After a verbal brow beating, Jones decided that Kathy's punishment was to strip down to only her underwear to show how fat she had become. After that, Kathy was sent to the back and pushed into the deep end of the pool. She then shamefully gathered herself and fell back into her place in the crowd. "I tried *to rule* with love, but people took advantage of that," Jones said in a hostile voice. "The only thing that people understand is fear." Looking back, this was a philosophy that Jones had with every person that he was ever close to. His only concern was "*to rule*." He just found the most efficient and effective way to do so.

As Jones became more violent and abusive with his congregation, his attorney's grew more and more concerned about the possible, and inevitable, legal implications. One of Jim's attorneys, Gene Chaikin, wrote up a release form that members were to sign before being disciplined. If the child being disciplined was under 18-years old then the parents would be expected to sign for them. Jones was now legally free to hand out beatings at will with no fear of reprisal. After this, Jones began to formalize the disciplinary sessions. He had a one-by-four-inch thick custom-made wooden board with a handle carved into it for spankings. A 250 pound woman named, Ruby Carroll, was assigned to perform the beatings, assisted by two guards whose jobs were to hold down the victims during the assaults.

One of the worst beatings, by far, was that of sixteen-year-old, Linda Mills—particularly considering the "offense." Linda was seen hugging her girl-friend. The problem was that Jim regarded this girl-friend as a traitor. Jim considered Linda's friend an outsider, because she only came to the church when she felt like it. Jones called Linda up to the front and ordered for her to receive *seventy-five* smacks with the newly acquired whacking board. He then asked Jeannie Mills (the girl's mother) if she agreed that the punishment was adequate. Jeannie knew that she had no choice but to comply with Jones. Jeannie and Al Mills sat in utter and complete horror as their daughter was held down and savagely beaten by her "friends." After every ten-lashes Ruby was ordered to pause to give Linda a few seconds to collect herself. Jones counted off all seventy-five whacks with nearly everyone standing in sheer terror. The monstrosity they were witnessing was unprecedented, even for Jones. Tears ran down the faces of members who were close to the Mills family. As the count paused at sixty Jeannie felt like she was going to throw up. Her thoughts of leaving the church and never returning were solidifying with each whack.

After the almost relieving seventy-fifth whack, Linda was handed the microphone, which she then thanked Jones publicly for disfiguring her bottom. Then, Sharon Amos (perhaps Jones' most trusted and loyal members) led Jeannie and Al into the kitchen area where Temple attorney, Gene Chaikin, handed them a stack of papers to sign. Collectively, the papers were a *release form* explaining that Jeannie and Al asked Jones to have Linda whipped. Forced once again to adhere to orders, they both signed the papers as their hands shook profusely. As they drove home with Linda in the back seat, no one spoke a word. Linda could not sit on her bottom, and later her bottom was described by Jeannie as looking like a hamburger. This was the straw that broke the camel's back for the Mills family. It was at that point that Jeannie and Al Mills decided to leave the church, for good.

Between the drugs and alcohol (mostly the drugs), Jones was becoming more and more of an emotional and psychological mess. He was having a hard time keeping it together. Not a very rational thinking man to begin with, he was now clouded by drugs and a continuing sleep disorder. Jones knew that he could not beat the elderly members physically, so *fear* became his greatest weapon for controlling them. He constantly told the members that concentration camps were being built to torture, rape, and murder the Blacks in America. If they left the church, he claimed that he could not protect them. Jones would reiterate this several times throughout the Jonestown era.

The Planning for Jonestown (1973 – 1976)

With help from the planning commission, it was official in October of 1973, that Jones and his congregation were going to attempt to acquire property in Guyana, South America in order to establish a branch of the church there. They had planned to continue operations in the United States as well, but the Guyana Mission, from what was known publically to church members, was going to house most of the congregation. In late December of 1973, Jones, Marceline, their sons, and about a dozen of the most trusted members stepped off of a plane at Mathews Ridge airstrip in Guyana, located about 130 miles from the capital city of Georgetown.

The group was met at the airstrip by Guyanese official, Emerson Mitchell, who was there to take them on a tour of the area and who had been ordered by his superiors to take good care of them. According to Tim Reiterman, the Guyanese saw the prospective move as a benefit to their country. Jones offered $2 million for the settlement, which was speculative because the Temple reported their grand total income as $396,000 for the year ending June 30, 1972, and permanent funds of just $260,000. Guyana had been desperately searching for a group to cultivate their untapped, resource-rich jungle area. Their previous two attempts to clear the jungle, plant crops, and build more roads and houses around Port Kaituma were unsuccessful. Perhaps the biggest reason for the Guyanese to want Jones and his followers to occupy the border area was because it would make it unlikely that Venezuela would choose to provoke any incidents with Americans. Venezuela and Guyana were going through a border dispute by what is known as in Venezuela as *Guyana Esequiba*, or the territory administered by Guyana but claimed by Venezuela—mostly unsettled jungle, but consisting of the western two-thirds of the country. Perhaps the biggest reason that Guyana rolled out the red carpet for Jones was the fact that several top American officials, which included then First Lady, Rosalynn Carter, wrote letters to the Guyanese government recommending Jones.

In any event, Jones and his followers spent two days in the Matarkai region, which consisted of Mathews Ridge, Arakaka, and Port Kaituma. After two days, Jones and his entourage headed back to Georgetown to settle the land lease with deputy Prime Minister, Dr. Ptolemy Reid. Jones assigned Archie Ijames to stay behind and get started working on the new promise land. Jones left an initial deposit of $100,000 before heading back to the states. Jones soon sent Temple attorney, Gene Chaikin and Paula Adams to help Ijames.

Once back in the States, Jones was up to his old antics. He posted a list up on the Church bulletin board with one-hundred names of people that he said were badly in need of reducing their weight. Jones also upped his fear rhetoric, claiming that the last days of the world were coming soon. Among Jones' claims were that Black newspapers were being forced out of business, drugs were being given to Black soldiers, and that the CIA brought heroin into the country to raise funds for its work. Jones also told countless stories of revolutionaries being arrested by the CIA, strapped down, and administered sodium pentothal in order to have them reveal secrets. This information would, in years to come, surface as truth, with sodium pentothal, commonly becoming known as truth serum used by the CIA for just that reason. How Jones knew countless stories of such events is unknown.

In December of 1974, the Temple asked for Guyana to provide them with a four-wheel drive vehicle, a ten-ton truck, and a four-wheel drive tractor and winch, and an assortment of tools and farming equipment. On their own they purchased a ten-ton dump truck and a mobile crane. By 1975, those Temple members who had stayed behind moved from Port Kaituma into Jonestown. In February of 1976, the government finally granted the Temple the lease for the land. The Temple had originally asked for 25,000 acres, but the lease granted them only 3,000 acres of land for the first five years and the opportunity to renegotiate at five-year intervals after that. The settlement would be called *Jonestown*, a name that Jones credited Emerson Mitchell of creating, even though it was Jones that created the name all along. The Temple was required to develop and occupy at least half the land within the first five-years and report on their progress. While the early settlers worked hard, things were good. Jones visited them briefly on two different occasions in 1976. Jones was still very busy running things in the States, but he would be sure to send the early Jonestown settlers hour-long tapes of his sermons to remind them of the cause.

Jim Jones had ordered Paula Adams to be the principal liaison between the Temple and Guyana officials. Paula was Debbie Layton's old college roommate and one of the most trusted members in the Temple. She spent most of her time in the Temple's Georgetown headquarters in Lamaha Gardens. There, Paula became sexually, and later romantically, involved with the Guyanese Ambassador to the United States, Laurence Mann, who was married at the time. According to Debbie Layton and others, the relationship occurred by design (ordered by Jones). Paula recorded many of her phone conversations and meetings with Mann, then later transcribed the contents of the conversations, and wrote reports of what she'd learned, and then sent them to Jones. This was yet another way for Jones to get information. This also gave Jones a hold over Mann, as the relationship could be used to blackmail him if necessary. Jones had hundreds of thousands of dollars stashed in Guyanese banks, and Paula would ensure that the money was secure; or at least she would provide word ahead of time if there was going to be any trouble.

CHAPTER 5 – THE X-FACTOR

Deanna and Elmer Mertle were elite members of Peoples Temple from 1969 to 1975. The couple changed their names to *Jeannie* and *Al Mills* after defecting from the church to void the power of attorney they had unwittingly given Jones. Both Jeannie and Al were very religious. As a young woman, Jeannie belonged to the Seventh-day Adventist church. It was there she met a man who she soon married, at age twenty-one. From that marriage came two children: Eddie and Daphene. Al married his childhood sweetheart, Zoe, after he finished college and his service in the armed forces. They had five children. Al and Zoe were enthusiastic supporters of the U.S. Bill of Rights, and they fought such things as racism and inequality avidly. Al once marched with Martin Luther King, Jr., in Selma, Alabama. Both Al and Jeannie later divorced their significant others and joined an organization called *Parents Without Partners*. It was there that they met, fell in love, and married six-months later.

After joining Peoples Temple in 1969, they both rose in the ranks fairly quickly, being educated White folks. Jeannie served as head of the Temple's publications office while Al was the official photographer. They decided to leave the group in 1975, after Jones had Al's sixteen-year-old daughter, Linda, brutally beaten on stage at a church function.

September, 1975

After Al and Jeannie Mills made the brave decision to leave the Temple, Jeannie had the daunting task of notifying them of their decision. She decided to call a high ranking Temple official to have that individual inform Jones. Jeannie did not want to tell Jones, personally, that she was leaving. So, she decided to call a top staff member of Peoples Temple and former T.V. news reporter, Mark Duffy. In order to not offend the highly-sensitive, highly-judgmental Jones, Jeannie knew that she would have to give a good excuse for leaving the church. She did not want to tell them the truth, which was that her and her family were leaving the church because they no longer believed in what they stood for. She had seen through Jones' guise of benign preacher. Al's mother had just given Al and Jeannie a rest-home business to run. Jeannie had also previously informed some other members of this, so Jones would be able to confirm that she was not lying. Jeannie decided that she would use that as their excuse to part ways with Jones and his followers.

Jeannie made the call to Mark and informed him of the situation. Jeannie said that their schedule was going to be too intense for them to continue as members of the church. Elite Temple members were elite for a reason. Not only were they Jones's most trusted, they were able to project many of the coercive characteristics of Jones. They all had the very sharp skill of projecting a hostile standpoint through a caring and understanding tone, passive aggressive to the extreme. Jeannie was very fond of Mark and they were good friends while she was a member. She made the mistake of breaking from the story and confiding in him. She wanted Mark to understand her true for their departure from the church. True to the nature of the elite, Mark relayed to Jones the true reasoning for Al and Jeannie leaving the church. Not only was Jim was not happy; he was insulted. According to Jeannie, Jones was concerned that their defection might make others question Jones and his motives.

The following evening, six trusted Temple counselors visited Jeannie and Al at their home. The counselors wanted to discuss why the couple was leaving the church. They sounded friendly and did not seem confrontational. Meri Crawford was one of the counselors. Jeannie and Meri were at one time very good friends. In fact, Meri had lived with the Mills family for several years, at one point. The Mills family was the reason that Meri joined the church in the first place. On that day, however, Meri was visiting as a counselor and had become a very different person by that time. She had risen substantially up the Temple hierarchy over the past few years, and she had become cold and distant as a result. The counselors advised Jeannie that they had come seeking the Temple's membership lists, which Jeannie had been holding as part of her church duties. Jeannie said that she had them upstairs. "Can we set a date to get them," Meri asked. Confused, Jeannie repeated that she had them upstairs and asked them if they wanted her to go get them. Oddly enough, the counselors ignored her request and then stated that they wanted to discuss Jeannie and Al's relationship. With their slick linguist tongues, they referred to the sexual assault documents that Jeannie and Al had signed, along with other document allegations.

These members were the carbon copies of the double-talking, slippery tongued, passive-aggressive Jones. By this time, Jones not only had his own rhetoric down to a science, but he now had many members of his finger-snap army projecting the same message without losing its effectiveness. Jeannie and Al denied all allegations. But the six counselors continued to voice their concerns. It was an eerie event; and it soon became evident that this was not the only reason for their visit. As Al and one of their children became more confrontational, the counselors suddenly got up, as if orchestrated, and left, without mentioning the lists that they had come for. As they locked up for the night they noticed the back door was wide open. When they went upstairs it was obvious that someone was rummaging around though their things. The membership lists were gone along with the deed to their property in Redwood Valley. Furthermore, some other items were also missing, including $80 in cash. "I wonder if they went through our house too," asked Al. They quickly drove to their home in Oakland, and as anticipated, family slides, their slide projector, several books and records, and a stack of Jones' sermons were missing.

The next morning, there was an envelope on their dining room table. It was a disturbing letter written in the double-talk that Jones and his followers had mastered. The letter was addressed to Jeannie and signed "Alice," a pseudonym for what was likely Jones himself. The letter was brilliantly written as not to outwardly threaten the family, but had the implications as if it had come from the devil himself. The wording of the letter made it seem as though it came from a good friend. This "good friend" was writing to Jeannie to inform her that one of her children had written to her and informed her that they had witnessed Al in a sexual act with one of their other children. Alice also wrote that one of the neighbors knows about it as well, and she informed the family to get some help. The most frightening thing about the letter is the care it took to write in a way that yielded no proof of who wrote it or the direct threat that was implied. Furthermore, the letter would make others question Jeannie's character before looking for a direct threat in it. Jeannie wasn't afraid up until that point. As she read the letter, however, she went into a panic.

Soon after the letter, Jeannie and Al were at a store across the street from a bank in Berkeley when a bomb exploded in the bank, leaving a hole in the wall and shattering glass in the store that they were in. Jeannie had kept some pejorative Temple photos and documents in a safe deposit vault in that Bank as insurance (in case they had tried to blackmail or threaten her). She believed that the evidence would help her prove the potentially violent nature of the church. Fortunately, none of the vaults were damaged in the explosion. They thought that Jones might have been involved, but wrote it off as a coincidence. That was until they received a letter the next morning on their porch. *"We saw you two near the bank last night,"* the letter said. *"We know where you keep your belongings."*

The Mills' were very strong people and their love for each other somehow would keep them going. But Jones did not give up easily and would keep a close watch on them for some time. For the moment, they persevered. They laid low for a few weeks and weren't bothered by the Temple. They were slowly trying to recover financially from the hit they had taken from the church. Things were rough and they were just making ends meat. Soon, they would receive a break. In early December of 1975, Al's mother asked them to take over the second rest home. Finally they would be making enough money, with both rest homes, to be able to save money. Moreover, the second rest home had a large attic apartment with five separate rooms. That would add the much needed security they desired and they could also move the children out of the basement and onto the third floor. The only contact that they had with the Temple at that point was occasionally seeing some members soliciting money in front of the local grocery store.

They would always acknowledge the solicitors in a jovial manner in an effort not to reignite Jim's paranoia. One day that's just what they did, unfortunately. Al had been a little too friendly, starting a conversation and asking a member some questions. Realizing the *sensitive nature* of the situation, Jeannie hinted to Al that this was not a good idea, but it was too late. Sure enough, the next morning there was a letter from Jones on their porch. *"Mildred said that you told the manager of the store that the church doesn't need any money,"* the letter read. *"We thought we were going to be friends, but we want an answer as to why you have done this."* They ignored the threat until two nights later; they witnessed eight Temple guards standing outside their kitchen window with arms crossed and malevolent looks on their faces. When they were seen, the guards got into their cars and drove off. They were there to send the family the message that they were watching and could get to them anytime they wanted. Jeannie immediately called the police and reported the incident. When the police arrived, Jeannie feared that giving them too much information would cause even more devious repercussions, so she told the police that the guards "represent a powerful group, and we don't want hassles with them."

Not knowing where else to turn, Jeannie contacted Mark Duffy to find out why they were continuing to be harassed. But Mark claimed that he had no idea about their present circumstances after reporting their departure. Jeannie was livid! The following day, they received another letter. This time Jones stated that they did not answer his previous letter and that he wanted to set up a meeting. Soon after, Jones called Jeannie and scheduled a meeting in front of the *Berkeley Public Library*. "We'll bring our attorney," said Jeannie. "No attorneys," Jim replied. "We'll meet as old friends."

Still very fearful and untrusting of Jones, the Mills' hired a private investigator (Joe Mazor) to stand nearby and observe the meeting. When they arrived they saw Dick Tropp (the resident Temple professor) stationed on the library steps. Much to their surprise Jones was nowhere in sight. Instead, it was Carolyn Layton and Temple attorney, Tim Stoen. Even odder was the fact that Carolyn and Tim did not say one word to them throughout the encounter. Instead, Carolyn wrote notes and handed them to Jeannie as her way of communicating. Tim just stood and stared. Jeannie was furious and expressed how Jim had lied to her about not sending an attorney. Carolyn passed her a note saying that Tim was not there as an attorney, but acting in place of Jim.

"Are you absolutely crazy," Jeannie cried out! "Tim is an attorney no matter who he is representing, he's an attorney!" Jeannie was trembling with fury. "Father does not lie," Carolyn wrote. "His character is above reproach." Jeannie and Al were utterly disgusted and they let them know about it, then turned and began walking away. Carolyn furiously scribbled on her pad and shoved a note into Jeannie's hand. The note said that Jim wanted to make a parting agreement with them that gave them the title to their Richmond property in exchange for one more Jones errand, which consisted of collecting rent from a few church properties. Not only was Jeannie infuriated at this point, Al's blood pressure was now rising as well. The Mills' had turned over a total of twenty-two homes to Jones and the church: nineteen of them had foreclosed, because Jim did not have them taken care of. Moreover, Jim had let the Richmond property become the worst property in the neighborhood. They vehemently declined the offer and left promptly.

The next morning, yet again, there was a note on their porch. Jim again expressed that he wanted to get together and straighten this out with them. Again, they cautiously agreed to meet Jones in the Alameda South Shore parking lot. On December 4, 1975, Jeannie and Al arrived first at the parking lot. Again, the shifty Jones did not show. Two car loads of Temple guards, however, showed up in his place moments after they had arrived. The guards asked them to pull to a more remote section of the parking lot, but Al refused. These people were the same men who Jeannie had been friends with and shared laughs with only months earlier. Now they were militant and hostile. The guards began to push Al and soon became physical with Jeannie as well. The situation was starting to escalate out of control until Al made a saving promulgation. "You guys go ahead and do whatever you want," Al screamed. "You're being watched!" This was not the case, but it scared the men just enough to have them back off. Amidst the continued threats hurled at Jeannie and Al, one of the men claimed that they were responsible for the bomb in the bank. They made it clear that they knew where they kept the incriminating evidence against the Temple and that they would get it soon. Jeannie tried to use good old-fashioned reasoning with the men, speaking to them in a rational manner, but there was no use. When they realized that their efforts were futile, Jeannie and Al quickly made their exit.

The next day, they received a call from Temple attorney, Gene Chaikin. They were still very shaken and decided that they were not going to be caught off guard again. As Jeannie spoke she quickly began taping the conversation. Gene began by emphasizing that the message was to show the Temple's good character and good intentions. Gene opened by proposing that they were willing to give the Richmond property back and that they were willing to keep the peace. He expressed his basic concern for her and her family. He also relayed the Temple's concern over rumors that Jeannie had been spreading lies about the group. Gene assured her that everything that the church had done in response had been purely out of self-defense. Jeannie defended herself, but the attorney side-stepped her logic and again emphasized that they wanted to keep the peace. The back-and-forth continued for some time, with neither party backing down.

Jeannie Mills was not the ordinary Temple member who was on drugs, a minority or poor. Sure, the congregation had several members that were scholars, lawyers, and other well-educated, but they were the minority of the group. Jeannie was a major contributor with her donations and a strong willed female. This scared Jones. Jeannie held her ground and reiterated that her threats were defensive. Suddenly and without warning, Jeannie heard a voice on the other end of the phone say, "We need to stop this nonsense." It was Jim Jones. He grabbed the phone and began explaining to Jeannie that he is not a monster, but a loving man. The two spoke cordially. They both reiterated their points. Jones could not combat Jeannie's logic or, frankly, her correct stance on the situation. Instead, Jones countered with his normal rhetoric, which included several distortions of the truth and a softening perspective, in an attempt to lull her into a false sense of security.

In doing so, he got Jeannie to explain the real reason for leaving the church. The conversation was long; with mostly Jones speaking long monologues of nonsense and Jeannie interjecting with valid points that were completely ignored. Jeannie seemed to throw Jones off with logic, but like many great orators, Jones just talked until either the individual wasn't listening anymore or was in compliance out of attrition. Whether Jones made sense or not, he continued talking. Often Jones would talk until he found a point. None of that mattered to Jones. What mattered was that he had to be in control, dominant. He demanded complete compliance from everyone.

Jeannie was not affected by Jones' rhetoric, nor did it affect her from making clear and valid points. Jones would deflect her escalating tone by replying with words like "dear" and "sweetheart" before rebuffing her statements or simply changing the subject. There was a short time when there was an even exchange of dialog, but that didn't play to Jones' strength; and he quickly went back to long-winded monologues. However, Jones seemed very personable and did address some of Jeannie's issues. Nevertheless, he did so in a way that sounded more like a politician, insincere.

As the conversation was coming to a close, Jones began to gradually change his tune and tried to appeal to Jeannie. He made the point that communication had broken down and was the reason for all the misunderstandings. Jones harped on, and distressed over, this point with the appearance of sincerity. He also made several references alluding to Jeannie coming back to the church, to which he did not ask directly. Jones' last words were informing Jeannie of the progress of their new mission they were building in Guyana. During this time, Jones was all about talking-up his new agricultural project that would soon be known as "Jonestown."

The conversation seemed to have resolved the situation between them. There was no indication that any further retaliation would ensue. But in reality, Jones was not being totally honest as far as his intensions. Jones would be the first to show his true colors and break the peace. Soon, more anonymous letters poured in. Some of them threatened of Jones' connections with the Muslims, the Mafia, and the Black Panthers; others threatened of his political connections. Rumors of Peoples Temple's success began to build, along with the mounting hype about its leader. Jones continued to build powerful connections and political clout.

Early in 1976, the Temple boasted a nationwide membership of 20,000. In reality, the truer count was closer to 3,000. Jeannie could attest to this as she was the one in charge of the membership files, which is probably the reason why Jim and his counselors so desperately wanted those records. The propaganda was running ramped, reporting that the Temple had trained eighty members to become registered nurses, when it was more like three. They claimed to have educated twelve lawyers, when it was more like two members still in law school. It was reported that 2 percent of the members were on welfare, when it was about 20 percent. Jones was able to get away with his many fabrications through his favorable affiliations with many in the media and by acquiring some hefty political alliances.

One of Jones' most loyal media connections was Dr. Carlton B. Goodlett—a medical doctor, publisher of the San Francisco newspaper the *Sun Reporter*, and civil rights activist for minority rights. Goodlett was a Black man who was regarded highly by the

Black community for his business acumen and political beliefs. The Sun Reporter was a weekly newspaper that catered to Black audiences. Jim Jones first came to his attention through conversations with former patients who had attended the weekly Peoples Temple meetings in the early 1970s in the Ben Franklin Junior High School auditorium. After hearing several of his patients speaking highly of the work that the Temple was doing in the community, and after being invited to a Temple service by one of his patients; Dr, Goodlett decided to see what the buzz was all about. Coincidentally, Dr. Goodlett was also invited to Peoples Temple enclave in San Francisco to treat several elderly patients who suffered from various forms of arthritis and were unable to travel to medical offices.

However, it wasn't until Dr. Goodlett began treating Lynetta Jones, Jim's mother, that he began a more intimate relationship with the preacher. It was 1972, and Dr. Goodlett was called to Mount Zion Hospital. Lynetta had been suffering from various complaints; including diabetes, high blood pressure, and hypertensive heart disease. In April of 1972, Goodlett and his newspaper awarded Jim Jones with the Sun Reporter Special Merit Award for his longtime commitment to equal rights. Dr. Goodlett also defended Jones against the attacks from Kinsolving. Along with Sun Reporter editor, Tom Fleming, they bashed Kinsolving, calling his attacks against Jones racially motivated. Dr. Goodlett also wrote a recommendation letter to editors of the Guyana Chronicle on Jones' behalf prior to the Temples first visit to the country in 1974. More importantly, Dr. Goodlett had allowed the Temple to use his medical license to open their physical therapy clinic in Church facilities. Furthermore, they had also used Dr. Goodlett's influence to get Larry Schacht into medical school. Schacht was a loyal Temple member, and would later be known as the head doctor in Jonestown.

Perhaps Jones' most important, yet most damaging, affiliation was that of San Francisco Mayor, George Moscone. In 1975, Moscone (Democrat) was the State Senator of California representing the 10th District in San Francisco County, and was running for Mayor of San Francisco. Moscone's opponent, conservative realtor John Barbagelata, had the White popular vote sewn-up. Moscone and his aides knew that they needed to canvas liberal areas, particularly areas with Black voters. With limited finances to do so, one of Moscone's aides suggested they call on the help of Jim Jones and his followers to help with their efforts. Assembly Speaker, Willie Brown, had the honor of contacting Jones for the task. Thrilled, Jones rallied his followers. Moscone's bid for Mayor also supported Joseph Freitas for district attorney and Richard Hongisto for sheriff.

Just before the election, hundreds of Jones' followers flooded Black neighborhoods. They also sent several hundred members to Moscone's campaign headquarters downtown. Moscone, Freitas, and Hongisto all won. Seeing as Moscone only won by four-thousand votes, Jones wanted Moscone to know that the Temple was primarily responsible for him getting elected, even if this was not necessarily the case. After the election Jones would ask Moscone to return the favor, and he would ask quite aggressively. One of Jones' top Temple members, Mike Prokes (former television reporter in Modesto, California and head of the Temple's public relations), was named to the committee that Moscone would use to screen names for one-hundred upcoming commission appointments.

For each post position, Prokes would put forward names of Temple members that he thought were qualified. None, however, were selected by Moscone. Not happy being overlooked by Moscone, Jones and Prokes complained that the Temple's earlier work to get him elected had not been recompensed. Trying to sooth Jones, Moscone appointed him Human Rights Commissioner in March of 1976. Seeing this as a lateral move, however (because of his prior appointment to the same position); Jones was still not happy. Jones ordered a letter-writing campaign of more than sixty members, flooding Moscone's office with letters stating that Jones' talents were being misused. Just minutes before Jones was to be sworn in for that appointment, he stormed into Moscone's office, with Prokes standing nearby to voice his dissatisfaction. After reaching an agreement, Moscone named Jones to the San Francisco Housing Authority on October 18, 1976.

Jones' publication, *Peoples Forum* was soon boasting a readership of about 600,000. In it, Jones continually posted photographs of himself with the most powerful figures in California. The paper became a "who's who of S.F. politics," and all of those photographed with Jones wanted to meet the great humanitarian and be photographed with him. Jones used this clout to bolster his own image. Jones was determined to become a household name and he was using the most powerful political and social figures in order to do just that. In one issue of *Peoples Forum*, Jones announced that the honorable Wallace D. Muhammad, Supreme Minister of the Nation of Islam, invited him to be the Keynote Speaker at one of their big engagements. In 1976, Jones picked up tremendous steam and he was at the peak of his popularity. In March of 1976, Jones was appointed to the San Francisco Human Rights Commission.

In September of that same year, a testimonial dinner was held in Jones' honor, which brought out most of San Francisco's most powerful political figures. Some of the distinguished guests included: Mervyn M. Dymally (Lt. Governor), Willie Brown (Assembly Speaker), George Moscone (Mayor), Harvey Milk (San Francisco Supervisor), Joseph Freitas (District Attorney), Angela Davis (American political activist), Eldridge Clever (Former Black Panther), among others. In October Jones was appointed to the San Francisco Housing Authority Commission. In November, Jones and Mayor Moscone had a private meeting with Vice Presidential candidate, Walter Mondale. In February of 1977, Jones was elected Chairman of the San Francisco Housing Authority Commission. In March Jones and then first lady, Roselyn Carter, sat together at Head Table of the Democratic Convention Dinner. Needless to say, Jones was at the top of his game and the peak of his popularity. But the house of cards was about to come crashing down in dramatic fashion, and lead him and his followers to a mass departure.

CHAPTER 6 – THE ROLLING STOENS

Perhaps there was no greater impact on the fate of Jones and Peoples Temple than the dynamic duo of Tim and Grace Stoen. Their history started in the world-class wine vineyards of Mendocino County, California. Grace Lucy Grech was a beautiful, exotic-looking, street-smart nineteen year-old-girl. Timothy Oliver Stoen was a 32 year-old, well-established bachelor when they first met in the summer of 1969. After meeting briefly in a chance encountered, the two met again later that fall at an overpopulation and pollution march, which ended near the City Hall Dome. The two hit it off and were soon dating.

Tim Stoen was a classic professional with degrees from Wheaton College in Illinois and Stanford Law School. The liberal Republican with black-rimmed glasses spoke of his aspirations of a career in politics, including one day running for Congress. At that time he had a private law practice in the area. Tim Stoen was a man on the way up, with the world at his feet. He drove a brand new burgundy *Porsche Targa* and lived in beautiful Berkeley California. Grace did not have such an affluent upbringing. She came from a working class family that struggled for economic mediocrity. Grace's mother was a Guadalajara native that came to America and married a butcher. Grace had darker skin because of her Maltese heritage and was often made to feel inferior as a youngster. However, Grace's adaptability, charisma, and good looks carried her through, and eventually she became vice president of her junior class and a basketball cheerleader. Grace managed to keep her head on her shoulders and planned to attend City College.

At the same time, a growing Peoples Temple had been rapidly gaining in popularity all across California, particularly in Mendocino County where they had two churches. Tim was first introduced to Peoples Temple back in 1967, two years before meeting Grace. Tim was a recent Stanford Law graduate and had taken a job working for the Mendocino County District Attorney's office. The state bar association had just asked him to "head an effort" to open a legal services center for the poor in Ukiah. Stoen missed city life and had planned to move back to the Bay Area, but he knew that this was an opportunity to use his years of schooling to aid in his passion for the poor. With Stoen's fundamentalist Christian background, he truly had a deep conviction for helping the less fortunate. He scoffed at those who attended rally's, gave a few dollars, and then went home to their mansions. He wanted to make a true different, and he wasn't afraid of getting his hands dirty to do so.

One of Stoen's first duties with the Legal Services Foundation was to renovate a suite of local legal aid offices. Through a recommendation from a friend, Tim called up the nearby church in Redwood Valley looking for volunteer workers. Tim told the church representative that he was looking for volunteers to start working on Tuesday morning. When he arrived early Tuesday morning, Tim expected to see no one there. Suddenly, he saw a line of 20-30 Black, White, young, and old people carrying paint, Tide, hammers, and nails. The workers hit the place like a blizzard, and what Tim thought was going to take two weeks they did in one day—and they didn't ask for anything in return or even a thanks from Tim. He was thoroughly impressed. This was his introduction to Peoples Temple.

Jones had served on the Legal Services' board of directors when Tim had interviewed for the job. Later Jones would introduce himself to Stoen and inform him that he was impressed with him during the interview. Jones specifically pointed out Tim's response to the board when asked to describe himself. Tim had told the board that he was "a theological conservative and social radical." A light immediately went on in Jones' head as the opportunistic preacher saw Stoen as high quality fresh meat. Stoen was just what Jones was looking for: a White elitist with a Stanford Law degree and a liberal-socialistic vision. Stoen and Jones became fast friends. Stoen admired Jones very much.

Stoen was a committed member of Berkeley's First Presbyterian Church, which he attended weekly. After some time Stoen accepted an invitation to attend a PT-service that was being held at the county fairgrounds in Ukiah. Stoen was truly impressed by the co-mingling of Blacks and Whites, which was a rarity at the time. The one thing that tipped the scales in the Temple's favor was the fact that Jones had adopted a Black child. Stoen thought Jones a very committed man to take on such a repudiated task—an 18-year commitment that was made more laborious by its geographic location at the time—racist Indiana.

When his work was done Stoen moved back to the Bay Area and bought himself a Porsche and a nice apartment. But Stoen soon found himself taking frequent drives out to the Redwood Valley Church to attend services, a two-hour drive from his Bay Area home. Tim and Grace continued seeing each other and their adoration for one another soon flourished into love. One day Tim decided to introduce Grace to Jim Jones at a Temple service. Grace took the two-hour drive with Tim for her first Temple service and an encounter with what would soon become her greatest enemy.

Grace was immediately awestruck by the casual mix of races and the loving atmosphere. It was easy for newcomers to see and feel that these people really believed in what they were doing. This was not your average church experience. After the opening act, associate minister, Jack Beam, finished the opening of the service. The silence soon turned to anticipation. The atmosphere and feverous pitch began to overflow and the crowd began calling for their "father." Suddenly a roar waved across the assembly. Grace looked incessantly to get her first glimpse of what Tim had come to admire so. Suddenly, like a rock band bursting onto the stage, a jet-black haired, handsome, charismatic preacher in a white robe appeared. His presence was undeniable. He spoke of issues that were relative to the day. Yet, Grace was still very skeptical. She could sense that something was amiss, as many others had felt at first.

Grace did not agree with some of Jones' outlandish tactics and was not as caught up in the spectacle as many others were. She was not impressed by his ritualistic healings, his outlandish prophecies, and she was repulsed by his money collection techniques. However, she was in love with Tim and he was completely enamored by Jones and his movement. The atmosphere, though, was contagious, and Jones had been making a major play for Tim for some time. Stoen had already made up his mind to join Peoples Temple at that rally in the summer of 1969.

Jones then sent two young members to Tim's apartment to get a formal commitment from him and the youngsters were very surprised how willing Stoen was to join and how inspired he had seemed. On January 9, 1970, in a letter to Jim Jones—which was more like a formal acceptance letter—Tim Stoen asked for the advice of Jones on what type of car he should drive, what kind of clothes he should wear, and questions related to material things.

Tim also knew the ramifications of such a commitment, but it was not easy for him to, in essence, completely give up these materialistic values. Tim was living the American dream—what some would never get to achieve—and he was about to give that up for a higher cause. He knew it was a huge commitment and perhaps he was just wisely showing Jones that he was ready. Jones never had a problem with treating each person differently. Jones was also a very good judge of character. He knew that if he accepted some of Tim's terms in the beginning, to draw him in, it would be easier to slowly take them away as time went on. Jones was shrewd and he knew that having Tim Stoen as a dedicated member was priceless, particularly at that time. The clout that Stoen brought to the Temple would be unprecedented. Tim would become a major gun in Jones' arsenal. Tim knew this as well. One day he took the long drive out to the Redwood Valley church, walked up to Jones and said, "You need me."

In the months since they had met, Grace and Tim had fallen in love. Before moving back to Ukiah, Tim had unfinished business. As cliché as it may sound, the young lawyer asked Grace Grech to become Grace Stoen, but there were terms and conditions that Grace would have to agree with. Tim asked her to dedicate one year of her life to the church, and then he would run for congress. Grace thought that the idea of dedicating one year to the church wasn't so bad. She was anticipating having children and getting a house of her own one day soon, so this was a small sacrifice to make for such a bright long-term future. With their agreement in hand and their love burgeoning, the two moved to Ukiah and joined Peoples Temple. Tim took back his job with the Mendocino County District Attorney, in the civil division, as the county government's legal advisor and representative.

On June 27, 1970, the two tied the knot in an elaborate Temple ceremony, even though Grace's parents had wanted a catholic wedding. Jones had won out again and took the opportunity to introduce the Temple to Tim's high profile friends. The wedding also carried local news coverage as their county's new assistant district attorney was getting married. Right from the get-go the Stoen's were the source of much jealousy among Temple members.

The Stoen's were allowed several materialistic things and special privileges that others were not. In a time when several members were living communally, The Stoen's had their own beautiful house. Tim Stoen rose up the Temple ladder, immediately becoming the Temple's attorney of record and chairman of the board of directors. Grace slowly worked her way up to the Temple ladder as well, becoming a Planning Commission (PC) member and eventually head counselor of the church council.

The first year of their marriage was a good one for the couple, though they did not see the grander plans of their leader. Tim was a hard worker and soon began taking on other duties, such as setting up a legal clinic sponsored by the Temple, which kept him away from home often. Tim admired Jones a great deal and he whole-heartedly embraced Jones' socialist ideals. In an essay, Stoen wrote an elaborate piece on socialism, claiming that "The socialist wants the wealth of the country redistributed so that everyone has his basic needs met." Tim even voluntarily donated 25 percent of his salary to the church. With each passing day he was becoming more committed. But as his commitment grew toward the Temple, his relationship began to suffer.

As a result, Grace started to resent her husband for the time that he dedicated to the Temple. The one year commitment had come and gone and there was no talk of quitting anytime soon. Grace, herself, had even been drawn in too deeply by Jones as well by this time. She was given more important church duties; she would soon become one of the most powerful Temple members. Tim grew more in awe of Jones as time went on. Jones' rhetorical skills were nearly unmatched and his deep conviction and megalomaniacal manner had Tim believing that Jones was a true messiah.

Tim was a huge church asset and would soon become Jones' right-hand-man and nearly his equal in alliance, though not in church standing. Tim had a church related education and applied for and had received minister stature. Soon after, Tim became a member of the Disciples of Christ regional board, which put a Temple member in a major position to ensure their continued standing with the organization. This happened all at a time when the Temple started gaining prestige and momentum. Tim was meeting daily with very powerful local politicians and lawyers and was passing on the word of Jones and the Temple, even shamelessly plugging Jones' healing techniques. He rose at 4:00 a.m., with his whole day planned out, and Grace rarely fit into those plans. This obviously put a huge strain on his marriage.

Grace was looked upon as an elitist because of the nice things that she had, but she was not apologetic about it. She believed that she had wanted these things all her life and she couldn't think of a reason why she should not have them. Though Jones had begun to grow on her, Grace was not as star struck of him as Tim was or any of the other adoring members, for that matter. She was repulsed by those who gawked over Jones. Jim Jones was certainly not above questioning in her mind and this is another reason why some members resented her. But it was hard not to like Grace. She was such a personable woman and had a special quality that made people look up to her. She soon became a very well respected and well liked member.

Though Jim Jones and Timothy Stoen made a great team, Jones was not content sharing any of the spotlight. His true intensions were always hidden and were always to undermined anyone who he saw as a threat—which was anyone that he saw as an equal or better—and break them down systematically and underhandedly. As Tim Reiterman stated in his book, *Raven*, "Tim Stoen's mere presence raised those old inferiority feelings in Jones. He was many things that Jones was not…But he was also naïve and prone to zealotry and idealism and Jones exploited that. Having elevated Stoen to the highest standing, Jones made his fall all the more calculating and cruel."

One day, Jones complained that too many women wanted him sexually and he asked Tim to help him with the burden. He advised that Tim would be doing him a great service by sleeping with Sharon Amos for the betterment of the cause. Somehow, Tim bought into this and went through with the deed. Sharon was not a very attractive woman, and compared to Grace, it was a big step down for Tim. Clearly planned all along, Jim informed Grace of Tim's infidelity in not so many words and left out the part about his own involvement. Jones caused problems like this with many members. He did it slowly and methodically, breaking them down through lies and manipulation over time. Controlling complete families was one of Jones' specialties and he did it through a "divide & conquer" strategy.

Unlike other members, the Stoen's household was not a traditional part of the Temple commune, though they did boarder children. Jones mainly used the Stoen home for emergency visitors whom he did not want subject to the culture shock of the church. As stated earlier, one of these visitors was Mark Blakey's mom. Jones would sometimes stop by the house to see Grace while Tim was away and he frequently called her on the phone as well. Tim's long hours away from home allowed Jones to build a private relationship with Grace. The closer he kept the Stoen's the easier it would be to manipulate them; and perhaps he was after Grace, attempting to add her as another mistress. Jones never got over the fact that Grace did not fawn over him like many other female members did and Jones no doubt saw this as a challenge.

Tim and Grace were in love and had sex as regularly as Tim's schedule allowed. Grace soon became pregnant and this brought a host of new criticisms from several other church members. In July of 1971, Grace received a harsh browbeating from several members at a PC meeting. Sharon Amos was one of the outspoken members who voiced her opposition to the pregnancy. Sharon ridiculed Grace harshly, saying that there were too many unwanted children in the world. This was something that Jones had taught his followers. Jones taught that having children was greedy and that adoption was the only acceptable option. With tears flowing from her eyes Grace confronted Tim about the allegations of infidelity. Tim's weak argument about doing it for the cause did not hold water with Grace. She told Tim how ashamed and embarrassed that she was and claimed that many of the Temple members were laughing at her behind her back. By this point, Tim had already slept with three other Temple females at the suggestion of Jones. Though they had problems, the couple was still very much in love and committed to try and work things out, especially with a baby on the way.

On January 25, 1972, Grace gave birth to a healthy baby boy who they named John Victor Stoen. Tim stood by his twenty-one-year-old bride at the Santa Rosa Memorial Hospital during the birth and later he would describe it as the most exciting thing he's ever experienced. The extended labor had taken its toll on Grace, however, and she was confined to bed rest for several days following the birth. On February 1, 1972, the parents received a copy of the birth certificate, which listed Grace as the mother and Tim as the father. However, unbeknownst to Grace, less than a week after receiving the birth certificate (Feb. 6), Tim Stoen signed a Power of Attorney form stating that he in fact was not the father, but that Jim Jones was. The document claimed that in April 1971, Tim had asked Jones to sire a child for him and his wife Grace. Of course, the document stated that Jones accepted the offer only after the insistence of Tim.

> *"I Timothy Oliver Stoen, hereby acknowledge that in April 1971, I entreated my pastor, James w. Jones, to sire a child by my wife, Grace Stoen, who previously, at my insistence, reluctantly but graciously consented thereto. James W. Jones agreed to do so, reluctantly, after I explained that I very much wished to raise a child, but was unable after several attempts, to sire one myself."*

This mystery thickens when Marceline's signature was found on the document as a witness. Later, Marceline would claim that Jones had asked her for permission to sire the child in advance. No one really knows exactly what happened or the real truth, but based on Jones' track record it is very safe to assume that the child was Tim's and that Jones had this document created for the purposes keeping a stron-hold on Tim and Grace. This was a very common type of manipulative tactic that Jones used to keep a hold on his members. Silently, however, most members appear to have felt that the child was in fact Tim's, although they would have never taken a stand against Jones at the time. Tim's dangerous infatuation of Jones had reached an all time high and his signature on that document marked the biggest mistake he would ever make. In Tim's defense, he believed that the document would serve as insurance—in the event that anything ever happened to him or Grace; the Temple would take custody of John. But Tim did not consult Grace on the decision. Furthermore, he never planned on telling Grace, nor did he think that she would ever find out.

On the other hand, Jones had a different agenda and the document, to Jones, meant that he had the Stoen's right where he wanted them. There also may have been several other reasons, such as a matter of breeding, as Jones knew that Tim had a superior intellect. Jones also longed for someone to mold into his own image from birth. His own biological son, Stephan, had already begun to form a dissenting opinion from Jim's own and this may have made him even more desperate to acquire someone to succeed him. John was treated accordingly by other Temple members. They seemed to sense Jones' projections of importance onto young John.

Once Jones made his claim on the child, he began to put more pressure on the Stoen's. By the second year of John's life, Grace was forced to quit school and work nights while, against Grace's will, Jones had talked Tim into moving John to the church to be raised communally. Jones was systematically developing a select few young ones to be raised in the communal lifestyle. His efforts were to have a whole new crop of children who would grow up knowing only the communal experience. John not only became one of them, but he was also Jones' own little project who was to be raised in his own image. Jones went to great lengths to persuade other members of Tim's importance and spoke very highly of Tim.

Grace buried herself in church duties and soon the elitist ridicule died down. Grace was putting in sixteen-hour days for the church and other members were forced to notice her dedication and work ethic. Jones took notice as well and rewarded her by promoting her to church council and then head councilor. Tim and Grace had officially become the most powerful Temple couple next to Jim and Marceline/Carolyn, of course.

Jones continued to poke into their marriage and he saw Tim as the easiest way to have an immediate impact. As Stoen was Jones' legal advisor; Jones was Stoen's marital and spiritual advisor. One piece of advice that Jones gave Tim was to "not pay a lot of attention to her. This will toughen her up and make her a better socialist." However, this only pushed Grace away and Jones knew that. Jones relied on this divide-and-conquer strategy as his major weapon against family ties. This methodical tactic soon took effect, and Tim and Grace soon split and moved into separate homes. Obviously, Tim and Grace had as much to do with the split as Jones, but Jones' involvement was certainly undeniably impactful.

After the split, Jones saw it as open season on Tim. Jones began to publicly humiliate Tim, making him publicly admit being a homosexual. This was the kiss of death in regard to having a political career in 1975. Up to this point, Jones had only subjected other members to this sort of public humiliation. Now, Tim was vulnerable and Jones knew that he could use that vulnerability to further destroy Tim's standing. The fact was that Jones had several ways and means of attaching his members to the church, whether through planned blackmail or coerced confessions; Jones put the fear of retribution into anyone who thought of leaving. This fear made the members easy targets for Jones' sick public degradation sessions. With his son John Stoen now looming over his head and the Temple being a large reason for the split between he and Grace, Tim was fully vested in the church and had become just another pawn in Jim Jones' sick game.

Like any true bully, Jones got a rush from seeing how far he could push people and he usually did so almost immediately after he had some type of damning insurance on them. With Tim it took him a while, but he eventually began to enforce his will on him as well. Jones began trying to convince Tim, as he did others, that every man was a homosexual. As much as he was still caught up in Jones' zealotry, Tim just could not bring himself to believe Jones about this particular promulgation. Jones continued to push Tim to have a homosexual experience and give in to his true nature. Tim respected and revered Jones so much so that he considered it; but when faced with committing the actual act, he could not bring himself to. He knew that he was inherently a heterosexual male.

Grace defects

Grace was growing more intolerant of the Temple by the day. She had grown even more intolerant of Jones, himself. In 1976, for Grace, every injustice that Jones committed was magnified. She contemplated leaving, but thought about her son John and played the waiting game—waiting for the right time. Eventually she knew that she would have to make a run for it and leave John behind for the time being. Grace could no longer bear to witness Jones' evil ways, manipulative tactics, sexual degradation, or his self-serving prophesies. Finally, in July of 1976, after witnessing several atrocities, including an elderly man vomited and urinated on for sleeping to long, as well as a hellish bus trip with Temple faithful; Grace decided she had, had enough.

Grace had just come back from the bi-weekly bus ride to the L.A. church. She was completely drained after holding in her objections to Jones cramming the buses full of members. Some members were forced to lie in the overhead compartments and others were even stored in the luggage compartments below the bus. She was thoroughly disgusted and ready to make her move. She could not live another day as a Temple member, but she knew to keep her silence until she was ready. During the long bus ride back to S.F., Grace pondered all the horrors she had seen and partaken in over the years. During her short six years in the church she saw her son become Temple property, public beatings, her marriage disassembled, her husband publicly humiliated several times by Jones, and she witnessed many of the poor members being treated like animals and fed poorly. She also had enough of working 16-plus-hour days as head counselor of the Temple.

Grace was not without sin throughout the Temple years, though. She knew that she had helped enable Jones to commit some of the atrocities. Grace had made her share of threatening phone calls for the church. As one of the churches notary publics, she had taken part in several coerced property transfers.

Only a month or so earlier, Jack Arnold Beam, son of Jack Beam Sr., had approached Grace, asking her to leave with him. Grace and Jack were good friends and she knew that she could trust him, but she was not ready to make her move at that time. Before Jack Jr., defected he told Grace to confide in his friend and bus garage co-worker, Walter Jones—known as, Smitty. Jack Jr., and Smitty had been talking about leaving for some time, but Smitty had stayed behind when his wife and family defected. Grace had spent a lot of time with Smitty and they grew close, both sharing a secret of one day leaving the church. Other members saw their alliance as a positive and did not make a fuss, believing that Grace would keep Smitty close to the church. However, it was Grace that was pulling him away.

After witnessing a brutal Temple boxing match, where a 40-year old female was brutally beaten by several members for saying that "Jones had turned them all into robots;" Grace told Smitty that she was leaving. Smitty asked if he could tag along. Grace fled the S.F. church and headed to the Redwood Valley Church, where she would gather her things. When nosily approached by members,

Grace told them that she was just getting rid of some garbage. Without even informing her husband, Grace and Smitty set off for the beach in Lake Tahoe where they spent the 4th of July. Despite Grace's departure in July 1976, Tim continued on as a Temple member.

The Temple held their 4th of July picnic, but the festivities were darkened by the highest defection that the Temple had encountered up to that point. Jones held an emergency PC meeting during the picnic in which he cursed Grace. Members were even more resentful of Grace's defection due to the fact that she was afforded so many more comforts than the rest of them. Jones was truly hurt by Grace's defection and it was something that he would never get over.

Grace had left the church hastily, but she did not want to hurt the church; she was just confused at first and wanted to gain her bearings. She left important records and unfinished business plans behind as to not hamper the Temple's business plans. She also left a note expressing her grief over leaving her son and other members whom she'd grown to love over the years. Jones was outraged, but Tim was stunned like a deer in head lights. Tim believed that Grace would return and was willing to give her time to cool herself off. Tim was not too far off in his thinking, and only one day after her defection Grace's guilt compelled her to call Jones from Nevada. Much like Jeannie Mills and other future defectors, Grace wanted Jones to understand her reasoning for leaving. However, Jones was incapable of understanding any other way of thinking than his own, particularly when it came to his sorest subject: defection. He was incapable of compromise in that respect.

The talk soon turned to her son John. When Grace demanded to speak to John, she was met by a cold reception from him. John was not even four-years-old yet, but Jones was still able to control him much like the others. Grace knew that John was being coached by Jones during the conversation. She didn't even think that it sounded like John, though she knew it was. Jones continued to throw it in her face that she chose to leave her son and there really wasn't anything that she could say to combat Jones.

Jones then asked Grace for a favor after reminding her who holds the key to her seeing her son. Jones asked Grace to make a recorded statement that he could play to the rest of the Temple members to make it seem like her and Smitty were on Temple business and had not defected. Jones advised her that the tape would buy him about a month, hiding the defections for that time. Grace reluctantly agreed, and after a few takes she had made a statement claiming how she missed everyone. She said that she was on official Temple business and that she would see them all in the promise land. When she was done she asked Jones for a favor in return. Grace asked to see her son. Unenthusiastically, Jones agreed.

In September of 1976, Grace pulled up to the L.A. church and swallowed her pride. The excitement of seeing her son John took precedence over her fear and embarrassment of seeing the two men that she had run from. As she entered the church, Jones and Tim greeted her. Jones did the talking at first, while Tim stood by still angry and hurt. John was happy to see Grace and they hugged and shared a moment. Both men asked Grace to return to the church, but she explained that she did not want to and that she was just there to see John. Grace handled herself well even though Jones and Tim both egged her on with indirect threats trying to get her to fold. Eventually Grace broke character and made a big mistake. Grace said something to Tim that was seen by him as a threat. Tim later informed Jones that he believed that Grace was going to take legal action against them in regard to John. The decision was then made by Jones to move John to Guyana. In October of 1976, four-year-old John Victor Stoen was sent to the promise land.

After almost two months of sobering solitude, Grace finally had a one-on-one phone conversation with Tim in November of 1976. Tim had realized that he was still in love with Grace, but nothing had changed. Tim was still Jones' mouthpiece and he showed no signs of any profound change. Quite the contrary, Tim sounded like he was reading from a script and Grace was very careful not to say anything that could be used against her in the future. Then, Tim broke the devastating news to Grace: John had been sent to Guyana back in October. Grace's heart sank and she felt like she had been hit by a bat! She tried to keep her composure, but her whole being had just been thoroughly rocked!

Tim informed her that she could travel to Guyana twice a year to visit John and that the Temple would pay for all expenses. He pleaded with Grace to come back to the church, to no avail. He admitted that he had made horrible mistakes in their marriage and promised that if she came back he would be a better husband. Grace was so overwhelmed with her son's departure that most of what Tim said was not really registering. She wanted nothing to do with the church or Tim. The only tie that they had was their son, who was now being used as leverage against her.

By February of 1977, Grace could not hold in her distain or her tongue any longer. She had taken all that she could take and her shock and disappointment soon turned to rage and determination. In a phone call with Tim they wrestled back and forth over having John come back to the States vs., stay in Guyana. Grace had finally snapped and there would be no more compromise any longer. She decided to take on an offensive position. She wanted her son back and she voiced her concerns to Tim in a threatening manner. Tim took the stance of Jim Jones, telling Grace that John was being bred for a leadership role in the Temple, but Grace would not have it. Equally as combative, Tim held his position. Grace knew what the Temple was capable of and was worried what they might do if she resisted their demands; but when all seemed lost and she was backed into a corner, she was left with no other options. She warned Tim that she was going to file for divorce and retain a court order to get her son back.

Neither side showed any signs of backing down. Jones and Tim consulted daily in the busy month of February. Jones knew they stood no chance in court to retain custody and that public and media pressure would surely hurt the Temple and cause unnecessary controversy. Jones demanded that Tim take a leave of absence from his job and move to Guyana. Tim agreed. That same month Tim hopped on a plane and headed for the jungle of South America, but with a back-up plan. Before leaving, Tim had his father set up a private bank account for him in Colorado and Tim obtained a backup passport in the event that Jones tried to pull a fast-one and take his away, as he had done with just about every other member. After years of being on the inside, Tim knew exactly what was going on in the Temple and he had a healthy fear and distrust of Jim Jones.

Jones had also been watching Tim closely and his intrinsically paranoid nature made him distrust Tim as well. Tim had left for Guyana on February 16, 1977, but his father had sent a letter to S.F. that was intercepted. Jones opened the letter and found check books with his new Colorado bank account information and was furious. It was a clear sign that Tim was being disloyal and may have had ulterior motives involved in his trip to Guyana. Jones now feared that Tim was planning on kidnapping his boy from Jonestown. Jones was livid! He was so upset that he chartered a plane to Jonestown to confront Tim. When Jones voiced his concerns Tim used the excuse that it was just his materialistic ways resurfacing. Jones gave Tim the benefit of the doubt and flew off soon after; but not before ordering other members to keep a close eye on him. Tim had no way of taking John out of Jonestown. He was being closely watched, but he would later claim that this was his intension.

Tim worked fourteen-hour days in the Saw Mill and kept his nose clean. He spent every evening with his son and he would later claim that it was "the happiest time of his life." This happy time that Tim described was a time in Jonestown before Jim Jones had moved there. The overall consensus in Jonestown at that time was that things were heavenly before Jones showed up. They all still worked hard, but the true mind control and abuse did not occur at that point. However, Jones still had his "eyes" watching and still called the shots from S.F. Jones learned that Tim and John were spending a lot of time together and he was not happy about this at all. After just one month in Jonestown, Jones ordered Tim to move to Georgetown, with the excuse that he would do paper work for the Temple and resume his legal duties.

CHAPTER 7 – HOUSE OF CARDS

The "Conn" Man

The Temple was on high alert after Grace's defection. Grace was facing the threat of Jones telling her that he would kill her himself. Grace went into hiding. Fearing for her life, she moved to a small city hundreds of miles from San Francisco. Jones continued to meet with powerful political leaders and attend gala events with politicians on hand as well as other popular figures. By the later months of 1976, Jeannie and Al Mills hadn't had any communication with any Temple members for some time. They had no way of knowing what was going on in the church. However, they both still feared for their lives. They were isolated. Most of their "friends" were in the church and they didn't know who they could turn to. Jones seemed untouchable.

One day, after a long day of work, Jeannie and Al were contacted by a long time friend and Temple member, Roz, who had lived with the Mills family at one time. Roz was fearfully curious of one thing: she wanted to know how Jeannie's ear was. Roz explained that when Jeannie defected Jim had put to a vote whether or not he should have her ear cut off in order to send a message to other "traitors." Roz had just left the church for many of the same reasons that Jeannie did. Roz explained that Jones had become even more bizarre and sadistic, and his disciplinary tactics had escalated. Jeannie was surprised to find out that several other members had left the church as well. Roz told her that other PC members, such as Joyce Shaw, the entire Purifoy family, and Grace Stoen were all recent defectors. Jeannie was delighted to hear the news. Roz gave her the phone numbers of these old friends. Before they hung up, they had decided to have a get together with those defectors and have a "traitor's party," as they called it.

Grace was a much more powerful Temple member than Jeannie, and her departure meant great embarrassment for Jones. This further tarnished his credibility with other Temple members. From the outside, Jones was untouchable and gaining in power; but he was starting to crumble from the inside. The only thing that could ruin him now were Temple members who chose to leave. The big problem with Grace's defection was that mostly all members liked and respected her. By just about all accounts, Grace was seen as a warm and approachable woman. It was a hard sell for Jones to try to make Grace out to be anything less. Grace was still very terrified of Jones and his wrath. Grace was determined to get her son back, and Jeannie saw a coalition building out of their hatred for Jones. But they knew that it was not going to be easy to convince anyone else of their stories; they hardly believed it themselves and they had been through it.

By January 1977, Jeannie Mills was infuriated over continually seeing Jones' popularity growing, while her and her family had to sit in fear of retribution from him. She knew what kind of man he was and the type of devious operation that he was running, and she couldn't bear to sit and do nothing while some of the most powerful leaders in the country continued to endorse him. Out of desperation, she contacted various news sources and political leaders to try and explain to them that Jones was not who he claimed to be or who they thought he was, and to warn them that their affiliation with Jones and the Temple would hurt them after he is exposed. Jeannie, though, was continually met with the same responses: they all thought that she was crazy. One man, however, decided to listen.

Only a few months earlier, Linda had also left the church. Linda was Al's daughter from his previous marriage. Linda's mother (also Al's Ex-wife) Zoe Kille had called Al to tell him that Linda had called asking that she pick her up immediately from the grips of the Temple. Linda later explained that she had left the church because she believed that Jim had gone crazy. She explained that the beatings and abuse had gotten even worse. The family still had other loved ones in the church and their crusade to stop Jones increased. One day Zoe suggested that the Mills' speak to her longtime friend; Dave Conn. Zoe believed that he could help. Dave Conn was no one, in particular, but he knew a lot of people. Conn had been a member of Richmond's Barrett Avenue Christian Church, which was, like Peoples Temple, part of the Disciples of Christ, a major American Protestant denomination. Conn, however, was asked to leave the church in 1965, because he was an activist for school integration and fair housing in Richmond. In fact, Al Mills had also been a member of that same church and had known Conn and was acquainted with him in those days. After hearing their story, Conn believed them and appeared genuinely concerned for their well-being. Conn suggested that they allow him to bring a reporter friend of his to record their story. He advised them that at least if anything were to happen to them they would have their story as evidence. A few days later Conn arrived with his daughter's boyfriend, George Klineman (a reporter for the *Santa Rosa Press–Democrat*). Grace Stoen was also in attendance.

Jeannie and Grace told them everything that they could. They explained about Jim's politics, his brutality and abuse, his threats, and so on. Klineman recorded everything. Both Conn and Klineman were astounded by the bizarre, horrendous stories and were both concerned for the safety of those involved. A few days later Klineman put them in touch with Jim Hubert, an investigator in the *United States Treasury Department*. They told Hubert all the same details about Jones and the Temple, adding that Jones was also shipping weapons to Jonestown in the bottoms of crates marked "agricultural supplies," and also that Temple members wore money belts around their waists in order to smuggle in cash. Hubert swore absolute secrecy about their involvement, promising that an investigation would ensue.

Although Conn had given his word that he would not share their stories with anyone else, he felt the need to warn others. In doing so, he took it upon himself to contact his former co-worker at the Chevron refinery, George Coker, who also happened to be a Native American. Conn knew that Coker had an affiliation with Dennis Banks, who was the leader and co-founder of the *American Indian Movement* at the time. Banks had been a vocal supporter of Jones over the years. Conn had seen a picture of Jones and Banks together, and not knowing the nature of their relationship, he thought that it would be wise to warn him that his affiliation with Jones could tarnish his movement.

Conn did not know at the time that the Temple had donated $19,500 to the Banks and his American Indian Movement back in early 1976, which was perhaps the biggest Temple donation on record. It has been alleged that at least some of that money had been loaned to Banks by Jones to bail Banks' wife out of jail. In any case, Banks was a Temple supporter and he was also indebted to them. Coker, a full-blooded Seminole, passed on the information to Lee

[Lehman] Brightman, a Sioux Indian. Brightman, a close friend of Banks, had actually shared the stage with Jim Jones at an April 1976, public rally in support of Banks (to help stop his extradition). Banks feared extradition to South Dakota, after being wanted in South Dakota on a controversial conviction for possession of arms in a riot "without intent to kill." Banks feared that if extradited it would lead to a trial and a death sentence. Brightman passed the word on to Banks and set up a meeting between him and Conn to discuss the allegations.

Conn met with Banks, Brightman, Coker, and a tall-dark haired girl at Brightman's house on March 23, 1977. According to Conn, Banks listened intently as he told them everything: the fake healings, the abuse, defectors' names, the Treasury Department's investigation into the gun and cash smuggling, and so on. Conn claims that he advised Banks to write a statement denouncing Jones and the Temple and have it notarized so that when Jones and the Temple inevitably fell he would have proof. He also advised him to gradually disassociate himself from Jones. However, in a statement in October of 1977, Banks claimed that Conn approached him and said he was working with the Treasury Department, and informed him of all the problems he had heard about Jones and the Temple and that his association with the Temple would reflect very badly on his extradition. Banks also claimed that Conn assured him that if he denounces Jones the rulings in his extradition would go in his favor. According to Banks, Conn urged him to meet with a Treasury agent, but Banks refused unless he was accompanied by his attorney, Dennis Roberts, to which Conn insisted that he meet with the agent alone. By the end of the three-hour meeting, both appeared to be at a stalemate.

On March 25, 1977, Jeannie Mills was reading through the San Francisco Chronicle and read an article explaining that Jim Jones had collapsed the night before at a Housing Commission meeting. Just as she was finished reading the article she received a call from Dave Conn, who sounding frantic and told her that he was rushing over to see her. As she waited for Conn to arrive she received a call from Grace. She explained that she received a strange letter on her porch the previous night, and she began to read it to Jeannie. The letter spoke of Dave Conn and all the things that he said to Dennis Banks, as well as saying, "The public will never forgive people who are unthinking robots." The letter ended by referencing Grace's son, John, and an indirect warning that her recent actions have put him in jeopardy.

Jeannie hung up the phone, walked to the porch and, sure enough, a letter was on her doorstep. It was almost the exact same letter as Grace had received, minus the mention of Grace's son. When Dave arrived he was insipid and rickety. Dave tried desperately to explain his story as Grace had arrived as well. Jeannie and Grace were furious with him as he explained what he had done. Dave also explained that his girlfriend had gotten a call in the middle of the night from a person saying he was going to burn their house down. Dave was in such fear that he had already moved into a new apartment. They called Jim Hubert and explained what had happened. He informed them to hold onto the letters and that he would pick them up so that he could check them for fingerprints. That night Jeannie received two more threatening letters.

Jones had heard about Conn's conversation with Dennis Banks the night before the Housing Commission meeting. It was said that it was that conversation, along with Tim Stoen's first defection, that caused Jim to collapse at the meeting. Tim Stoen had returned to the Temple for a short time after his first defection. Jones talked him into returning to the church, but for Stoen it was hard from that point on to hide his disenchantment with the Temple. Jones never trusted Stoen again after his first escape from the church, and he had other members keep a very close watch on him. On June 12, 1977, Tim Stoen had finally had enough. He slipped out of Georgetown, Guyana on a plane headed for New York. He briefly returned to San Francisco to see a girl that he had been dating, but he was shocked to find out that she was engaged. He then withdrew to Colorado and later to Europe to clear his thoughts. His defection would be one of the central reasons for Jones' subsequent mental breakdown.

Grace and Jeannie felt that all had been lost and it appeared as though Jones had won. They believed that it was just a matter of time before Jones retaliated, whether against them or their families. Yet, little did they know, they had pierced through Jones' seemingly unpierceable armor. The big mess-up by Conn turned out to be their saving grace. Jones' paranoia, as well as Jeannie and Grace's tenacity was starting to take their toll on Jones. Jones' drug use was also escalating and his mind, once sharp and witty, was becoming clouded and more irrational. Jones' next move, in essence, sealed his fate, opening the door for Jeannie, Grace, and others to take him down.

The Wild, Wild "New West"

One day back in 1976, Marshall Kilduff, a reporter for the *San Francisco Chronicle*, started discussing Jim Jones with his colleges, unsure what to make of the charismatic preacher with political clout. Although Jones had claimed that he never wanted to hold a political position, doing so had opened him up to a closer inspection and possible scrutiny. After being approached by Jones at a commission meeting, Kilduff got to thinking. Jones tried to intimidate him. Kilduff wanted to know more about Jones. He decided to do a profile story on Jones, nothing to hard hitting.

In 1976, when Jones was appointed to the Human Rights Commission, San Francisco Chronicle reporter, Julie Smith, had been assigned to write a story about him. But when Julie began conducting research and doing interviews, Jones began a furious letter writing campaign to the Chronicle, sending hundreds of letter and making hundreds of phone calls, in an effort to thwart any possible attempts to expose the abuse and mayhem that was occurring in the church, even though that was not Julie's intention. Coincidentally, Julie received phone calls from her own friends asking her not to do the story. When the story finally ran on April 26, 1976, "*The Unusual Leader of an Unusually Active Church*," it had been edited down to the bare essentials by higher-ups at the newspaper.

Kilduff would have a hard time convincing any newspaper editor to release a negative story on Jones unless he had something that couldn't be denied, a real Pulitzer piece, *per se*. Kilduff had tried for many months thereafter to do a piece on Jones, but he was met with much resistance from Jones and the Temple. When he was finally given the green light to do the story in March of 1977, by *New West Magazine*, Jones' people got to New West's editor, Kevin Starr, and the story was again squashed. Kilduff then got *San Francisco Magazine* to agree to publish his story, but when he finally wrote it, they rejected the piece because it lacked substance.

A couple of months later Rosalie Wright replaced Kevin Starr as editor for New West. Rosalie decided to publish the piece, under the guidelines of revising it and adding new material. They also assigned one of their own reporters, Phil Tracy, to assist Kilduff. They concentrated on Jones' political rise to power, raising questions of hostility, paranoia, and secrecy regarding the Temple. Yet, the story again had little in the way of substance to answer these questions. Jones, however, did not know this. In his paranoia Jones believed that Kilduff and Tracy were working with Dave Conn, Jenna Mills, Grace Stoen, and others in an effort to portray the ugly truth of mistreatment and abuse in the Temple. Jones went into a complete panic, and coordinated a fierce letter writing and phone call campaign with his members and supporters. They sent hundreds of letters and made hundreds of phone calls each day in protest of the article.

Meanwhile, Jeannie began getting phone calls from a current Temple member who continually provided her with information about when the Temple shipments to Guyana were being sent from San Francisco. With each of these tips Jeannie contacted Treasury Department agent Jim Hubert, expecting that he would investigate and bust Jones for the illegal contraband that was being sent outside the country. She even went as far as to drive by the Temple after these calls came and she witnessed large flatbed trucks sitting outside the church packed with crates headed for Guyana. Still, Hubert did nothing. After several failed attempts with Hubert, she started to believe that either he didn't believe her or someone above him was preventing the investigation.

Jones' harassment of New West offices caused more harm than good. Finally, on June 11, 1977, San Francisco Examiner political columnist, Bill Barnes, published an article entitled *"Yet-to-be printed story builds a storm,"* which raised the question: what does Jim Jones have to hide? The article also quoted New West's editor, Rosalie Wright, as saying, "I feel threatened" by the numerous letters and phone calls coming from the Temple. Jones' own paranoia and false assumptions had turned what was likely to be an innocuous political profile into a vicious cycle that would ultimately lead to his downfall. Jones had, in essence, blown the whistle on himself.

After reading the article Jeannie finally made the call to Phil Tracy to tell him her story. After so many failed attempts and still fearing retribution from Jones, Jeannie was reluctant at first to give her real name. She explained to Tracy that it was vital that she remained anonymous. Jeannie told him everything, and Mr. Tracy handled it like a pro. Their first conversation lasted for an hour and a half, and Tracy made Jeannie promise to call him back. On June 18, 1977, the S.F Chronicle printed a story about a *"strange break-in at the magazine."* The report claimed that a Peoples Temple file had been tampered with. Fortunately, only Kilduff's first copy had been obtained by the intruders, which only spoke of Jones' political clout. Jeannie immediately contacted Tracy after reading the article and informed him that this was the work of the sinister Jim Jones. Mr. Tracy assured her that all his notes were safe. Four days later police issued a statement claiming that there was no evidence of a break-in, reinforcing Temple supporters' belief that New West was on a witch hunt with no substance to draw from.

Mr. Tracy pleaded with Jeannie to give her real name and publicly testify to her statements. "Until someone has the courage to come out publicly, the atrocities will continue," Tracy explained to her. Jeannie took some time to think about it and the serious risk this would cause. They truly believed that if they came out publicly they'd be killed. After talking it over with Al she decided this was the chance she had been waiting for to make her stand. Jeannie told Grace, who was in a custody battle with Jones to get her child back at the time, and she agreed to tell her story as well. They also agreed to be photographed and soon, they were joined by 10 other members. Kilduff, Tracy, and the others all met up at Jeannie's house to discuss their stories. What they heard went far beyond what they had expected. They finally had a story that would bring down this house of cards.

Back in June of 1977, Jones was becoming frantic about the rumors of the Kilduff *exposé*. Being overly paranoid, Jones called an all night meeting with four of his most trusted female members, where he explained to them that he wanted to expand the letter writing campaign and phone calls to New West. Jim's plan was to put even more pressure on and flood New West with an even more extreme letter writing and phone call campaign, informing them that Kilduff's impending attack was unwarranted. Each of the participating members were given a stack of quarters and told to go to various pay phones throughout the San Francisco area to make calls so the calls were not traced. They made calls to the secretaries, the vice president, the marketing department, and all other departments at New West. They even contacted Rupert Murdoch, who was the owner of New West Magazine at the time.

Jones was worried that the article would be released before all his members were able to flee to Guyana. He was also fearful that he would be arrested and brought up on charges and would not be able to leave the country. The difficulties that Jones was having with the migration was that he had sent 400 members to Guyana the previous month and Guyanese officials wanted a halt on anymore incomers from the group in order to review the swell of immigration applications. Jones, however, offered to deposit $500,000 into the Bank of Guyana, and suddenly the halt was lifted.

Another difficulty had to do with transportation. Due to the forthcoming article, Jones feared that the media was now keeping a watchful eye on the S.F. airport, so he didn't want to use that route any longer. This meant that he would have to bus members to anonymous cities for departure. Regardless, Jones had the evacuation in full effect. The biggest problem that the article posed, however, was the fact that the land was not fully cultivated and would not be for a few years. This meant that the rushed exodus would certainly mean over-crowded circumstances. Jonestown was not ready to accommodate 1100 residents at that time.

The editors and advisers of the magazine received as many as 50 phone calls and 70 letters a day from Temple members, as well as some from local politicians and Temple supporters. Many of the calls and letters that New West was receiving were to the affect, "We hear you are going to attack Jim Jones in print; don't do that. He's a good man who does good work." Even prominent Californians called with a similar message.

Tape *Q579* is believed to be one of the hundreds of calls made by Temple members to *New West Magazine*.

Female Temple member: Well, I've been uh, around San Francisco a long time, I was born and raised here, and I'm interested in your magazine, I've read it here and there, and I just recently found out that uh, one of your reporters is— seems to be doing a lot of uh, (pause) talking and it's about a situation that I happen to know a little bit about. Uh, I understand he's saying a bunch of negative things about uh, this Peoples Temple group, and I know for a fact—

Receptionist (New West): Okay. Let me stop you— Let me stop you right there.

Female Temple member: Yeah?

Receptionist (New West): Okay? We've been inundated with calls on this. Uh, the guy is not our reporter. All right? He is a reporter, he's just free-lancer [Kilduff]. We have not committed to do any article, we have not signed anything, uh, we have not committed ourselves either way. Uh, it— it wasn't even an assignment that we've given him. Okay?

In early July of 1977, Rosalie Wright, editor of *New West Magazine*, called Jones—with Maria Katsaris and Debbie Layton present—and read him the article that was scheduled for publication on the August 1st. As she read the article, Jones interrupted her several times in order to refute the allegations. "Shall I continue," she said, as she informed him that she was reading him the article out of courtesy and there was nothing he could do about its release. As he listened his mouth became dry and his stress level reached an all time high. Jones paced back and forth in angst listening to what was, in his mind, surely his worst nightmare being realized. The more she read the worse the article painted the Temple. Jones sat through the testimony's of defector after defector, getting more and more bothered with each sentence. "Fuck these bastards," Jones furiously scribbled on a little note pad that he passed to Maria and Debbie. Rosalie finally neared the end of the article, reading the section that gave numerous reasons why Jones and his Temple should be investigated. Jones sucked down a few of his prescription pills and scribbled one final note as he wrapped up the call with Rosalie:

"We leave tonight. Notify Georgetown."

The biggest concern now was how to get 500 plus members shipped over to Guyana. Jones got right to it, wasting no time. Jones stayed up that whole night preparing for their decampment. Debbie and ten PC members, including Jim's wife, Marceline, were left behind to maintain and eventually close down shop in the States. Debbie would not leave for Jonestown until early December. Jones immediately headed for Guyana days later, where he set up in Georgetown, receiving constant updates on any monkeyshine from the press. All messages were communicated in "secret code" via amateur HAM radio broadcasts from S.F. to Guyana. For instance, when Jones said over the radio that he needed more "Bibles," he wanted "guns." In fact, the Temple developed a complex glossary of terms, or codes, that they would use while communicating on amateur HAM radio, virtually breaking every restriction and regulation of the FCC.

A rally was held for Jones on July 31, 1977, on Geary Street. Jones' most important supporters were on hand: S.F. Assemblymen Willy Brown, S.F. Mayor George Moscone, S.F. Supervisor Harvey Milk, and Carlton Goodlett. Jim Jones, himself, spoke. Although in Guyana at the time, Jones transmitted his speech by radio long-distance. The article was released on August 1, 1977, "*Inside Peoples Temple*." The first part of the article profiles Jones and his political ties. It opens fairly affably for Jones. However, the second part of the article tells the stories of ten defectors. Furthermore, the third part provides several reasons why Jones should be investigated. All and all; it was a devastating blow to Jones.

The article caused quite a big stir. The contrast between the Temple's public image and its private practices was indeed an eye-catching read. So good, in fact, that other reporters kept digging, looking for more dirt on the Temple. Kilduff and Tracy had become local celebrities, of sorts. A second article went into preparation almost immediately after this article was released. The next day Jones read aloud his resignation as Housing Commission chairman over the radio. New West smelled blood. Capitalizing on knocking Jones to his knees and sending him running with his tail between his legs, they published several more articles. The first was published on August 7, 1977: "*Rev. Jones: The Power Broker; Political Maneuvering of a Preacher Man*." The second was published on

August 14, 1977: *"The Temple, a Nightmare World."* These articles, particularly the last one, did even more damage to the churches' already teetering reputation. In Jones' absence and isolation in a foreign land, his supporters would slowly fade to almost nil.

Mass Exodus & the "Six Day Siege"

By April of 1977, Jones was making several trips to and from Guyana. He continually bragged to U.S. members how great it was there. Jones always returned with video to show U.S. Temple members how happy everyone was there and what the land looked like. Undoubtedly, the Guyana members were told what to say, but none the less, he piqued the interest of all U.S. members' with his video propaganda. By April there were about 600 people residing in Jonestown, including Mark Blakey, who'd been sent over early to help with the construction. Jones told U.S. members the exact opposite of what it was going to be like for them in Guyana. He claimed that the work hours were short, food was good, and the sleep was plenty.

Jim's son, Stephan Jones had moved to Jonestown in January of 1977, eight months before Jim had moved there. What Jim said about Jonestown was actually accurate before his own arrival. It was only when Jim moved to Jonestown that it was truly run like a military camp. As Stephan recalls, Jonestown was a very different place before Jim moved there. Work there was still hard, but when they were off, their time was "their time." Stephan claims that before Jim moved there, it was the "best time of his life." However, when Jim arrived, the place changed overnight and work went from being a means of production to a "means of control." The food became thoroughly inadequate when Jim arrived and even when work ended it was still Jim's time.

Jim had been preparing for his evacuation long before the New West article. Jones' departure is most commonly referred to as a "mass exodus," and many believe that he took 1100 members to Guyana in one trip. However, there were about 600 members already in Jonestown by April 1977, and more were being shipped every few weeks. The mass exodus occurred over a period of about three months. Twenty-four-year-old Maria Katsaris was the Temple's financial secretary at the time. Teri Buford and Debbie Layton

Blakey were her assistants. Jones and his financial team had been closing various Temple bank accounts and wiring the money over to Guyana. The assets of the Temple were plenty, equating to about $10 million by 1975, and had grown since then. They were also receiving a total of $65,000 a month in social security checks for the older Temple members. This money was also transferred to Guyana. Church properties and homes were also put up for sale to fund the Guyana property lease, which as an investment totaled $5 million. In order to sneak money or "transfer" money across the border, all members were given $5,000, which is the legal limit. However, some of the older and unsuspicious looking members were given as much as $20,000 to smuggle past customs. There was also several hundred-thousand dollars shipped over in crates.

Jones also used the relationship between one of his most trusted members, Paula Adams, and Guyanese Ambassador to the United States, Laurence Mann. Paula's relationship with Mann helped them get through Guyanese bureaucracy in many areas. Mann helped with the money smuggled in by Temple members, aiding them in depositing the money in Guyanese banks. Well before the New West article was released, Jones had been preparing for such an event. Jones had urged his followers to get their passports ready and get the necessary shots needed to enter the country of Guyana. Jones began sending his followers to Jonestown in May of 1977. He ramped up his efforts in June, July, and August as his fear of the potential New West fiasco grew near. By July there were more than 800 members residing in Jonestown; by September there were approximately 1,000. Jones kept the San Francisco Temple active, and he communicated with them often by radio: getting news updates, supplies, food, clothing, and a host of other items.

After Jones moved into the interior, he soon sent for Carolyn Layton and their son, Kimo Prokes. Both would live with Jones once in Jonestown. Eight-hundred members were residing in Jonestown when Jones arrived and that number would soon grow to one-thousand. By August of 1977, Tim Stoen had joined forces with Grace Stoen in the battle with the Temple over custody of John Victor Stoen. Things were looking good for the couple initially, as on August 26th Grace was awarded custody by a California court. A few days later her attorney, Jeffrey Haas, travelled to Guyana to get John back. Jones, however, refused to return the child. So, Haas went to the court there in Georgetown and obtained an arrest warrant for both Jones and the child. He travelled to Jonestown with Guyanese Supreme Court Marshall, Billy Blackman, to retrieve the child and arrest Jones. When they got there, though, Temple members claimed that Jones was not there, and they refused to accept the warrants. Blackman was forced to nail the warrant papers to a wooden wall.

Although Jonestown had won this round they were thoroughly panicking about how close the Guyanese Government had let Haas get to them. Jones would use the incident to play on the fears of his followers. In early September, Jones told his followers that there was a sniper attack. Days later Jones let loose ear-piercing sirens and alerted everyone to the pavilion area. Jones claimed that the camp was under attack by armed forces led by Tim Stoen. Jonestown guards ran about with guns searching for these mysterious forces while other members were given weapons and ordered to surround the encampment. At one point Jones even screamed over the public address system that he had been hit (shot). This fake invasion ordered by Jones lasted for six days, and came to be known as the "six day siege."

The warrant was never signed, however, and the Temple's lawyer successfully argued that the court had no evidence that the Stoens had revoked an earlier standing grant for Jonestown resident, Joyce Touchette, to serve as the child's guardian. That was reversed, however, on November 18, 1977, when a California Superior Court judge in San Francisco issued an order awarding custody to Grace Stoen, as well as visitation rights to Tim. The judge rendered the ruling that Grace and Tim had previously authorized Touchette and other Temple members to serve as the child's guardian null and void, and he ordered that Jones must "immediately deliver the minor John Victor Stoen" to Grace Stoen. The order also authorized Grace to initiate contempt proceedings against Jones.

Meanwhile, Debbie Layton had been busy tending to her mother, Lisa, who was fighting cancer. Jones began realizing that Debbie's attention had been focused on her mother's condition and this angered him. He began questioning her commitment to the cause. He also required her to perform a task of great importance to him in an effort to have her refocus her energies on the Temple. Jones told her that Lisa's condition would miraculously improve once she was closer to him, and he started to make preparations for their arrival in Jonestown. Jones ordered Debbie to contact a high-ranking Guyanese official, who was visiting the United States, and give him a message on behalf of Jones. The message to the Guyanese official centered on the ongoing John Victor Stoen custody battle and the pending court case against Jones. She relayed the following message:

> *"Unless the government of Guyana takes immediate steps to stall the Guyanese court action regarding John Victor Stoen's custody, the entire population of Jonestown will extinguish itself in a mass suicide at 5:30pm that day."*

Although a California state court did not have any jurisdiction in foreign lands and could not compel Guyanese courts to do anything, Jones still wanted more insurance against any further legal action. In fact, Jones again started a furious letter writing campaign; this time aimed at stalling the Guyanese courts from any further action against him. A local Georgetown paper even picked up the story, claiming that the judge had received so many threatening calls and letters that he had excused himself from the case. The article also acknowledged that the judge wasn't even sure which side that the threats were coming from, but that he wanted no part of it any longer. At that point Grace and Tim Stoen had to start all over again, this time with a new judge. The Stoens continued the fight for their son, making several more court appearances and even another trip to Guyana. Unfortunately, Jones refused to relinquish him.

On December 6, 1977, Debbie and her mother Lisa started their perilous journey to the promise land. Each was saddled with $10,000 and dreams of what they had heard was the most beautiful place in the world. As they set off on their journey, they both hoped that it was everything that they had dreamed it would be. Their first stop was New York, where they would have a big dinner and a bottle of wine that they promised they would not speak a word of. From there they would embark on a life changing experience that only one would return from! With high hopes and even higher expectations, they left feeling excited and confident that they would finally find the true happiness that was so elusive to them in the United States.

CHAPTER 8 – INDIANA JONES & THE TEMPLE OF DOOM

The trip to Guyana—Jonestown in particular—was a wretched one, indeed. The long, laborious journey was more than just disorienting and disconcerting; it went straight to the heart of traumatic. The *first-leg* of the trip kicked off with a long plane ride from the United States to the Guyanese capital, Georgetown. Before entering Georgetown, which sits near the edge of the ocean, there was what seemed like an endless amount of jungle to those flying overhead. Once passengers touched down at the Timehri Airport and stepped onto the ground below the heat was immediately recognizable. The sweltering tarmac aggressively ate away at the rubber soles of shoes and the heat was so thick that many felt the need to brush it away from their faces. Passengers then entered a terminal where they were goaded towards customs agents, at which point they were thoroughly searched. At the airport they were met by other existing resident members who drove them to Temple headquarters in mud soiled vans. The view was lined with old, neglected sheds and shacks, down the narrow, one-lane mired road that led the passengers into town.

Partially clothed children and meager living accommodations were witnessed as they passed through the poorer section of town on their way to the capital. Slender black and brown people proudly showered the streets of the capital, some with suits and brief-cases. Although it did not seem like a capital city, the streets were at least paved and more populated than all other areas. The historic city of Georgetown was inhabited by a mix of descendants of British, East Indian, Caribbean, Spanish, and Amerindian people. Passing through the center of the capital, the van turned onto another dirt road, where houses were about a block apart. Shortly after that, members pulled into the driveway of 41 Lamaha Gardens, the "Peoples Temple House" (a.k.a. Peoples Temple Headquarters) located on the outskirts of Georgetown and owned by Jim Jones. The house functioned as a *way station* for Temple members moving to and from Jonestown. Sharon Amos resided in the house along with her two adopted children, Christen [age 7] and Martin [age 6]; while Sharon's biological daughter, Leanne [age 21], resided in Jonestown.

Once in Georgetown, it was quickly apparent that things were dramatically different from the States. Guyana was Jones' ideal situation, his dream—a socialist country that welcomed him with open arms. Jones' power there was much more immanent. Instead of meeting with small city mayors and assemblymen, he was meeting with diplomats and the Prime Minister. Jonestown was even represented at a meeting of the ruling party of Guyana, the *People's National Congress* (PNC). The atmosphere in Jonestown had become much more militant, as Jones turned his once, sect, to a cult, and by this time to a militia. Smiling and laughing was not promoted. The change was noticeably different in comparison to back home. Jim's evolution had been complete; from his days of locking his friends up in the garage to becoming the absolute ruler of his people.

The trip up to this point was a cake walk in comparison to what was ahead. From there, it was time to travel into the interior: Jonestown! On the *Second-leg* of the trip, members were ushered to the Georgetown docks where they boarded an old seventy-two-foot tug boat named, "the *Cudjoe*." The trawler set out onto the Caribbean Sea, which is located at 9-22°N and 89 to 60°W, headed for the Kaituma River. Their journey would end after a treacherous thirty-two-hour voyage. Bouncing around the sea, members were continually drenched from pouncing waves crashing onto the deck. Clothes were soaked with sea-water and vomit and no one was spared from the seas' asperities.

As the boat entered the mouth of the Kaituma River, the *third-leg* of the trip had begun; only eight more hours to go. The raging waters changed from crashing blue-green waves to calm, dark, muddy waters. During the final few hours of the boat trip, the *Cudjoe* captain, Tim Sweeney announced that he would be confiscating any outside correspondence brought in and that any communications would be reviewed by the Jonestown *Clearing Committee*. This was the first sign of things to come and what to be expected in Jonestown. Yet, no one knew exactly what precarious conditions awaited them. After the long and arduous boat ride, members arrived at Port Kaituma. A flatbed truck waited to take them on the *Fourth and final leg* of the journey.

Port Kaituma was about eight-miles away from Jonestown—about a forty-five minute ride down a remote and hole-ridden dirt road. Debbie Layton and other members claim that this was the most "agonizing" part of the trip. By this point members were completely impoverished. The one-hour ride that was ahead of them was only slightly dulled by the anticipation of getting ever closer to the "promise land." The agony of the ride was mainly due to the rough terrain of the unpaved jungle road. The cement-less, mired road had its own impressions of "pot holes" that grabbed the truck like long arms reaching out of the ground. The tires rolled and spiraled like a vehicle stuck on ice, struggling to move forward. The road was very narrow and surrounded by trees and jungle in every direction. As the truck trudged on through the carved out pathway and crept closer to Jonestown, a white sign hanging from a tree appeared reading, "GREETINGS Peoples Temple Agricultural Project." Jonestown was still out of sight, but evidently near.

When the truck finally rolled up upon signs of civilization—in the form of lights swinging from tall poles—the excitement stirred like a kid on Christmas. The truck drove parallel to the Jonestown encampment and came to a stop in an open area with a long wooden walkway that led to a large open-sided tin-roofed-tent known as, "The Pavilion." Dark green military tents and wooden huts were in clear view of arriving members.

Entering Jonestown

The new arrivals were not greeted by smiling faces and the warm welcome of a utopian society, but rather with a distant look and a cold disposition. The residents all had the look in their eyes of isolation and confusion, of people who had no contact with the outside world. There would be no honeymoon for the new arrivals. Their shattered expectations would be almost immediately realized. Every member entering Jonestown during and after the exodus had the exact same reaction: disappointment and fear. Newbies were led to a tented area where they were met by the Jonestown *Greeting Committee.* The very formal process was more like an interrogation from customs agents rather than a hospitable greeting. Committee members dumped the belongings of new arrivals onto an examination table and openly riffled through and discussed the contents. Upon commencement of the inspection, the committee made a full report of each individual. Most everything was confiscated and the newbie's were given only four T-shirts, four pairs of socks, a toothbrush, toothpaste, four pairs of underwear, and a bar of soap. All of the confiscated belongings were stored in a shed on the compound and precious items were set aside for Jones to sift through for his own personal use. Just another example that Jones' vapid socialist ideals were meant for everyone but himself—he was exempt. This was a clear indication of his dictatorship society. Yet, only a small example in comparison to what was to come.

Tour of Jonestown

Jonestown was an impressive sight to see. The camp was built by members whom labored long hours in the hot sun, building this fortress from scratch, clearing the jungle for more than a quarter of a mile—or 900-acres.

Entering Jonestown, facing SOUTH:

The main entrance to Jonestown was a long wooden walkway that led through the garden area past the *first Well* and the *first Generator*. A few 100ft later was the *Playground* on the left, and the *Banana Stand, Dinning Tent,* and *Kitchen,* on the right. Just before the playground was a footpath that veered off to the right. This small pathway led to the *Bakery, Vegetable Stand, Smoke House, Herbal Garden,* and *Cellar cooler* all located on the right. One the left of the pathway were the first set of *Showers, Doctor's office, Infirmary, Laboratory, Pharmacy,* 6 *Troolies* (cottages with walls made from woven troolie reeds/leaves), and at the end of the path was the first of three sets of *Bathrooms*.

Just past the playground was a small footpath laying perpendicular and crisscrossing the main walkway that provided the option of making a left or a right. To the right and several 100 feet down the footpath was the *West House*, Jones' living quarters; which is where the road ended. To the left led to the rest of the camp. Making a left on the walkway, the playground would immediately be on your left and the *Office* would be on your right. As we continue down the road, we would soon have the *Radio Room* directly on our right and the *Pavilion* on our left. A few more feet up on our right were two big *Educational Tents*, one behind the other.

Continuing forward, we would soon come to the first of five *Dormitories*; the number three dorm being behind that on the left. From there, the road split to the right, angling north-east of the direction we are walking. As we make that right and walk a few feet forward, we would see on our left the number four dorm, the number two dorm, and behind that were the *Showers*. From there we have the option of continuing straight or making a left. Going straight ahead a few 100ft would lead to the *Basketball Court*, which was on our left, and just past that was a huge section of land that held the *52 cottages* and the *Tower*; the road ends there. If we decided to make a left at the split instead, we would see the number five dorm a few feet up on the left, and at the end of the pathway, the *East Guest Houses*; numbering three; as well as the infamous *Well* close by. If we go back to the entrance on the main walkway and continue straight past the playground without turning left or right, we would soon come upon several resource sheds on the left: the *Supply Shed*, *Tool Room* and *Garage*, *Saw Mill*, and behind that, the *Warehouse*. Additionally, there were three bathrooms, two generators, 2 wells, 2 showers, a *brick factory*, and a *soap factory*. Jonestown also had *The Cuffy Memorial Baby Nursery* located right next to the basketball court. The nursery housed the 33 children that were born in Jonestown, and it was run by Marceline Jones. This was Marceline's pride and joy. She was very proud of this facility in particular. It was a great inspiration to her.

Before Jones' arrival people truly believed that Jonestown was a utopia. Prior to Jones' arrival members watched entertaining movies from Georgetown. However, when Jones arrived that was replaced by soviet propaganda shorts and documentaries on American social problems. Scholastic studies and lectures turned to lessons focused on Soviet alliances and reports from Jones that Blacks were being corralled into prison camps back in the U.S. As more and more poured into Jonestown during the mass exodus conditions started to deteriorate quickly. Buildings fell into disrepair and weeds encroached on fields. Conditions had become so overcrowded that mission administrators complained to Jones that "more room" needed to be added. Construction was sped up, but the already overworked crew could not keep up with the influx of incoming members. When approached by administrators about the overcrowded conditions Jones coyly said, "Make room."

The rules in Jonestown were unwritten, yet very clear: keep to yourself, don't speak of your inner thoughts or fears, and assimilate completely into the group without a hint of individuality or distain. Learning the ropes quickly was of the utmost importance. Becoming a trusted member was the ultimate goal. Members were honored for reporting words of disloyalty of others, or the fears expressed by others, or discrepancies with Jones' rules or life in general in Jonestown. Jones often had many members pose as potential defectors, instructing them to tell pre-selected individuals that they were thinking about escaping. If the pre-selected individuals (who were normally close friends or family members of the subject) did not report the potential defectors, they would be punished severely. This type of mind control exercise ensured that individual members could not trust other members, even if they were family. The worst part of the disciplinary process was being isolated and looked down upon by peers. Although, it could be argued that being enclosed in a dark, muddy hole was far worse.

Public punishment and embarrassment were far worse for Temple members while in Jonestown. Jones' idea of socialism had turned his flock into zombie-like followers who were stripped of their former identities and all independent thought; they lived in fear. Jones often had members write themselves up for capitalistic thoughts, or worse; he had them write things that they feared the most. When they would get out of line in any way, Jones used those admissions against them. If you were afraid of snakes and fell asleep during one of Jones' never ending speeches, you could be sure that you would be spending time with a not-so-nice snake in the very near future. Or, if you didn't like rats and you were late for a meeting, you could be pretty sure that you were going to spend the night in a rat infested hole. Certainly after being tortured and desensitized by Jones' foul tactics members were then excited to see others receive cruel and unusual punishment as well, as it was then seen as fair.

There was a special disciplinary crew known as the *Learning Crew*. This crew primary function acted as a "re-education crew" for any individuals not following orders. This included not working fast enough, being perceived as having a poor attitude, complaining, and a whole host of other acts that Jones deemed rebellious. Jones maximized every disciplinary technique to its fullest and made the techniques work for him and against others. For example, if three people on a five person crew wrote someone up for something and the fourth did not then the fourth person would be punished along with the assailant and sent to the learning crew. This kept alliances from forming. It also pitted mother against daughter and father against son. The system helped perpetuate the strength of its leader.

Everyone was watched and written-up. If someone's pace slowed, they were written-up and sent to the learning crew. While on the learning crew, members worked twice as fast. They were not allowed to talk to anyone or smile. They slept under armed guard and ate separately from the rest of the community. To illustrate the severity of the situation, guards on the learning crew carried rifles. Every new arrival was expected to work hard labor, except for the very young and the elderly; but that also was negotiable. As if the learning crew was not harsh enough, Jones had *The Box, The Well* and *The Medical Unit* as other chambers of torture.

The Box was a small ditch dug-out of the ground that had a custom-made cover which sealed it. Sometimes even children were sentenced to for days on end. One man was sent to the Box for ten-days. The six-by-four-foot space was hot, dark, and for people who had a hard time with claustrophobic areas; it was an absolute nightmare! The unlucky prisoners dinned on only mush and had only the bugs to keep them company. Some former residents of Jonestown report that while in the box, members were forced to listen to a tape recording that repeated over and over again, "I'll be a changed person when I get out." *The Well* was just that: a well that held water at the bottom of it. The legend of the well in Jonestown is that Jones would send unruly members there in the dead of night. There he would have them hung them upside down over the well and lowered in. Someone was usually unknowingly stationed at the bottom of the well to scare the victim as they gasped for air from being dunked under water repeatedly. *The Medical Unit* had a dual function: performing routine medical services and serving as a menacing torture chamber in which unruly members were involuntarily drugged until they were incapacitated. This was the worst punishment of all for disruptive, uncooperative members. The medical unit was stocked with large quantities of psychoactive drugs used for behavioral control and modification.

Jones played the worldwide news over the public address system every morning, waking most out of some much needed sleep. Later, Jones would test members on what they had heard and learned from these reports. The news was played in order for Jones to convince the members how bad the rest of the world had become and how lucky they were to be in Jonestown. There were absolutely no freedoms in Jonestown. Each day, for each member, was planned out and full. If a couple wanted to have a relationship in Jonestown they had to plead their case in front of the *Relationship Committee* (RC). The RC would determine whether the couple would in fact be allowed to engage in a lasting relationship. The process, however, appeared very bureaucratic by design, as the RC's determination process usually took about three-months to return a verdict. Many of the members who were traveling from the United States to Guyana were expected to smuggle either money or weapons. Many of the weapons were smuggled into Jonestown in the luggage of members who seemed inconspicuous. The guns were not smuggled whole; rather, they were smuggled in piece-by-piece and assembled in Jonestown. Some of the weapons, among other things, were also smuggled in by boat.

The Security Staff at Jonestown numbered about thirty-five members and was led by head of security, Joe Wilson. There were extensive fire-arms trainings for security staff members in Jonestown as well as back in San Francisco. Joe Wilson, Tome Kice, Stephan Jones, and Calvin Douglas were just some of the firearms instructors. Jonestown security members were rarely armed, but there were special occasions when they would arm themselves at Jones' request. The only time that security members were always armed was during special events or during disciplinary functions, such as public beatings, during learning crew work or during the infamous *White Nights*. *Hut-C14* was a building in Jonestown where heads of security resided and many operations were coordinate. Weapons were frequently seen carried in and out of Hut-C14, but no one has ever confirmed whether or not there was a secret weapons storage there or not. The security heads that were responsible for issuing weapons were Joe Wilson, Johnny Brown Jones, Johnny Cobb, Calvin Douglas, and Bob Kice. Stephan Jones was known as the weapons expert in Jonestown and was an expert marksman. Stephan was also in charge of cleaning all weapons. Two armed security members were always stationed at Jones' house, which was known as the West House, in the south-east corner of Jonestown. An armed security sniper was also often seen atop the Jonestown tower.

In addition to the known security force in Jonestown there was also a secret security force present, known as *Roaming Security* or "roamers." The responsibility of the *roamers* was to observe (spy on) members on the suspect list as being "negatives," which included all those who had been publicly disciplined and those who had expressed a desire to leave Jonestown. They also kept a close watch on those that were being held against their will. Bob Kice was in charge of the daily roaming security. The rest of the roaming security members were unknown to the rest of the residents in Jonestown. It was well known that just about everyone in Jonestown wanted to leave the moment that they arrived, but they also immediately realized that there was no way out. Jones had also confiscated all passports, making a trip back to the states almost impossible even if a person was to escape. Moreover, over 30 miles of jungle separated Jonestown from any other civilization. One wrong turn in the jungle and the person(s) escaping would die for sure. Jonestown was an armed prison camp. This was almost immediately recognized within the first ten-minutes of entering; which was by then too late!

Jones often planted roamers among the workers in an effort to build their confidence. Many times Jones would specifically target certain individuals and have a roamer befriend the targeted individual and then ask them certain questions in order to test their loyalty. If they answered unfavorably they would be written-up and punished severely. If they spoke of plans to escape they would be dealt with in the most extreme manner, in an effort to break the individual's spirit. Jones used the excuse that he had the knowledge that the FBI and the CIA had infiltrated Jonestown and that members from both agencies were among them. This may not have been far from the truth; although, Jones may have been one of them and well aware who the others were. Write-ups were submitted to Rita Tupper, Eva Jones (no relation to Jim), Rochelle Hochman and Maria Katsaris.

The *Letter Writing Committee* (LWC) was headed by Rita Tupper, who described herself publicly as a violent revolutionary. The LWC was in charge of doctoring and reviewing letters written by Jonestown members in efforts to sensor any sensitive or threatening information from reaching the outside. Every letter that came into Jonestown or went out of Jonestown had to be run by Tupper first. Any members that did not comply with the rules of letter writing were reported and severely beaten, drugged, and or ordered to do things at gunpoint. Antagonists were also put on the list of "negatives" and were ridden harder and watched closer by roaming security members. Note: Unruly members were rarely beaten by one man. Sometimes one person was beaten by upwards of twenty men. Joyce Touchette also held a high ranking in the LWC. Amoung the many rules in Jonestown, one stood out: "never criticize the settlement when writing back to the United States." This was the cardinal rule!

Field workers were expected to work in the field from 7:00 a.m. to 6:00 p.m., six days per week, and on Sunday from 7:00 a.m. to 2:00 p.m., with one-hour for lunch and one-hour for dinner. They were also required to attend rallies that started at 7:30 p.m. lasting until midnight, every night. Work days and work assignments were coordinated by Charles and Joyce Touchette. While working to cultivate the fields, Debbie Layton claimed that they were being patrolled by uniformed armed guards with access to 200 to 300 rifles, 25 pistols, and a homemade bazooka. Many witnesses claim that the number of guns that were in Jonestown numbered a total of approximately 200. Weapons also included cutlasses [machetes], which Jones had a surplus of, and a number of crossbows, longbows, and combination bows stored in a crate next to the metal warehouse. There were also hundreds of rounds of ammunition (Note: a round is not a single bullet, but is as much ammunition a weapon will hold. This amount varies from weapon to weapon. The term has been misused so often that now even police and military personnel refer to a single bullet as a round. It is similar to ordering a round of drinks at a bar).

Jones had told the members that the farm was not expected to be self-sufficient for another three years and their current source of food was not coming from the fields. It wasn't long before Jones realized that he had made a huge mistake in choosing to migrate to

Guyana. Jones understood at some point that no matter how hard they worked, the fields would never be cultivated enough to provide for the community. The diet consisted of rice for breakfast, rice water soup for lunch, and rice, gravy, and beans for dinner. Two or three times a week they were served vegetables, and on Sundays each individual received one egg and one cookie. On the few occasions when outside visitors, whom Jones wished to impress, came into Jonestown they were treated to meat and vegetables, which included all members. During these visits members were drilled on what to say to keep up the image of a utopian society.

The meetings scheduled in Jonestown consisted of Marxist/Socialism classes on Tuesday and Thursday nights. The members were tested on Sunday from the previous Tuesday and Thursday lessons. Russian classes were also implemented as Jones had been negotiating with Russia for possible exile for the group. Not only were these classes to help members get accustomed to the possibility of their new country, but it was also to impress Russian dignitaries who would visit Jonestown. Not many members took Jones serious in regards to his sentiments of moving to the Soviet Union. Many believed that it was just another ploy or part of Jones' manipulation strategy. It would be safer to assume that Jones was planning to move to Russia with a few select members after extinguishing the community in a mass suicide/murder.

In April of 1978, the Temple's PR staff—led by Mike Prokes—reported to the Russian Embassy that the agricultural project in Jonestown was not going as planned. The constant foraging, burning, hoeing, planting, ranking, and clearing land, was not having the effect that was expected or desired. The jungle had its own ideas for what would grow and would not grow. The jungle had fought off each cultivation attempt. It was a battle that they could not win. Consequently, Jones instructed the PR staff to offer the Russians several million dollars for their safe passage to Moscow. Jones was also considering Cuba as another outlet. Later, Jones would even suggest that he would even take safe passage in Tanzania, Libya, or Uganda if they'd have them.

Jonestown was sold to its people as a utopian, socialist society where everyone would be treated equally. Elite members, however, only worked eight hour days and did not have to wait in Long food lines, while the others found themselves in far worse situations. Coincidentally, ninety percent of the elite, inner-circle members were White. The security force did not have to work menial labor jobs and existed primarily to discipline other Jonestown members. The security administered most of the initial beatings, especially on those expressing their displeasure with Jonestown or those who slacked during working hours. After the initial beating from security force, the ones receiving the disciplinary actions were often called up to the stage at a later time to face a public berating and possibly another beating.

Members who took on the extreme measure of leaving Jonestown were dealt with in an equally extreme manner. Those who attempted to escape Jonestown were hunted down, dragged back to the camp, and put on *Public Service*. Those on public service were shackled with leg irons—which are synonymous with the slavery of Blacks in America from 1625–1791—and kept under armed guard. Their punishment also included extended work hours and they would be last to eat meals. Only Jim Jones could determine the length that an individual served on public service. Tommy Bogue and another member escaped Jonestown on November 1, 1977. They were caught a few days later and brought back to Jonestown, where they were shackled together with leg-irons and made to work 18-hour days while sleeping under armed guard for three-weeks. People were made to believe that the security force in Jonestown was to protect them against mercenaries and other possible invaders when in reality its main function was to prevent against escape and to enforce Jones' strict disciplinary code.

Most members quickly came to the realization that the only way out of Jonestown was by death. Immediately after entering Jonestown, Joyce Touchette commandeered all passports and money. Escaping into the Guyana jungle was the least a member had to worry about. Just about every individual in Jonestown also had a family member present. Before a person attempted escape, they would have to be ok with the fact that their loved ones would be held under armed guard and virtually held hostage for the remainder of their lives. Jones often taunted members, claiming that all roads leading to Jonestown were one way. Even if an individual worked their way up to trusted member and was assigned to Georgetown, no one in their family was let out of Jonestown. While in Georgetown members were not permitted to speak to anyone outside the Temple unless they were specifically assigned to do so. In the rare cases that a wife and a husband were let out of Jonestown, their kids would be left behind as insurance.

Jones' health began to deteriorate dramatically while in Jonestown, even though he was the most cared for individual in the community. This did not slow Jones down a bit, however, when it came to his maniacal tactics. Day in and day out Jones came up with different tactics of conditioning that made his followers walk on egg shells. Jones no longer cared about being loved or ruling with love; he wanted to be feared. Jones' speeches were also becoming more maniacal and militant. He constantly fired up his congregation with militant speeches.

Jones: If by any chance you would make a mistake to try to come in and take any one of us, we will not let you, you will die, you will have to take anybody over all of our dead bodies...Don't ever say hate is my enemy. Love has practically caused me to get you destroyed. If I had hated a little more, just a little more, we woulda had a little less trouble. As I look at my faults, analytically. Sure you gotta love. Principle! But don't say, 'hate is my enemy I've gotta fight it day and night'. Love is the only weapon? SHIT!! BULL SHIT!!! BULL SHIT!!! MARTIN LUTHER KING DIED WITH LOVE! KENNEDY DIED TALKIN ABOUT SOMETHIN HE COULDN'T EVEN UNDERSTAND, SOME KIND OF GENERALIZED LOVE AND YAH KNOW HE NEVER EVEN BACKED IT UP. HE WAS SHOT DOWN! BULL SHIT!!! LOVE IS THE ONLY WEAPON IN WHICH I'VE GOT TO FIGHT; I'VE GOT A HELL OF ALLOT OF WEAPONS TO FIGHT! I'VE GOT MY CLOTHES, CUTLASSES [Machetes], I'VE GOT GUNS, I'VE GOT DYNAMITE, I'VE GOT A WHOLE LOT TO FIGHT. I'LL FIGHT!!!!!! I'LL FIGHT!!!!!! I'LL FIGHT!!!!!! I'LLLLLLLLLLLLLLLLLLLLL FIGHT!!!!!! I WILL FIGHT!!!! I WILL FIGHT!!!! I WILL FIGHT!!!! I WILL FIGHT!!!!

Crowd: (cheers uncontrollably!)

Jones: Let them hear it in the night!!!!!

Crowd: (cheers sounding more like screams of excitement and rage, uncontrollably!)

Jones: I'LLLLLLLLLLLLLLLLLLLLLLLLLLLLLLLLLLLL, ah yes we'll fight! Let the night roar with it! Let it roar! They're out there; they hear us [speaking of the "imaginary" mercenaries who were allegedly monitoring them from the jungle]!! We'll kill them if they come!!!

Waiting for the Right Moment

Much like several members in Jonestown, Debbie Layton began to struggle with her sanity. She was mentally and physically exhausted, suffering from malnutrition, and in constant fear of punishment. Debbie tried to visit her mother whenever possible, but was always in fear of how Jones would view her visits. Lisa was against the over-working of the members in the fields and the lack of protein they received. She was also against the long meetings and the extensive punishments, especially against children. Lisa voiced her disapproval to Debbie and informed her that she wanted to go to Jones in protest. Debbie pleaded with Lisa not to, as she knew the consequences would be harsh. Lisa was receiving two eggs a day because of her cancerous condition and would always share one with Debbie. Lisa was worried about Debbie and knew that she was not getting the proper nutrition. Lisa would not let Debbie leave her quarters until she shared an egg with her.

At first, Debbie was not really eating. The food smelled heinously, partly because of the iodine and other chemicals put on the food to protect it against jungle plagues. Another undesirable quality of the food was the insects that would regularly make kamikaze dives into it while people were eating. To make matters worse, food lines ran deep. Members who showed up just a few minutes late for dinner sometimes waited on a line of 300 people or more. Moreover, the meals consisted of rice and gravy, sometimes soup, and rarely were the members served meat. Right from the very beginning Debbie wanted to leave Jonestown. She wanted to confide in her mother of her thoughts of leaving, but she just knew that it was dangerous. She trusted her mother, but there were just too many reasons not to tell her. She knew that even if she did have a chance to escape and confided in Lisa, that Lisa might get worried and start to cry. If Jim saw her tears he would know get suspicious. There was also the idea that Lisa may think that Debbie was sent by Jones to test her. There were just too many bad scenarios for Debbie to confide in anyone about her feelings of leaving. Furthermore, she did not have a plan. Debbie had also been building up trust in Jones and by the request of Carolyn, had moved in with Jim's three sons and his daughter-in-law, Beth, who was married to Jim's adopted son, Lew.

One day in late February of 1978, Debbie fell very ill while working in the field and her sanity began failing because of it; she began to hallucinate. She was sent to the medical unit—not for punishment, but—for care until she was relatively healthy again. Seeing the severity of her condition, Jones assigned her to work in the radio room. Debbie was very good at this particular job and over time became the quintessential worker in the radio room. Eventually, she would become the person in charge of all communication from Jonestown to Temple headquarters in Georgetown. Radio room shifts consisted of two different shifts, both with vastly different codes. The first shift was from 7:00 a.m. – 6:00 p.m. The second shift was from 7:00 p.m. – 4:00 a.m. Up to that point, Maria Katsaris was working the day shift and the night shift was run by Jim and Carolyn. After thorough training on both shifts, Debbie soon took over the day shift in place of Maria. During this time, Debbie regained the Temple stature that she had once risen to back in the States, and she was once again part of the Temple's elite inner circle.

Debbie was looking forward to returning to the United States. It was the only solace that she had and it kept her focused. Some of the other more trusted members were told that they would be sent back to the United States after a brief stay in Jonestown; but once there, most knew immediately that they were not going to be let out of Jonestown. Before she had arrived Jones had promised Debbie that he would be sending her to the U.S. to run the S.F., radio room. She was originally told to accompany her mother Lisa to Jonestown and stay for about a period of two weeks until Lisa was acclimated. One evening while on shift in the radio room, however, her worst fears were realized. An angry man had contacted the radio room and vehemently demanded to speak to his mother and sister, who were residing in Jonestown at the time. After several attempts to stop the man from talking to them, even attempts by Jones himself, they finally allowed him to speak to them. The man again got very angry when he heard Jones trying to couch his family members on what to say. The man began to berate Jones and Jones finally disconnected the communication. It was at that point that Jones informed Debbie that she could never return to the U.S. Debbie tried to conceal her disappointment, but she was devastated. Her whole world had just come crashing down in that one instant! Now there was truly no escape. She was trapped like a rat in a cage. The only comfort she had was the thought that her quarters held guns—due to Jones' sons living with her—and she thought that she could always shoot herself if she could not escape.

Later that day, Jones had requested Debbie's presence in the radio room. As Jones was asked for more guns to be sent to Jonestown and instructing Temple leaders in S.F. how to answer the flood of questions from reporters, Carolyn pulled Debbie aside to have a word with her. Carolyn advised Debbie that she and Jim had decided to have Debbie chaperone the youth group into the capital the following morning. Debbie was in shock! She desperately tried to disguise her excitement and tried to act as nonchalant as possible. Debbie even went as far as calmly offering up other members to go in her place to hide her eagerness. Carolyn played right into Debbie's plan and advised her that the decision has already been made and she was going to be the one to go. Debbie was chosen for two main reasons: she was a very trusted member at that time and she was young and would blend in well with the other teenagers. Debbie would be accompanying 15-children to Georgetown where they would perform a cultural dance presentation entitled *Dance of Freedom*, held at the Guyanese Cultural Center. Staying true to his character, Jones had ulterior motives under the surface. The main reason for the visit was to personally deny and refute claims that the children were being mistreated and held against their will. Debbie was sent to watch over the children and ensure that none of them gave away the Temple's dirty secrets.

When Debbie got into bed that night she wondered what she would tell her mother or if she would ever see her again. One small slip-up could mean disaster for her. With absolutely no plan she played out all of the scenes in her head. She truly believed that this was her only chance at survival and a normal life; there was no other way. On the other hand if she failed, she knew that it was not without dire consequences. Death would be easy in comparison to some of the other torture techniques that Jones had been known to bestow upon others. The evidence was sitting in a coma-induced haze in the medical unit and the screams from the well and the box. She promised herself that she would not tell anyone of her plans, not even her dear old mama.

As she walked to Lisa's cabin in the morning to say goodbye, Debbie remembered an incident that occurred when a man named Rick told his son Jeremy that he'd figured a way out of Jonestown. Possibly thinking that he was being tested, Jeremy reported his father, and his father was dealt harshly to the learning crew. Debbie knew that so many people in Jonestown were unhappy and wanted to leave, but were too afraid of each other to do anything about it. Debbie also wondered about her brother Larry. She knew that if she could not get to him first that he would be told lies about her and that he would immediately be sent to Jonestown.

Debbie entered her mother's cottage and quickly advised her of the assignment to Georgetown. Lisa sensed something was wrong and different about Debbie on this particular morning. Debbie tried to conceal it, but Lisa knew her daughter all too well. As Lisa began crying, Debbie realized that no words of her escape plan were needed, it was understood. Debbie was unable to speak as Lisa finally acknowledged that the two would never see each other again. Debbie made her push towards the pavilion when suddenly Jones appeared out of nowhere, and pulled her into the radio room for a private conversation. He reminded her how important her mission was and, using a psychological stamp of manipulation, he reminded her how Lisa depended on her for her health. As the bus began to drive off, Jones looked on as the children began to wave goodbye to him. Before Jones was out of site, Debbie saw him turn and begin walking towards Lisa's cottage. Terror ran through Debbie's body. Would he try to manipulate Lisa into giving her information? There was nothing she could do at that point, so she sat back and let her exhausted body slip into autopilot. Mud spattered her face and arms as she took one final glance at her five-month prison. She looked at the same things on the way out as she did on the way in, but with what seemed like a completely different set of eyes.

Debbie knew that she needed to quickly come up with a plan for escape. With no money, passport or contacts, she couldn't just up and run away. She knew that she had to appear as though she was all business so that she was not ordered right back to Jonestown. After completing a few tasks, Jones ordered for her to stay in Georgetown as the coordinator of all PR activities. Now it was time for her to formulate a plan for escape.

CHAPTER 9 – CALL TO FREEDOM

Debbie's resiliency surfaced just when she needed it the most. She was now in position to exploit her stay. Everyone was excited about the upcoming performance of the children. Sharon Amos was particularly interested, but someone had to stay at the house and man the radio room during the show. Debbie knew that this was her first chance to set her escape plan in motion. This was the opportunity she had been waiting for. Debbie suggested that since she had seen the show performed several times in Jonestown already, Sharon go to the event in her place while she stayed behind to guard the home. Sharon graciously agreed.

On the night of the performance Debbie wished them luck as they all spilled into a van and sped off for the Guyanese Cultural Center. Debbie cautiously waited until the vehicle was out of sight before making a phone call to her sister, Annalisa. However, she knew that the call was not without risk. She knew that Jim was always one-step ahead of his conspirators and that he had ears everywhere. She worried that there might be a bug in the room. She also knew that in the States it took two-minutes for calls to be traced. As she dialed Annalisa, she cautiously looked at the clock, making sure that the call would stay under two-minutes. Moreover, even the international operator who would connect the call was a suspect.

The phone rang ten-times before Annalisa's four-year-old son answered. Debbie tried to remain calm as she told him to get his mother and that it was an emergency. The seconds seemed like hours as she waited for what was her one chance at freedom. Finally, a frantic and worried Annalisa got on the phone. After Debbie calmed Annalisa down, she informed her that everything was fine and that she was calling to tell her that she was sending her a letter that would explain everything, which would be mailed the following day. Debbie reiterated to her a couple of times to tell no one of their discussion. She had also managed to keep the call under two-minutes.

The children were soon ordered back to Jonestown a few days later and Debbie was forced to play the waiting game in regard to sending the letter to Annalisa. Debbie was staying at the house with three very trusted members: Sharon Amos, Paula Adams and Karen Layton (her brother, Larry's wife). It was impossible up to that point to mail the letter. No one was allowed to leave the house unless accompanied by at least one other member. About three-weeks after her arrival in Georgetown, Debbie still had no concrete plan for escape and time was running out. But soon enough, Debbie would get the small window she needed, along with some overheard vital information.

One night at around midnight an emergency call came over the Georgetown radio. It was a distress call from Jonestown informing them that one of the children had an accident and needed immediate medical attention. Mysteriously, the caller advised that a child was "accidentally" hit over the head with a baseball bat. Assuming that the baseball bat story seemed a little suspicious, Georgetown members were instructed to call the ambassador at home and advise him that the child had fallen from a play structure and needed to be airlifted to Caracas for emergency medical treatment. Sharon had the honor of contacting the ambassador. As Debbie listened to Sharon on the call, she received a miracle and vital information that would aid in her escape. The ambassador informed Sharon that they could issue a passport in fifteen minutes in the event of an emergency. Sharon assigned Debbie to go to obtain the emergency passport for the child. Sharon had to stay behind and man the radio. Debbie's plan was slowly forming, but destiny would need some time to take shape.

On April 30, 1978, at 7:00 a.m., Debbie made a slight detour into the Pegasus Hotel and made a call to Annalisa from a payphone there. Annalisa was wise to the Temple's workings and had a plan to get Debbie out. Coincidentally, Annalisa's husband, Ray, was headed to South America a few weeks later on United Nations business, and Annalisa had planned to request Debbie as a baby-sitter. The next day, Annalisa's telegram arrived at Temple headquarters at noon. Debbie showed it to Sharon first then read it aloud to Jones over the radio. The flight was booked for May 12, 1978. Annalisa had booked the flights and the hotel reservations just in case Temple members confirm the arrangements.

However, Jones not only didn't bite, but instead claimed that Annalisa was going to try and kidnap Debbie. Consummately suspicious, Jones said this to gauge Debbie's response. Debbie knew this and had no choice but to affirm. She knew that she could not sound as if she was involved in this plan in any way; this meant acting indifferent to Annalisa's suggestions. Just as expected, Jones asked Sharon to verify the reservations. He then shrewdly said that it wasn't safe for her in the capital any longer and ordered her to return to Jonestown on the *Cujoe* during its return visit from the embassy on May 11, 1978. Flushed of all emotion and frankly shattered; Debbie had no choice but to comply. Jones also ordered Debbie to call Annalisa and personally decline to let Annalisa know that he was onto her. Cleverly, Annalisa knew that Debbie was being coerced and being watched as they spoke on the phone. She told Debbie to "roll her eyes in disgust" as she just listened. She told Debbie that the flight was booked on the 12th of May, Pan Am, Georgetown to Caracas, and that the Caracas to New York flight was booked under her middle name in case the Temple was monitoring flights to America. Debbie would have to endure ten-more secretive, cunning, and agonizing days before departing from hell.

Debbie got another huge break in the form of Sharon accompanying the consul into Jonestown on May 10, 1978, where she would remain for the next few weeks. Taking Sharon's place would be Lew's wife, Beth. Even though she did not want to lie and betray Beth, she knew that it would be relatively easier to do in comparison to Sharon, who did everything by the letter of Jim's law. Plans soon changed and Debbie and Beth were ordered to go to the American Embassy to tape record and blackmail the American Consul on the 12th of May at noon. Beth agreed that Debbie should go alone at 10:00 a.m., to arrange the meeting on the 12th of May. Debbie's plan was to inform the consul that she was in danger, obtain an emergency passport, and go to Pan Am to pick up her ticket, all before noon. She would then meet Beth back at the embassy in time for the meeting.

When Debbie arrived at the embassy, she informed the secretary that she needed to speak to the consul and that it was an emergency. As she sat waiting, Daniel Weber, the Vice Consul, approached her and introduced himself. Debbie informed Daniel that she had an urgent message that she must personally deliver to the consul before noon. Time ticked by very slowly as she sat in wait for the desperate help that she needed. When the consul—Dick McCoy—finally arrived, Debbie told him everything. She informed him about the suicide drills, the poor diets, the beatings, and even the impending blackmail attempt. As the bureaucracy took its course, Debbie feared that she would not make it to Pan Am to get her ticket before Beth arrived at the embassy. When the red-tape was finally behind them, the consul and vice consul had prepared an official-sworn-paper-statement for the record, detailing all of the injustices occurring in Jonestown per Debbie's statement.

Debbie quickly signed the statement and was given an emergency passport, which she asked them to hold for safety purposes. Debbie informed them that there should be no contact between them until she would meet Dan (vice consul) at the Pegasus Hotel at 8:30 p.m., at which time he would drive her to the airport for her departure. She also informed Dan that she had been in the country for five months and that she knew anyone in the country for more than three-months needed "tax clearance" to leave. Dan told her not to worry about it and she rushed off to the Pan Am office to get her ticket, with no time to spare. When she arrived, she was horrified to find that there was no ticket waiting for her. With tear filled eyes, she begged and pleaded with the ticket agent to no avail.

Quickly rushing back to the embassy, Debbie arrived just in time to meet Beth for the noon meeting. As the meeting commenced, the consul nearly blew her cover. Luckily, Beth later accused him of being CIA and assumed that he must have been monitoring their transmission and broke their complex codes. Unfortunately, Debbie was not able to inform the consul or vice consul of her misfortune at the Pan Am office. Beth had arrived before she could advise them, and she had not time to let them know after the meeting as she left with Beth. When they returned to the PT house, Debbie soon realized that the people that she was dealing with at the embassy were complete morons and did not understand the magnitude and danger of her situation. A Temple member named Jack told Debbie the embassy called and said that she should pick them up the following day from a man named, Dan Weber. Every member in the house looked at Debbie with a puzzled look on their faces and questioned the situation. Compromised yet again by the embassy, Debbie played it cool and acted indifferent. As the curious chatter died down, Debbie—now a bundle of nerves—had even more worries and concerns.

Debbie knew that she needed to get to a phone somehow and contact the consul. She figured that she would at least not be flying that night, because she had not received a plane ticket. She knew that she had to break-free of her comrades for a few hours and contact the consul. Quick thinking, she grabbed a bottle of *Johnny Walker Red* and convinced Beth and Karen that Jim had assigned her to give dentist, Dr. De Costa, a bottle of whiskey as a "thank you" for going to Jonestown and giving free dental care. At 8:50 p.m., she hitched a ride with the welcome committee, who were headed to the airport to meet and greet new arrivals.

After Debbie was dropped off at Dr. De Costa's house, she presented him with the bottle of whiskey and asked him if she could use his phone. She warned him that what he was about to hear was going to sound bizarre and that she'd explain later. As she got the consul on the phone she noticed the desk-clock read 9:20 p.m. The consul was awestruck by the call. He advised her that Dan had been waiting for her at the Pegasus Hotel for almost an hour. Debbie explained that she had presumed that the earlier call from Dan was to inform her that the plan was postponed until the next day, but the earlier call was to inform her that Pan Am found her ticket and that Dan had it in his possession. The consul called Dan to let him know that she was on her way and her new accomplice, Dr. De Costa, graciously gave her a ride.

For some strange reason, Debbie thought that it would be a good idea to go back to the house to change her clothes. As they pulled up to the PT house she pled with the doctor to wait for her, and she hurried inside. She quickly grabbed a pair of pants and a towel and swiftly scurried quietly towards the door. Jack and Karen were sitting in the radio room in plain view and Debbie was spotted by both as she made her way down the stairs. Karen stepped outside and intensely questioned her, but Debbie had come too far to be denied that point. She gave her a brief excuse and never stopped walking towards the car. Karen suspiciously looked on as Debbie leaned into the window, making believe that she was handing the doctor the towel. Suddenly, she opened the back door and dove into the back seat and said, "Quick! Hurry! Get me out of here!"

At 9:50 p.m., the most helpful Dr. De Costa and Debbie arrived at the Pegasus Hotel; where Dan intercepted them, took Debbie, and raced her to the airport.

Dan made good time and they made it to the airport at 11:10pm. Coincidentally, the welcome committee and new arrivals were still at the airport. Debbie panicked when she saw them and hid behind a pillar. The members quickly spotted her and looked on with suspicion. Debbie made it seem as though she was on a secret mission, and the other members were happy to do their part not to interfere. She seemed to be in the clear, or did she? Approaching the gate, Dan handed the customs agent her passport. The agent looked at it and said, "no one leaves without "tax clearance..." The rude customs agent was not impressed with Dan's credentials or Debbie's begging and pleading. Meanwhile, Temple members still looked on as they continued to try to sort out the problem. But as they were doing so, the plane that Debbie was supposed to be on flew off into the night. Debbie would have to remain in her personal hell for at least one more night.

Since Debbie could not go back to the house, Dan suggested that she stay at the Tower Hotel for the night. She knew that her nightmare was far from over. She knew what was happening all around her: that Temple members were probably digging-up her confession papers; lies were being told to Larry and her mother; someone was waiting at the embassy for her; the post office would be watched; a point man would be driving around all night looking for her; and members were being instructed on how to abduct and drug her. She feared that Larry would be ordered to Guyana before she had a chance to contact him. If she could have just taken that flight she may have been able to contact Larry in time. Now the Temple had time to formulate plans against her. She was alone, afraid, and in a strange land. Much worse, people were hunting her down. Even though she was getting help from Dan and others, she knew she was basically alone in her struggle. How could they ever understand the world in which she had just escaped from? Albeit it was happening just around the corner, it was inconceivable to outsiders.

Dan escorted Debbie as she checked into the hotel. They brow-beat the clerk about her having complete anonymity. The plan was for Dan to pick her up at 8:00 a.m., sharp, where she would fly to America with the consul. Debbie had her first true taste of freedom that night. She walked around the hotel room naked, smoking a cigarette, and took a long shower. She felt exuberant as she tottered between the crisp, clean cotton sheets. But the nightmarish-memories soon came flooding back in and it wasn't long before the memory of Jonestown sucked her back there, working her into a nightmarish frenzy. So much so, that the slightest noise in the hallway sent her running for the cover of the bathtub. Completely exhausted; she waited and listened intently, expecting a Temple crew to break through the door at any moment and take her back to hell. One moment she was waiting to be attacked, the next moment she opened her eyes. It was morning and the phone was ringing. She realized that she had just spent the night in the bathtub. The call was from the hotel: Dan had arrived and was waiting for her.

Dan was there bright and early and informed her they would have to go to the post office to get tax clearance before going to the airport, an unwelcome detour for Debbie. She was not happy about this at all and she knew that someone from the Temple would be waiting for her there. Dan tried to sooth her worried mind, but he just didn't understand the Temple's true nature. The reality of the situation was that Jones told no one of her defection. Only a choice few knew. Like with Jeannie Mills, Jones feared that if people knew that such a trusted member had defected it might cause and upheaval and other members might start to question his leadership skills. He no doubt learned this from the Stoen's defection. Jones' plan was to first try to coerce her into coming back. His last resort likely would have been to drug her and kidnap her, if applicable. Either way the objective of Jones was to get her back to Jonestown before any word of her defection was revealed.

Debbie entered the post office, and was soon waiting on line to get her tax clearance. There was still no sign of any Temple patrol. That was until a Temple member named Dierdra came out of nowhere and sat down next to her. Sounding as if she was possessed by Jones, himself, Dierdra used the old familiar double-talk that Debbie knew all too well. She tried desperately to persuade Debbie to return. Much like Jeannie, Debbie assured her that she would keep her silence about the Temple, but that she just wanted out at any cost. Relentlessly, Dierdra continued to try to persuade and talk her down, but Debbie was determined to never return to Jonestown. Soon, Debbie was in a small cubicle answering questions solicited by a postal agent. After about an hour of questioning, Debbie had her tax clearance and was one step closer to freedom. One more obstacle stood in her way, time!

Dan ushered Debbie back to the embassy with a few hours to kill. She would be forced to wait until they were ready to migrate to the airport. Debbie overheard the consul talking on the phone to someone inquiring about her whereabouts. They knew where she was and they knew about the consul's pending flight. Soon enough, she had talked herself into calling Jones. She figured that if she didn't call, Jones would assume that she had something to hide and that she would speak out against him. She wanted to assure Jones that she was not going to be a threat—that she just wanted out. Dan allowed her make the call.

Jones spoke with his predictable double-talk and manipulative tactics, trying desperately to diffuse the situation and have Debbie willingly return to Jonestown. Almost identical to the call with Jeannie Mills, Jones tried to talk her down like only he could. The only difference between Jeannie and Debbie was the fact that Jeannie was older and not as naive. Jeannie stood her ground verbally with Jones, Debbie just *yes'd* him to death, placated him. After a kind-hearted, yet, smooth tongue lashing, Debbie actually began to negotiate with him. Jones offered her many options, from meeting with Marceline in the capital to migrating to a safe haven in England. Debbie began to topple and wilt, agreeing and giving ground to Jones. She could not believe that Jones had her agreeing to things that she was not actually going to go through with. As she began to collect herself, she realized that the call was a bad idea. Jones wouldn't take no for an answer; he just continued to offer suggestions and rhetoric filled speeches. But she knew what Jones was capable of and that she would no doubt face his wrath, regardless of how pleasant he sounded at that time.

Finally, Dan ended the madness and urgently said that it was time to go and catch the plane. Debbie agreed to call Jones in six hours, knowing full-well that she would never speak to him again. The whole ride to the airport, Debbie looked to see if she was being followed. After a short hassle by the same cantankerous customs agent that wouldn't let her board the previous night, she was finally let go. Somehow, she found herself waiting alone for the plane. Seizing this temporary opportunity, two members approached from out of nowhere. The well orchestrated intercept was coordinated by

Beth and Karen. They quickly defended Jones, reminding Debbie that she was making a big mistake. The consul spotted Debbie defending her decision and quickly grabbed her arm. He pushed her to the front of the line, where she soon walked up the steps of the *Pan American World Airways* Jet. She looked over her shoulder frequently until the plan took off and touched ground in the S.F. Bay area. She never once believed that she would make it out of the country. Once in the confines of the United States, Debbie immediately went into hiding.

CHAPTER 10 – CONCERNED RELATIVES

The Kilduff and Tracy exposé opened up the flood gates for Temple opposition. The article started a local media frenzy. Reporters began digging for more dirt on the Temple and Jones. Articles focused on Jones' bizarre practices, abuse, and the abduction of Tim and Grace Stoen's child. Ironically, Jeannie was not killed for her participation in the Kilduff and Tracy article; instead the threats stopped all together, likely because Jones had fled to Guyana prior to the articles release. Some of Jones' political supporters continued to maintain their positive positions about the Temple amidst the media backlash. For one, they probably didn't know just how bad it had gotten for members. Second, they were likely fearful that if the public began to believe the dirty secrets of the Temple that their public support for Jones over the years would inevitably lead to political suicide for them as well.

For example, in February of 1978, S.F. Supervisor Harvey Milk sent a letter to then President Jimmy Carter explaining that Jones had "undertaken constructive remedies for social problems which have been amazing in their scope and achievement." Milk then went on an offensive against the Stoens. "Timothy and Grace Stoen, the parties that are attempting to damage Rev. Jones' reputation and seriously disrupt the life of his son, John, have both already been discredited in the news media here [S.F.]." Finally, Milk indirectly urged the President to help "halt" the actions of Timothy Stoen.

Once the New West exposé was released, however, Jeannie smelt blood. The article gave her renewed strength and vigor to continue her fight against Jones. Her fear began to slip away and death to her became second to helping those tangled in Jones' maniacal web. Moreover, she wanted Jones nationally exposed for who he really was and she pressed for a national inquiry into his organization. Jeannie vowed to see the fight against Jones through to the very end. Jeannie began contacting former members who had moved out of the area and were not aware of the local media storm being waged against Jones. Most were happy to come forward and help with the fight against Jones. Trying to encourage other former members, among other reasons, Jeannie and Al filed a million dollar lawsuit against the Temple for fraudulently steeling property from them.

Not long after, several relatives of those in Jonestown began inquiring about how to get their loved-ones back. Most believed that they were being held against their will. Those in Jonestown who were fortunate enough to speak to their relatives were watched closely while doing so, as well as being coached on what to say. Jones was also careful not to let any letters slip through to the States that might show any traces of unhappiness or fear. There were so many relatives coming forward to Jeannie and Al that they decided to form a group; they felt that together they would have more of a chance to fight Jones than they would individually. They would call the group *"Concerned Relatives."* Tim Stoen became the primary legal representative for the organization.

In April of 1978, fifty-four members of the group signed a petition pleading with the U.S. government to investigate allegations of human rights violations in Jonestown. Wanting the Temple to know of their actions immediately, they dropped a copy of the petition off at the S.F. church. They also distributed the document to the press, members of Congress, and members of the State Department. Among the many accusations in the petition was a Temple document threatening mass suicide, prohibiting relatives from leaving Guyana by confiscating their passports and money, and by stationing guards around Jonestown to prevent anyone from escaping, and physical intimidation and psychological coercion as part of a mind-programming campaign. The following day Temple attorney, Charles Gary, told the press that the people in Jonestown don't want anything to do with their relatives in the states, and that they are perfectly happy in Jonestown and that they are there of their own free will. From May – July (1978), Tim Stoen filed three lawsuits on behalf of former Temple members and family members of Jonestown residents against Jones and others in the Temple leadership. The Temple and Charles Gary countered, filing a suit of their own against Tim Stoen, claiming that Tim had led to a "personal vendetta" against Temple leader Jim Jones and its leaders.

Congressman Ryan Takes Notice

On November 13, 1977, Tim Reiterman, a reporter for the San Francisco Examiner, published an article entitled *"Scared Too Long."* The article detailed the death of Sam Houston's son, Bob, beneath the wheels of a train on October 5, 1976, one day after he had told Jones that he was leaving Peoples Temple. Sam Houston, of San Bruno, California, believed that his son's "accidental" death had something to do with Jones and his decision to leave the church.

Bob Houston was a full-time member of Peoples Temple in 1972, when he married another member, Joyce Shaw. The two rose quickly up the ranks to become part of the Temple's elite and Planning Commission members. Shaw worked as legal secretary for the Temple, and her and Bob ran one of the church's small communal houses, taking care of a dozen needy children, as well as Bob's two daughters, Judy and Patricia, from a previous marriage. The two lived in a Victorian house on Potrero Hill. Shaw, however, watched as Jim Jones had changed from benign preacher into a megalomaniacal monster. Joyce worked as a legal secretary for a law firm and Bob worked as a brakeman at Southern Pacific Rail Yards.

On New Year's Day 1976, the Temple was holding a planning commission meeting, with all 120 members present. It was early in the morning, as they had celebrated New Years Eve there. Jones began passing out glasses of wine to each member in celebration, which he claimed came from grapes in the church's Mendocino County vineyard. After watching all members chug their wine, Jones told them all that it was laced with cyanide and they'd all be dead in 45 minutes. Screams and cries rang out as people braced for death. Later Jones explained that it was just a test of their loyalty to the church. It was at that point that Joyce knew that she had to leave the church.

After that incident Joyce Shaw started planning her escape from Jones and his cult. She knew that she had to be careful and cautious because Jones had warned the PC members several times that he would kill anyone who tried to escape. Shaw was smart and resilient, though. She began by secretly moving a few possessions at a time to a friend's house. She did so when she went to do the laundry so that she could drop off some possessions but still return with some, which looked less conspicuous. On July 16, 1976, Joyce left work and took a bus to Ohio to live with her parents. There she called Bob and begged him and the kids to leave the church and come to Ohio. Bob was being watched closely, however, after Joyce's defection, and he had to play it cool. Finally Bob worked up the courage to tell Jones that he was leaving the church, but he died in an unexplained accident at his job the following day. The children's biological mother, Carolyn Houston Boyd, began taking care of the children, but she soon defected as well, and the two girls were soon sent to Jonestown. Shaw returned to San Francisco and joined Jeannie Mills and the Concerned Relatives.

Tim Reiterman's article caught the attention of California Congressman, Leo J. Ryan, who read the story in November of 1977. Ryan paid particular attention to the story because Sam Houston (an Associated Press photographer) had been an old friend and constituent of his for twenty-five years. Ryan visited Houston at his home and Sam explained to the congressman that Jim Jones was holding his two grandchildren (Bob's daughters, Judy and Patricia) in Jonestown against their will and the will of their mother, Carolyn. Congressman Ryan assured Sam that he would do everything in his power to help him retrieve his granddaughters.

The next few months were ripe with negative new stories about Peoples Temple. Moreover, there were several former Temple members that had filed lawsuits against Jones and were trying to get him prosecuted. Jim Jones' long-standing reputation as a benign preacher who helped the poor and had political clout was quickly disintegrating. Aside from the Stoens and the Mills family; the Medlock family was also trying to get Jones prosecuted. They claimed that Jones had threatened the elderly Black couple with death if they did not turn over their property to the Temple.

Meanwhile, the final straw was about to break this camel's back. After several months of hiding, Debbie Layton Blakey was finally ready to expose Jones. Once again it was Marshall Kilduff with the breaking news. His article, *"Grim Report From Jungle,"* in the San Francisco Chronicle on June 15, 1978, detailed the story of Debbie Layton through her affidavit, one month after her escape. Debbie indeed told a grim tale of what life was like for those in Jonestown. She claimed that "everyone there wanted to leave." She would later tell Jeannie Mills that at least ninety-percent of those in Jonestown would leave if they thought they'd be safe in doing so.

She also noted the armed guards, the extensive collections of weapons, the poor diet of those residing there, and mass suicide rehearsals.

Several members started sending Congressman Ryan letters asking him for assistance. In the letters they spoke of social security irregularities, human rights violations, and that their loved ones were being held in Jonestown against their will. The cumulative effect of all of this rushed Ryan to a decision to do something about it. Congressman Ryan decided to invite one of the Concerned Relatives, Clare Bouquet, to speak with him personally about her and her group's concerns. Among other issues, Clare's son, Brian, was one of the people in Jonestown at the time. The meeting went well, and Ryan promised her that he planned to investigate the situation in Jonestown as soon as the November election had commenced. Ryan explained that he did not want to exploit the issue for his reelection.

Jeannie Mills was ecstatic when Clare told her the news. In August of 1978, Congressman Ryan finally met with a group of Concerned Relatives. Ryan assured them that he planned on taking a group of people to Jonestown to investigate the compound. Previous to the meeting with Ryan, Jeannie and Al had started the *Human Freedom Center* (HFC) in Berkeley, California. The center was a non-profit organization set up to help those who escaped cults. It was a place to help "deprogram" the brainwashed minds of those who had been subjected to lies and abuse for so many years. The organization was funded by the nursing home that Al and Jeannie operated as well as a few generous donations from friends. One of the first official jobs that the center had was to help Ryan's aid, William Holsinger, coordinate the Guyana trip. The U.S Government was most likely not going to pay for anyone other than the official *codel* members, so it was up to the HFC to raise funds for the trip. Congressman Ryan had specifically hired Holsinger to look for possible violations of Federal and California State laws.

The details of their investigation led Ryan to request a meeting on September 15, 1978, with Viron P. Vaky, Assistant Secretary, Bureau of Inter-American Affairs, U.S. Department of State, and other State Department officials. By the time of this meeting it was clear that Ryan's curiosity of going to Guyana had turned to an obsession. After meeting with State Department officials on October 2nd and 25th, Ryan formally requested permission to go to Guyana on October 4, 1978, by writing to the House Foreign Affairs Committee Chairman Clement J. Zablocki's. Ryan had a particularly good chance of being approved from the get-go, as he sat on both the *Foreign Affairs Committee* and the *International Operations subcommittee*. He used these credentials to help try and persuade Zablocki into approving the trip. In his letter to Zablocki he wrote that he had become increasingly aware "of the problems related to protecting the lives and property of U.S. citizens abroad."

Congressman Ryan received permission for a congressional delegation visit to Guyana. As a result, Ryan decided to send a telegraph to Jim Jones on November 1, 1978. In the correspondence to Jones, Ryan cordially explained his reasons for the visit and asked Jones for his cooperation. Ryan met two more time with State Department officials on November 9th and 13th. At one of these meetings with State Department officials Ryan raised concerns about people being held against their will and the mass suicide drills held in Jonestown that was reported by Debbie Layton Blakey. One official called the threats "nonsense."

It was clear right from the beginning that Jones and others associated with the Temple would give Ryan a hard time, and they would try and delay, and even try and stop, the trip from taking place. Ryan also contacted the Hon. John Burke, U.S. Ambassador to Guyana, and Guyanese Ambassador to the U.S., Laurence Mann. They advised Ryan that the Temple wanted him to work with their legal counsel, Mark Lane, on the appropriate arrangements for the Ryan Codel visit. Mann, having his own dubious links to Jones, informed Ryan that they could not force Jones to allow him and his delegation into Jonestown.

Head Temple attorney, Charles Gary, was not happy about the fact that the Temple had assigned Mark Lane as the mediator between the Temple and Ryan's delegation. He was even more appalled the way he found out about Ryan's visit. It wasn't until early November—when Gary read a San Francisco Chronicle article about Ryan's visit—that he first found out about Ryan's upcoming trip to Jonestown. Livid, Gary threatened to quit his position as the Temple's chief attorney. Gary detested Lane and refused to work with him. Matters between the two were only made worse when

Lane wrote a letter to Congressman Ryan on November 6, 1978, outlining "logistical difficulties" of Ryan visit to Jonestown. In essence, Lane was attempting to, at least, delay Ryan's visit with the relatively threatening letter, which was certainly the wrong approach to take with the rather unshakable congressman.

Lane indirectly called Ryan's trip a "witch-hunt." Lane also mentioned that he wanted to be in Jonestown for Ryan's visit, but his schedule would not allow, and he requested for the visit to be delayed until they could work out the scheduling details. Ryan wrote back on November 10, 1978, with a rather hard-hitting letter to Lane. In it, Ryan explained that he was "not impressed" with Lane's threat of the likelihood of the U.S. government suffering an "embarrassing situation" if Ryan went ahead with his visit. Ryan also explained, in not so many words, that he would be visiting Jonestown with or without Lane in attendance. The letter from Lane only piqued Ryan's interest even more. It made him suspicious that they were trying to hide many things. Charles Gary was even more furious when he read the letter that Lane sent to Ryan. Gary claimed that the letter made it seem as though the people in Jonestown were not happy there. He believed that the move was strategically disastrous, only bolstering his belief that he should be running things.

Ryan's "Official Codel" *("Codel" is an abbreviation for an official Congressional Delegation traveling overseas)* consisted of Mr. James Schollart, staff consultant for the House Foreign Affairs Committee; and Miss Jackie Speier, Ryan's personal assistant, whose expenses were not paid for by the U.S. Government. Ryan's trip was to investigate allegations of human rights violations, individuals being held against their will, money and passports being confiscated from individuals, mass suicide rehearsals being conducted, and that seven attempted defectors had allegedly been killed. Ryan was quoted as saying, "The mission is to find out whether or not Jonestown is a jail." Ryan's attempt to keep the trip quiet failed as word spread quickly and attracted a host of anxious anti-Temple enthusiasts and opportunistic journalists. By the time Ryan's codel of 3 departed, they were accompanied by 9 newspaper and media men and 18 delegates of the Concerned Relatives.

5 Officials:

Leo J. Ryan, U.S. Congressman

Mr. Neville Annibourne, Guyanese Ministry of Information Officer

Mr. James Schollart, staff consultant for the House Foreign Affairs Committee

Jackie Speier, Ryan's top aid

Richard Dwyer, deputy chief of United States mission in Georgetown

*(Dwyer and Annibourne met the group in Georgetown, Guyana)

9 Media Members:

Don Harris	NBC News Correspondent
Robert Brown	Staff Cameraman with NBC
Tim Reiterman	Reporter for the San Francisco Herald-Examiner
Robert Flick	NBC Field Producer
Charles Krause	Reporter for the Washington Post
Ron Javers	Reporter for the S.F. Chronicle
Gregory Robinson	Staff Photographer for the S.F. Examiner
Steve Sung	NBC Sound Technician
Gordon Lindsay	Former free-lance reporter for the National Enquire, working as an NBC Consultant

14 Representatives of the Concerned Relatives:

James Cobb Jr., 28, Black, Male, former member who went to Jonestown

Carolyn Houston Boyd White, Female, who went to Jonestown

Anthony Katsaris White, Male, former member who went to Jonestown

Beverly Oliver Black, Female, former Temple member who went to Jonestown

Grace Stoen, 28, White, female, former member who stayed in Georgetown

Mickey Touchette, 27, White, female, former member stayed in Georgetown

Clara Bouquet, 50, White, female, one of the organizers of the Concerned Relatives stayed in Georgetown

Nadine Laurel Houston, 60, White, Female, member of Concerned Relatives stayed in Georgetown

Walter Wayne Pietila, 25, While, male, former member stayed in Georgetown

Tim Stoen While, male, former member stayed in Georgetown

Steven Katsaris White, Male, Stayed in Georgetown

Sherwin Harris White, Male, Stayed in Georgetown

Howard Oliver Male, Stayed in Georgetown

Bonnie Lois Burnham [aka Bonnie Thielmann] 23, White, female, former member stayed in Georgetow

CHAPTER 11 – THE FINAL DAYS I

"Some leading scientists say we have to have euthanasia. Oh, no. Oh, no. Who's going to decide who and when a person's going to die? We must never allow that because this is the kind of thing that ushers in the terror of a Hitler's Germany. We must not allow these kinds of things to enter our consciousness."
                                                                    -- Jim Jones

November 13, 1978 – Monday

Nightfall set over the jungle commune of Jonestown. James Warren Jones sat in his commander's chair in the radio room. With his right hand mildly shaking, he reached for a bottle filled with barbiturates: drugs that act as central nervous system depressant. His mind raced with the thoughts of the forthcoming Congressman and his entourage. He knew that he could not keep up this facade for much longer. Intense pressure was now collectively being put on him from external enemies. With negotiations for a possible exodus to Russia, Cuba, or even England pending, he had grown tired of being chased from continent to continent.

Moreover, Jones' whole fleeting existence rested in the hands of those closest to him: his members—those he had been readily abusing. It was easy for Jones to get people to like him while he was in the United States. But in Jonestown there was no new audience. It was the same people every day and every night. As a result this made Jones use more radical tactics in order to keep the attention of his people. He did so, primarily, by creating more of a sense of fear and desperation among his followers. His constant need for acceptance and dominance drove him to demand more and more of his followers, through more extreme measures, while in Jonestown. Jones had created an environment that neither he nor anyone else could thrive in any longer.

Moving at a turtle's pace, Jones raised his right hand and slowly griped the microphone. Suddenly, a series of sirens sounded that could have awoken the dead. Somberly, yet sternly, Jones begins to speak; "White night, white night, white night, everyone report to the pavilion." Figuratively, the sirens as well as the white night call both signified a life and death situation. It meant that the community was being threatened and an immediate course of action needed to be taken. Literally, everyone knew what this really meant by now: get up, put on some clothes and rush to the pavilion for what will most likely be an all night affair; and don't be late or you will face harsh punishment. It meant just another sleepless night for many who were already at their breaking points. Their bodies had been worn, battered, and torn from the rigorous field work and the unmercifully hot sun.

As the crowd assembled at the pavilion, Jones took the stage pacing around languorously like a prize horse that had lost a step. For the first time the guards, who were well known community members, surrounded the assembly armed with rifles pointed in toward the crowd. Members felt particularly uneasy at this meeting. Every other meeting the guns were pointed outward, at the so called "enemy." Members looked on puzzled, feeling like they were being held at gunpoint. Jones had a different look on his face and carried himself a bit differently on this day.

During this particular white night, Vern Gosney was on hand with his young mulatto son, Mark. At age nineteen, Vern married his Black girlfriend, Cheryl Wilson, even though he was an openly gay male. As an interracial couple they faced discrimination often. Not only did the first church they consulted about a wedding turn them down, but their families also rejected them. In 1971, however, the couple met Jim Jones. They were immediately taken by the Church's interracial religious congregation with core values of social service and social justice. Jones welcomed them with open arms and the couple soon moved into the communal housing system the church had built in nearby Redwood Valley. In 1973, Cheryl was left brain-dead by an overdose of anesthesia during a cesarean-section while delivering their son, Mark. Left with no family and a new son, Vern grew even closer to Jones and his welcoming congregation. Gosney had no choice but to turn Cheryl over to her mother for continued care. Vern and Mark spent the next few years living in Peoples Temple communal houses around San Francisco, where Mark was primarily taken care of by an elderly Black lesbian woman named Edith. They moved to Jonestown on March 19, 1978.

Vern turned and smiled at Mark, who was standing a few feet away. Mark had been staying with Edith while living in Jonestown. This is because parents and children were not allowed to live together in the "utopian" society. Mark smiled and waved back, not realizing the severity of the situation. Vern's smile, however, was a faint one; fighting back his feeling that impending danger was near. Vern wanted to leave Jonestown the moment he got there, like many others; but he knew that he was not free to do so. Vern's angst had been growing for some time prior to this day, and he was now itching to make a move. After the meeting everyone returned to their cabins for some much needed rest. Vern, however, could not sleep. Tossing and turning, he pondered the future, incessantly. He was confused and scared, but knew that he had a small window of time to make a move.

Not many Jonestown members were aware of the congressman's impending visit. It was, for the most part, kept under-raps until Jones could figure out a way to use Ryan's visit to manipulate his congregation. By November 9, 1978, the whole community was well aware of the Ryan's visit, as Jones had 600 members sign a petition saying that they did not want the congressman to enter their community. "I wanna see how many of you will sign right now, right now, and say 'no, no; I will not go back! No, I will not see any of my relatives!' Jones clamored. "This is what you have to do, because if your relatives come with Congressman Ryan, if your relatives come with him, then your relatives are no better that he is." One of the many philosophies of Jonestown was, "Anyone can leave at anytime," but Vern and the rest of the members knew that this was not the case. It was just another one of Jones' many double-talking, rhetorical techniques. Everyone knew by this point that any mention of leaving—even the slightest hint—would mean sure alienation, severe punishment, and possibly death.

That night Vern Leaned over to his roommate, Keith, who slept in the bed next to him, and said, "We gotta get out of here, we're gonna die here man." This was a very risky promulgation, especially because Keith had recently been caught trying to escape. Keith was punished so severely that it seemed to have deeply affected his psyche. This might have worked in Vern's favor, though, as Keith was nearly catatonic and didn't want any part of another escape attempt. Keith appeared as though he did not even hear Vern; he simply rolled over in his bed and stared off into space with a blank expression. Vern's admission to Keith made him even more anxious and fearful, however. Confiding in a cabin-mate while others were sleeping meant sleeping with one eye open and looking over your shoulder for a while. But Vern was desperate.

Tim Reiterman was home doing some last minute packing with the hope that he would be able to sneak in a short nap before catching a red-eye flight to New York later that night. Suddenly, he received an urgent call from the Examiner advising him that he had an emergency message from Al Mills requesting a call back at the *Human Freedom Center*. Al told Reiterman that he was concerned about Tim Carter (a high-ranking Peoples Temple Member); informing Tim that the Temple may have kidnapped him. Allegedly, Carter had escaped from Jonestown days earlier and traveled to the *Human Freedom Center* seeking protection from Jones. Mysteriously, though, his reason for escaping Jonestown was to get dental work in the states, because he needed two root canals. Carter swore hatred towards Jones and cried for his wife and child that he left behind in Jonestown. Naively, the Mills' and other defectors believed him. Carter had been missing at that point for 4-days.

Reiterman, however, was rightfully skeptical of Carter's motives and questioned Al about the incident. Apparently nothing seemed odd about Carter's speech and his mouth wasn't swollen. To make matters even more bizarre, on Friday afternoon, November 10, 1978, Carter asked Mills about the Ryan visit to Jonestown, and soon after getting this information he went missing. He was scheduled to go to the dentist the following day, Saturday, November 11, 1978, but he never showed up. Reiterman knew at that moment that Carter was "a plant." He was there to get information about Ryan's visit, on a special mission sanctioned by Jim Jones. Nonetheless, Carter was back in Jonestown and would be there for the subsequent finale.

November 14, 1978 – Tuesday

All media members were cautiously optimistic about their trip to Jonestown. The team of media members was certainly an all-star cast of veterans, except for 21-years old Greg Robinson. There was no assurance that any of them would get into Guyana, let alone get into Jonestown, especially Reiterman and Robinson, who both lacked entry visas in the country. NBC was most definitely their best-bet to get into Jonestown and the rest of the media members knew that the NBC members were their ticket in. All of the media members vowed to stick together. Ryan and his Codel informed them that they were not going to wait for any media member who got left behind. They were together, yet on their own.

One of Ryan's aids admittedly told Reiterman, "It's a game of chicken between us, the Temple, the State Department, and the Guyanese government." Jonestown was so inaccessible that if Jones did not want them in, they would not get in. Not understanding the true exclusivity of Jonestown or the true nature of the geography, the media members naively planned to charter a plane to Jonestown themselves from Trinidad if they were not let into Jonestown through bureaucratic means. Charles Krause, the Buenos Aires correspondent of the Washington Post, would join the rest of the media members in Guyana, on the last leg of their journey.

Once at the airport in S.F., the media members were met by the Concerned Relatives, who joined them on the red-eye flight to New York. While in S.F., Grace Stoen and Jim Cobb were getting ready to board the plane when they both noticed at least one Peoples Temple member watching the group as they departed. This was a tactical maneuver by Jones not only to intimidate, but to gather information. The group hopped on a *United Airlines* flight in San Francisco at 10:00 p.m. (on Nov. 13), and arrived in New York at approximately 5:30 a.m. (on November 14). They then caught a *Pan American* flight from N.Y. to Guyana.

Every relative on board had a loved one or more in Jonestown, and they all had the same story: they all had not seen or heard from their loved ones and wanted to make sure that they were all "alive and happy." Other than Ryan's codel and the media members; Bonnie Tielmann was the only individual who did not have a relative in Jonestown. Bonnie was traveling with Tim Stoen and had lived with Jones in Brazil. She was still a friend of Marceline, and it was Tim's hope that at least Bonnie would be let into Jonestown. Once in New York, the group was met by Steven Katsaris, his son Anthony Katsaris, and Grace Stoen. Some of the members had traveled to Guyana more than once to see their relatives but were unsuccessful. Most were pessimistic from prior experiences and they all felt that this was their best and possibly their last chance to see their loved ones.

Many obstacles and warnings had been issued, and there were still more to come for the group. Ryan was happy to have such reputable media sources accompanying him on the trip. He had hoped that the media's presence would both add security and force Jones and the Temple's public relations department to be more diplomatic. At least, Ryan had planned to have the media film the trip in the event that Jones did not let them in. Before the group boarded the plane in New York, a Guyanese Official warned them that they would be turned back upon arrival in Guyana, and he urged them not to get on the flight. However, this was a very determined group of individuals and they were not going to be dissuaded at any cost. "We'll take our chances," Reiterman told the official.

Tim Stoen had acknowledged that he was going to get his son John Victor Stoen back even if it cost him his life. The Stoen's had been bringing the fight to Jones for some time by this time, and the Stoen's were still the greatest source of anxiety for Jones. Congressman Ryan believed that it was his job to inspect things personally. This was not a new thing for Ryan. "If I had my way, every congressman would go overseas to find out about what was going on over there," said Ryan in Washington in a 1973 interview in an unrelated incident.

After the group boarded the flight to New York headed for the South American Province of Georgetown, Guyana, all members casually socialized and tried to settle in for the long, laborious journey. Ryan took the window seat and went over briefing papers with Schollart, who sat on Ryan's right, and Speier, who sat between them. The media roamed around talking to the relatives and getting their stories and perspectives on the situation. Relatives mulled over pictures of loved ones in Jonestown and they all shared their best stories of their loved ones. As the plane was nearing the airport in the Guyanese capital, Congressman Ryan stood up to address the passengers.

"Folks, folks," Ryan casually called for their attention. "We're about to land in Georgetown. It's been a long road for many of you. Your loved ones are down there and I just want to let you know that we are going to do everything we can to assure that their safe, happy, and being well looked after." The relatives looked on with a skeptical, yet hopeful gaze, hoping that Ryan could deliver what he was promising. Ryan's confidence was contagious, but this was no ordinary crowd. These people had been through hell and back several times throughout this ordeal. "In other words, we still don't have an official invite?" Sherwin Harris asked, as if he already knew the answer. Ryan then made a bold and presumptuous statement in a final effort to win over the trust of the whole group. "Let me tell you something right now, not as your congressman, but as your friend. We are going into Jonestown and if any of your family members want to come home, well then by God, we're gonna bring them home."

The relatives lightly applauded the congressman's efforts, even though they remained a bit skeptical. Not because they felt that he was lying, but because they knew Jones. Moreover, they knew that Ryan was not fully aware of what Jones was capable of. The media did not seem to be phased by the confident and motivational words of Ryan. Reiterman looked over at Don Harris and smirked as if to acknowledge that Ryan was just displaying typical rhetoric for a government official. Yet, everyone in the group knew that there was something different about this man. Ryan was no ordinary congressman. They could feel that he really did care and that he was sincere.

The congressman nodded in acknowledgement and began walking back to his seat. Overwhelmed by the moment, Sherwin stopped the congressman and thanked him and showed his gratitude for his role and effort in the trip. Ryan accepted graciously and quickly turned his attention to the pictures of Sherwin's daughter in his hand. "Leanne?" Ryan asked. Leanne was Sherwin's 21-year old daughter who had moved to Guyana with her mother and Sherwin's ex-wife, Sharon Amos. Sherwin was choked-up for most of the trip, especially when he spoke of his beloved daughter.

As the rest of the group went on with what they were doing, Sherwin quietly explained his present circumstances between he and his daughter. Ryan knew all too well as he had a few daughters of his own. In an attempt to give Ryan more background on the lunacy of Jones, he told the congressman a story of his ex-wife Sharon, whose name is actually Linda Amos. Jim Jones knew another woman named Linda that he had a falling out with and he had a particular distain for the woman. Consequently, Jones wanted no one else to be called Linda in his presence or otherwise, so he ordered that she be referred to as Sharon Amos, who was arguably Jones' most loyal follower.

The plane touched down at the Timehri Airport in Georgetown at approximately 11:30 p.m., on Tuesday, November 14, 1978. Stepping off the plane, the group immediately felt the ominous Guyanese heat that occupied the land. With the group safely on the ground, Congressman Ryan was immediately whisked away to safety by several Guyanese police, in a body guard capacity. The media members all vowed to stick together, especially with Ryan being escorted out of their presence two minutes into the trip. The group had naturally formed clicks and it was the media, the relatives, and the officials who would form three-mini groups among the main group. They were all basically going to the same place, but would all stay closer to the mini-clicks rather than as a whole group. Ryan would be solo a few times throughout the trip, leaving the group behind to meet with other officials and Temple lawyers.

As Ryan was escorted smoothly past customs, the rest of the group endured casual interrogation at the immigration station. Sly-tongued Reiterman immediately struck up a conversation with a U.S. Embassy Official, and soon he and Robinson suavely worked their way through customs. Waiting on the other side of customs were two very foreboding figures; big Jim McElvane and, just as intimidating, Sharon Amos. They stood expressionless, and the look in their' eyes could have cut glass. Sharon was obviously not the same woman she had been before meeting Jones, and was by comparison even further removed from reality since moving to Guyana. She barely acknowledged Sherwin—her ex-husband—as he walked right by her. Sherwin described Sharon as the type of person that would strap on dynamite and take out a whole room for Jones. Sharon certainly shared Jones' insolence for the group and Sherwin alike. Family was the enemy in Jones' eyes. Jones believed that family relationships were sick and unhealthy; and in reality, it was he who built that similar relationship with his own family. He made his wife share him with the cause, several other women, and his sons plotted daily to kill him.

As the group began to depart they noticed that there was one man missing from the group. They turned around just in time to see Ron Javers—who had lagged behind—being harassed by customs agents and guarded by a policeman. NBC members doubled-back to help Javers, as they had the most legitimate paper-work, and the rest of the crew scurried on. Apparently, Javers was detained for a currency violation and an improper entry visa. Consequently, Javers would be held overnight at the airport for what was later described as "orders from higher ups."

The remaining media members proceeded through the city on route to the Pegasus Hotel—a luxury hotel located in the heart of Georgetown with views over the Demerara River, the city, and the Atlantic Ocean—where they had previously booked and confirmed hotel rooms. However, when they arrived at the hotel the concierge advised them that there were no vacancies. Despite the group making a fuss and complaining, they were forced to spend the night in the lobby. The Concerned Relatives arrived shortly after and soon joined the media members in the lobby. "Cold beer" was the only desire of Reiterman and his cohorts at that point; and they would have to settle for Banks beer (Guyanese brew). Miss Speier and Mr. Schollart had no problem registering at the Pegasus Hotel, and Congressman Ryan spent the night as a house guest of U.S. Ambassador John Burke.

Throughout the trip, media members took every opportunity to call back to their respective offices to file stories, updating and detailing their experiences up to that point. After Reiterman filed his "arrival story" at around 4:00 a.m., a room was provided to him and Greg Robinson. However, there would be no sleep that night. Their comfort was short lived, as the ringing of the phone brought unwelcomed bad news. The call was to notify them that their passports were in violation. Shortly after, an immigration officer straight out of the twilight zone strolled up wearing an orange motorcycle helmet, and with a few short strokes of his pen he reduced their stay from five-days to 24-hours. The officer then advised them that they would have to visit the security chief from home affairs at 8:00 a.m., which was just an hour or so away.

Gordon Lindsay was the wily veteran and unofficial NBC guide of the trip; he knew his way around. Moreover, on his previous trip to Guyana he endured the same treatment and led the men to the Home Ministry office. The media representatives were not sure what to make of the lack of support and indifferent approach displayed by the American Embassy. This type of aloofness was very unlike the embassy, especially when a U.S. Congressman and a high profile media staff were involved. The American Embassy did finally come through, however, setting up a meeting for the media with the Chief Information Officer of Guyana. That meeting paid off for them, and their visas were extended for five days. Javers was also released after a 12-hour detainment at the airport. Things were looking up for the group.

It appeared as though Jones and the Temple had been pulling strings to make the group's trip as inconvenient as possible. From the moment they arrived they were harassed, denied previously confirmed rooms, one member was detained, and there was an attempt to shorten their visas. Whether this was a coordinated effort from the Temple or not, the trip had been a complete nightmare for the group thus far. As far as what was to come, the Temple would undoubtedly play a major part in the remainder of the trip, causing a plethora of delays and distractions. The Guyanese government assigned a "press escort" to the media and arranged a press conference in which Vincent Teekah, Guyana's Education Minister, publicly denounced Burnham's support of Jones and the Temple. Teekah went on record as saying that the Guyanese government did not recognize Jonestown, although his statement was not exactly forthcoming. Jonestown was not only given the emergency code by the PNC (Guyanese political party) in case the country was under attack, they were also used by the PNC as a deliberate attempt to establish Guyana's ownership of the territory claimed by Venezuela. Jonestown was also represented at several PNC meetings. Peoples Temple House was on high alert at that time. Sharon contacted Jones from the radio room of the PT-house to inform him that the delegates had arrived. "Come in Jonestown, this is Georgetown," said Sharon. "Go ahead Georgetown," Jones anxiously answered. "They're here," she answered disappointedly and in a stern voice. "They are determined to get in."

November 15, 1978 - Wednesday (Q 320)

Lying in his bed praying for some help; Vern Gosney felt a strangling sense of hopelessness. Suddenly, a very loud series of sirens rang out into the jungle night: another *White Night* distress call from Jim Jones. White Nights were held about 2-3 times per week, and sometimes several nights in a row, depending on the circumstances. In the weeks leading up to the impending delegation visit, these rallies were just about held on a daily basis. Everyone in the camp was on edge. Jones wanted to continue to pound instructions into the minds of his members. Jones only fueled and intensified the congregations fear and anger towards the congressman, media, and family members. Whatever Jones was doing to drum up anger in his members was working. The festering up of these feelings implanted by Jones was shown commonly in public announcements by members.

Jean Brown: My name is Jean Forester Brown. I believe in Jim Jones. I believe in socialism, but I do not believe that it is possible any longer in this country to effect change and to bring about socialism without violent (Pause) revolt, and I am pledged by everything that I hold dear that... I will stick a grenade or a bomb in my body and go to the Senate (Pause) or the Congress of this country and blow myself and this government up...

With all members in the camp being on edge, they walked in an orderly fashion to the pavilion. Gosney slowly walked towards the pavilion amidst a flock of Temple members, when, suddenly, he was approached by a young Black female by the name of Monica Bagby. During the course of their discussion, Monica cautiously said to Gosney, "I've gotta get out of this place." Gosney was completely caught off guard by her candor, and he wondered if it was a set up. He had seen her around the camp, but the two had never had a conversation before this. Sensing Gosney's apprehension, Monica revealed that Gosney's roommate, Keith had informed her that Gosney had confided in him about leaving Jonestown. Gosney was very nervous and untrusting of anyone at that point. He had worked very hard to keep his cover and keep a low profile while in Jonestown. He had built up a reputation as a hard worker with no resistance to the cause. Moreover, Gosney felt that Monica could have been sent by Jones to test his loyalty and get him on record as a possible defector. "Do you have a plan," Gosney asked, probingly. Monica looked at Gosney with a disappointed gaze, "hell no, I thought you did."

As they arrived at the pavilion, Jones was again discussing Congressman Ryan. Unexpectedly, a chill came over Gosney along with a life saving thought that rung in his head like a dinner bell: his chance for escape, the congressman!

The group was exhausted from the grueling trip and from the drama of their hotel rooms being delay. Just about everyone in the group slept straight through the morning of November 15, 1978, and awoke at around 4:00 p.m. Once the group had coordinated and gathered, they all headed over to 41 Lamaha Gardens in Georgetown; which, again, was the Peoples Temple house. When they arrived, they were met by Temple member, Mary Ann Casanova, who was standing outside. Mary Ann—a Caucasian 40 year old female with glasses—was a trusted member of the Temple and, along with Paula Adams, she was in charge of coordinating the Temple's shipments from Guyana. Mary Ann approached the group immediately and informed them that they were not welcome there and told the relatives not to even get out of the car. Beverly Oliver spotted two Temple females that she recognized and went over and started conversing with them. When Beverly finished speaking with the females, the group returned to the hotel.

Later that night, Sherwin Harris checked into his room at the Pegasus Hotel with only one concern: to see his daughter, Leanne. He immediately called Sharon to make arrangements to meet Leanne the following day. Leanne had been sent into Jonestown and all efforts were to keep her there until Sherwin left. But Sherwin was determined to put intense pressure on Sharon until she allowed him to see their daughter. Sharon accused Sherwin of trying to tear her and Leanne apart with his visit. Sherwin was not so much concerned about going to Jonestown or what was going on there. He simply wanted to see his daughter. Sherwin was not afraid of going into Jonestown to see his daughter if necessary. Sherwin was committed to make things right between him and Leanne like never before. The long flight only fueled his desire. Sherwin believed that from the moment of her birth, his daughter's life depended on him and he was determined to fix their estranged relationship. He had her at a very young age, but none the less, she was his world.

November 16, 1978 – Thursday

(Congressman shows up at the PT-House at midnight) Q050

First thing in the morning, Jones sent a message to Sharon Amos at Temple Headquarters in Georgetown ordering the return of his Son Stephan and the basketball team. Sharon relayed the message to Stephan, who was furious with the request, and he stormed into the radio room to speak with his father. "I want you to come home," Jones ordered. "Why," Stephan asked. "Why? You're needed here, is why! Mac [Jim McElvane] and [Jack] Beam are coming back first thing in the morning. I want you to be on the truck with him; the whole damn bunch of ya." Stephan then tried to reason with his father. "Look, you said it yourself, we're good PR, dad. That's all there is to it. We're having a good time. We're playing basketball."

Jim Jones stepped away from the microphone and began pacing around the room, voicing his frustration to no one in particular. His relationship with Stephan had been strained to the point of an argument at every encounter. The Temple basketball team had done the impossible, getting to the championship game to play against the highly touted Guyanese National team. They were a serious underdog in the tournament and it was quite impressive how far they had gotten already. The Guyanese Nation team was one of the best teams in the Caribbean. The game was scheduled to be played the next night. Obviously, they were very excited, and it was going to take a miracle to have them return to Jonestown before playing the game. Furthermore, Stephan believed that Jim was just being his paranoid self again and overreacting.

An empathetic Marceline then got on the microphone. "Steven, I think you'd better come back. You don't know what's happening here, Steven. We really need you." Jim was pacing back and forth in the room, visibly distraught and continuing to murmur unpleasantly. "We're staying mom," Stephan said firmly. "We're going to go up against the national team tomorrow. How's it gonna look if we just high-tale it outa here. Besides, you don't need to speak for him." This drove Jim over the edge, and he began knocking down papers and screaming. "Well, it's up to you," Marceline calmly replied. Realistically, Marceline did not want Stephan there through the tension filled period. She was just speaking to appease Jim. "No! It's not up to him," Jim erratically screamed. "I don't want him to have anything to do with that congressman or the relatives. I want him back here now! You don't give a damn what happens here," Jones screamed at Stephan. Jones was now losing control mentally and physically and Stephan's disobedience furthered his decent.

Back at the hotel, some of the members were drawn outside by an old Guyanese man who was making a speech outside and drawing a crowd. The old man looked like he may have been a former Guyanese parliament member who enjoyed the sound of his own voice. Suddenly, out of nowhere, a group of Temple members appeared by the seawall. Six Black and two White men approached and engaged the group in conversation. It was the Temple basketball team. Stephan Jones and Coach Lee Ingram were amount the men. Ingram was a Black man in his late twenties standing six-feet tall. Ingram asked the group why they were in Guyana and what their intentions were. The relatives pled their case to him as Ingram stood silent for most of the conversation.

Bonnie Burnham [aka Bonnie Thielmann] came out as the group and the team were conversing and immediately recognized Stephan Jones. They had been almost like brother and sister years earlier, as the Jones family had taken her in for a short time. Stephan and Bonnie hugged and conversed for a long period of time. Stephan told Bonnie that the team was there to play a series of basketball games and were probably in town for about a month. Stephan commented that there may be some difficulties with having some of the relatives enter Jonestown. It was very clear that he was alluding to Tim and Grace Stoen. When the two groups had finished speaking, the relatives returned to the Pegasus Hotel excited about their encounter with the team. At no time did the team indicated to them that there would be any trouble overall with their visit. Some relatives, however, were skeptical and questioned whether the team had been there to spy on the relatives and get information in order to relay to Jones.

Later that morning, Ryan had insisted that Ambassador Burke and other Embassy Officials meet with the relatives for the purpose of hearing their allegations. They met at the embassy building for about an hour. Emotional relatives told their stories with tears in their eyes. Despite their dramatic tells, the embassy withheld taking sides. Relatives shared their determination with Burke and vowed to go to Jonestown with or without his help. Burke claimed that due to certain legalities, there was nothing that he could do. Burke remained polite and cordial, but offered little help or true comfort, and the relatives left the meeting frustrated and disappointed. Temple attorneys, Mark Lane and Charles Gary, were scheduled to arrive sometime in the evening and the Temple was not going to budge until their lawyers were present.

Despite Ryan's confident attitude and shrewd negotiation tactics, it was beginning to seem as though the Temple gates had figuratively been raised. Ryan and his party were scheduled to travel to Jonestown later that day, but the Temple's efforts to stall the congressman and his delegates were wearing on the already weary group. Ryan was forced to reschedule the plane (a 20 passenger plane reserved by the Embassy, originally chartered to go to Jonestown on Thursday, November 16th) until Friday, November 17th. Time was running out for the group and they needed a miracle. Congressman Ryan kept busy, using as many different angles as possible to improve his position. Ryan made a courtesy call to Guyanese Foreign Minister Rashleigh Jackson to discuss United States-Guyanese bilateral relations.

Then, Ryan made an unannounced visit to the People's Temple House at 41 Lamaha Gardens in Georgetown. He took Charles Krause of the Washington Post with him, but Krause did not enter the headquarters. Most of the media members were enraged over the fact that Krause was brought along and that they weren't. This later led to a confrontation where Don Harris told Ryan that the group was not sure that they could trust him. Tensions were running high, but Ryan settled them down by hosting a dinner party for the entire group in the Pegasus dining room later that night. There, Ryan reassured the group one final time that things would work out. After dinner, Ryan explained the details of the trip to the relatives for the following day. He informed them that there were not enough seats to accommodate all of the relatives and left them with the decision of which members would represent the Concerned Relatives in Jonestown.

The Final White Night! Q050

Jones held his final White Night on Thursday November 16, 1978, to prepare for the impending visit from the congressman and his delegates. The pavilion was tense as Jones prepared and readied his members for their arrival. Angrily, Jones spoke blasphemous about the constitution of America; citing that it somehow gave the congressman the right to come all way out to Guyana to check up on them. "I do not know whether we will receive any guests tomorrow or not. I'm not so inclined to, um, be told when to receive guests. We came 6,000 miles to establish ourselves here with a certain amount of autonomy." Jones ignited the crowd and re-affirmed that the guests were not welcomed in Jonestown.

> **Jones:** He says the Constitution– the Constitution gives him the right to come down here and see us, because we're American taxpayers. The Constitution doesn't give him any right to go anywhere that he's not invited. We didn't elect him…They push us clear up here to the last corner of the globe, practically, all over this continent; we're right up here at the last point, right on the border of Venezuela. Now if they want a lot of hell here between Venezuela and Guyana, I'm liable to annex with whoever I feel like tomorrow. I'm sick of this shit, and I'm liable to sail the Russian flag. I don't know what the hell I'm gonna do. But I– I do know this– I know this, that I didn't come to be pushed around and be told what I'm gonna do, where I'm gonna go, and who I'm gonna be visiting with." (Applause…)

Jones worked the crowd into a frenzy; as he arrogantly said, "So you want to see your congressman tomorrow, stick around, he may come in. I don't know how long he'll stay, and I don't know what necessarily will take place or what kind of sequential arrangement. But I can assure you that if he stays long enough for tea, he's gonna regret it." Applause showered the pavilion.

After the meeting, Vern, Monica, and Vern's roommate (Keith) held a secret meeting in Vern's cabin. Together they had coordinated a plan to secretly slip the congressman a note saying that they wanted to leave and asking him for his help for a safe departure from Jonestown. "This is our last chance," said Vern. Taking a vote on the involvement of the two, Vern called out each of their names. "Monica?" Monica looked at Vern and shook her head up and down with no doubt. "Keith?" However, Keith just felt it too risky of a venture. He was still overwhelmed with fear of Jones' wrath from his prior escape attempt and he shook his head side to side, wanting no part of the risky proposition. Vern pulled out the paper and pen and began to write the note. Simultaneously, Monica turned to Vern and said, "What about your son Vern?"

Like someone had scratched metal on a chalk board; Vern froze. "If I tell him, he might report us," he replied. Though his son Mark was only seven years old, Vern had a very legitimate concern. Though Vern later admitted that he wasn't thinking clearly, this shows the fear drummed-up by Jones and the chaotic spin that he injected into the community. Jones was very consistent in his tests and often encouraged children to spy on their parents and elders and report any suspicious or devious conversations. Aside from this, Vern also believed that his son would be better off in Jonestown, due to the fact that he was a Black child of a mixed-raced marriage. Jones would often report to his members in Jonestown that Blacks were being put into concentration camps back in the U.S. To some degree, Vern believed Jones' fear tactics about Blacks in the U.S., and he also remembered vividly what it was like from prior experience. Pondering the question about his son, Vern continued on writing the ten-word note:

"Vernon Gosney, Monica Bagby, Help us get out of Jonestown."

November 17, 1978 - Friday

On Friday morning Charles Gary and Mark Lane finally arrived at Peoples Temple House, and Gary was steaming mad. He had, had enough of Jones' constant flip flopping back and forth between letting them in and not letting them in. Gary and Lane exited the car and saw a stone-faced Sharon Amos there to greet them. Gary walked to the back of the car to open the trunk to get his bags. "The only God damned reason I came here was to take Ryan to Jonestown. Who the hell changed it Sharon, you?"

"Jim did," she replied. Gary and Lane both grabbed their bags and Sharon led them into the house. In the mean time, The Concerned Relatives continued to show their determination and continued placing unrelenting pressure on officials to allow them into Jonestown. Several members of the group made a stop at the United States Embassy to speak with Embassy Representative, Dick Ellis. After that they stopped at the office of the Guyanese Prime Minister. No one knew just what Jones was going to do, but the pressure was mounting. Many top officials had by then become involved, and it was bringing Jones and the Temple more negative attention than they had wanted or anticipated.

Along with Sharon Amos, Gary and Lane went to the Pegasus Hotel and had a private meeting with Congressman Ryan. After the brief meeting, Lane and Gary emerged from the private session and announced that Ryan had gone back on his word when claiming that he would go into Jonestown alone. Ryan had told them that he also wanted the media and the relatives to go in as well. By late Friday morning Ryan advised the attorney's that he and his group were leaving for Jonestown at 2:30 p.m., regardless of Jones' willingness to allow them or not. He also assured Lane and Garry that he would leave two empty seats on the plane for them if they decided to accompany him. After a few hours of negotiations the attorney's were painted into a corner and sensed Ryan's undying determination and they knew they had to get Jones to concede. Gary was a little more experienced than Lane, but both were good attorney's and well versed in controversial cases. Although they were both experienced; Gary was more skilled in social relations. Lane led more by intimidation and an in-your-face type of negotiating style, which didn't really work in Ryan's case or in reasoning with Jones. After a few hours of negotiations, Gary decided to give Jones a call on the radio and give him an ultimatum.

Back at Peoples Temple House, Sharon summoned Jones on the radio. Ryan and others were not allowed into the room; only Gary, Lane, and Sharon were present. Jones was barely coherent and began rattling off what seemed like Temple mission statements. "Listen Jim," Gary proceeded, but was cut off by Jones as if he were oblivious that anyone was speaking to him. Jones continued in a calm, slurred, and drugged sounding voice. "I'm a righteous man and we are a righteous people and the traitors they...they've come to destroy us..." Gary began to pace back and forth shaking his head side to side in disgust. He was fed up with Jones' attitude and just wanted him to listen to reasoning. "Jesus," he uttered as Jones continued on like a broken record.

"...We cannot allow them. They... they've come to steal our children..." Gary leaned over the microphone and tried again to get Jones' attention, "Jim...? Jim...?" Jones continued on, unfazed. Gary was growing angrier and more impatient by the moment as he began to pace back and forth again, scratching his head. Gary had finally had enough and proceeded with a speech to Jones that would change the course of history forever.

> *"Jim, cut it! Now what I'm going to say is very simple. You've got two alternatives. Now the first is, you can tell the congress and the United States to go fuck themselves; you can tell the media to go fuck themselves, which is what you've been doing all along over my objection. You can tell the concerned relatives to go fuck themselves; but if you do that, I cannot live with it. It's the end of the line."*

Jim listened intently as Carolyn Layton walked in the room and handed Jones two white pills that he immediately ingested. Gary then changed his vocal tone to a much softer one while he relayed the second and, which in his eyes was the more plausible option.

"Now the second alternative is what I've been urging you to do all along. You can let the media in; you can let the congressman in; you can let the relatives in; and you can let them see for themselves what a beautiful place you have there."

Jones paused for about a minute of awkward silence while giving the matter serious consideration, with the CB radio in his left hand, holding it firmly to his lips. Sharon sat steady throughout, expressionless, seeming indifferent to the entire process. Gary leaned over the radio anticipating Jones' next words. Finally, Jones answered in a confused and distressed manner, "Come down... I - I - I don't know what I'm gonna do... Just come down."

The only thing left to do was for the Relatives to appoint the representatives that would get to go into the interior, as there was only room for only four of them. The selection process was a hard one, only made easier by the Temple's demands to have a racially balanced group. The *first* chosen was the resourceful Jim Cobb. *Second*, and by default the only Black woman, Beverly Oliver. *Third* was the unofficial group's leader while in Guyana, Anthony Katsaris. *Finally*, Carolyn Houston Boyd, the daughter of Ryan's old friend, Bob Houston. Including these four, there were nineteen people headed to Jonestown:

- Mr. Ryan
- Miss Speier
- Deputy Chief of Mission of the U.S. Embassy to Guyana Richard Dwyer
- Mark Lane
- Charles Garry,
- All nine media members
- Mr. Neville Annibourne, a Guyanese Information Officer

The remaining Relatives were disappointed, but understood the plight of the situation. Anthony and Steven were both planning on going inside and actually had planned to unwittingly abduct their relative, Maria, if she was not willing to leave on her own accord. Naively, they had planned to drug Maria, sequester a vehicle, drive to Port Kaituma, steal a plane, and fly to Trinidad. A very lofty, unrealistic strategy; this is further proof that Jones' paranoia, however manic it had become, was not far off base. Unfortunately, this radical act might have gotten the whole group murdered in Jonestown, and it was probably best that this didn't come to fruition. The two tweaked their plan to a more reasonable one. Steven was a psychologist and he gave Anthony some psychological advice, as Steven believed that Maria was thoroughly brainwashed. Steven instructed Anthony, as a last ditch attempt, to give Maria a cross that she had adored as a child as a tool of persuasion.

All media members rushed to file their last stories while in the seclusion of the jungle. The Relatives all shed a tear and one last embrace before getting onto the plane. From the Timehri Airport in Georgetown, the plane left for Jonestown at approximately 2:30 p.m., for a 155 mile trek to the northwest (Friday, November 17, Guyana time, 12:30 p.m., Washington, D.C. time). Meanwhile, back at the Pegasus Hotel, Sharon gave Sherwin the word he was looking for. She informed him that Leanne was going to Georgetown to meet him the next morning. Sherwin made arrangements with Sharon to have Leanne meet him at 2:00 p.m., the following afternoon at a local café called, Lamaha Gardens. Sherwin was relieved that he would not have to venture into Jonestown; though if Leanne did not show up at the scheduled time and place, he was fully prepared to do so.

As the group flew over the miles and miles of jungle, the remoteness became evident. Reality steadily crept in, and it was soon obvious that this place would have been impossible to get to without proper clearance. The group had no idea what they were walking into. The psychological state of Jonestown was bad enough, but if they had heard the tapes of Jones and other Temple members hurling threats and talking so incredulously about the group's motives, they may have thought twice before trying to enter. If they had heard all of the names that Jones had called them in the recent white nights— snakes, shit-heads, mother-fuckers, lyres, etc—they may have re-thought their positions.

Every person had a different agenda: The media just wanted a juicy story that would go national; the congressman and his party believed that they could use the congress and the United States to bully Jones and allow them entry to check on the people; and the relatives just wanted to see their loved ones and possibly bring them home. The poorly timed and poorly planned trip was escalating so fast and out of control, that no one, on either side, was able to think straight or properly process the magnitude of the situation. Jones was a very dangerous man in a very dangerous position. Moreover, if he was part of a clandestine CIA experiment, he would have known this was the end of the line for all of them. Regardless, this current group was the greatest threat to Jones and his community. Jones was literally working his members into such a frenzied state that it would have been impossible to escape without incident. But it was too late for that. The plane was on the way and both groups had a date with destiny.

Jones' P.A. Announcement (Q050):

In preparation for the forthcoming delegates, Jim Jones made a P.A. announcement to inform and instruct the members of Jonestown what to expect, how to act, and what to do and what not to do. The very delicate situation called for Jones to recant his previous violent outpour in order to deflate his congregations' anger for the group, which by now was become quite incendiary. Jones had not slept in eight-days and was running on fumes, adrenalin, paranoia, and most of all, drugs. Throughout Jones' speech, there are several tells that truly open up the world to the inside working of the Temple and confirm certain previously disputed information. One thing is for sure: Jones had changed his tune from violence and complete lack of respect and distain towards the on-comers, to a careful, covert, and a more cautious approach. Just a day earlier, Jones talked about robbing the media of their equipment once they approached the gates and shooting the congressman in the ass. At this time, however, Jones was telling his congregation to be cordial, polite, and proceed without incident. Still one thing remained clear: Jones' true feelings for the group never swayed. He believed that the group was coming to destroy him and his community, steal the children from them, and report lies about them, regardless of what they found.

At about 1:30 p.m., after Jones had given the "ok" for the congressman and his group to come to Jonestown, Jones addressed and instructed the community with a 15-minute speech that built up like a tornado. One thing was for sure, Jones sounded more alert than he'd been in close to a year.

> *"Come to rest for just a few minutes, to get some rest; lay down, rest, groom yourself so you look well; dress the very best you can. We will probably not be seeing these people before five o'clock."*

There were a few points that Jones emphatically reiterated throughout the speech, and rest was one of them. He wanted his members well-rested and alert. Jones wanted everyone to be ready and everyone at the pavilion like actors taking their places when the show starts.

> *"You should not have anything to say if they give you a letter; take the letter; don't open the damn letter; turn the letter in to Rita Lennon, uh, 'cause they'd say anything and everything. Don't even act like you're that anxious to hear from them. Be friendly; be cordial, if anyone comes in. You don't know who's coming in at this time. But we urge you to go and rest in your rest homes"*

> *"Now we don't want more of them crawling on in a couple of weeks. That's the thing– anything, anything to avoid more of these suckers coming in, because somebody's tensions are going to flare. Someone's tensions are going to flare. So please listen, go home, we will notify you a half an hour before they come in, and then don't waste your time, be under the pavilion, and we'll have an entertainment show, our entertainment show, and a good meal prepared for everyone"* [Loud yelling interrupts, unintelligible].

> *"Have the place cleaned up as possible. There should be everything cleaned up, there shouldn't be anything laying around, this place should be spot cleaned. They're in the process where they could take the first hour to uh, do something about that so the place*

looks spot clean as– uh, uh, clean as it can be, but then get to rest, get to rest, get to rest."

"Please listen to what I am saying; I am trying to save us our babies. Who in the hell cares about us, it's our babies that we're thinking of. We do not want to see all of our children sacrificed over a jackass from San Mateo. Please listen to me. I am listening to our attorneys. These people are trying to set us up. And as far as your relatives coming up to talk to you, be civil, but don't, uh, don't get engaged into long conversation with them."

No Turning Back

Port Kaituma held a small dirt airstrip about eight-miles away from Jonestown where the group's plane had intended to land. At about 3:00 p.m., the group came upon the airstrip, but the airstrip was unserviceable. According to the pilot, there was a Temple dump truck sitting in the middle of the landing runway, obstructing the plane from safely touching down. The plane climbed back up and planned to land in the small mining town 30 miles away called, *Mathews Ridge*. The unexpected detour would mean that the group would not be able to enter Jonestown until the following day. Spirits ran low and frustrations high as word reached the passengers. The media members coerced the pilot into flying them over Jonestown, where they took several pictures and got a good look at the encampment. Suddenly, the pilot decided to double-back to the small airstrip where he serendipitously found the runway clear for landing.

The pilot miraculously maneuvered the plane and landed on the dirt airstrip to thunderous applause from passengers. They quickly departed from the plane and all looked around and got their bearings. A flatbed truck soon pulled up carrying four Temple members. Among them was the ever present Jim McElvane, head of security at Jonestown, Joe Wilson, and the Temple's PR representative, Mike Prokes, who was carrying a tape recorder. Seeing the truck headed toward them, they began unloading their gear for the impending truck ride into Jonestown.

The group gathered their gear and headed toward the oncoming truck, when suddenly another truck appeared on the airstrip heading toward the group. A man got out of the oncoming truck wearing a Guyanese army uniform and sandals. With the rest of the group witnessing, the dark skinned man exited the truck. "I'm Corporal Rudder from the Guyanese defense force [Guyanese Regional Official assigned to the Northwest Territory]," the man said to Ryan.

"Thank you very much for meeting us," Ryan Graciously replied, as he extended his hand to Rudder. The two men exchanged a firm hand shake.

"I've been instructed to inform you that only Mr. Gary and Mr. Lane are to board the truck for Jonestown," Rudder said. Determined not to be sidetracked, Ryan raised his right hand and placed it on Rudder's left shoulder.

"Look, we're a congressional delegation and we're here to inquire into the health and welfare of the people of Jonestown. We don't intend to break any laws."

"My instructions are clear," Rudder replied.

"Well who are you getting your orders from?"

Rudder sighed in frustration and politely instructed Ryan to return to the plane. Sensing a possible incident, Gary stepped in.

"Congressman Ryan and his assistant here can come with us," Gary said calmly.

"Mr. Gary, I've been told…"

"Never mind what you've been told, I'm telling you. If you catch any grief I'll be right there, congressman." Gary signals Ryan to board and escorts him to the truck.

"What about the others," Ryan asks Gary. Gary looks at Ryan as if he was lucky to be going himself. "I'm working on it."

Herbert Thomas of the Ministry of Regional Development—slightly confused himself—stepped forward and announced that they are neutral and invited the remaining crew into town where they could wait for word back from Jonestown. As Mr. Ryan, Miss Speier, Mr. Dwyer, Mr. Annibourne, Mr. Lane, and Mr. Gary boarded the truck, Gary advised the rest of the group that he would try to get them in the following day at the latest and warned them sternly, "Don't try to come on your own." With that, Ryan got into the front seat of the truck and the rest of the crew jumped onto the back of the flatbed and were off to Jonestown.

Thomas's invitation was short lived, as word soon came back from town that they were confined to the airstrip. Confused and frustrated, all that the remaining members of the group could do is wait and hope that Gary and Ryan would go to bat for them and somehow get them a safe pass to Jonestown. The Guyana sun loomed over the group and their only shade was the wing of the plane. Corporal Rudder and his assistant, armed with a 12-gauge shotgun, guarded the refugees. Rudder allowed them to get some beer while they waited and Banks beer yielding the only perk of the situation. After about an hour and a half, Rudder and Don Harris went into town to talk to Rudder's superiors and the group was left alone with the 12-gauge toting assistant.

While they were gone, Beverly Oliver and the armed assistant became fast friends. The assistant spoke of several bizarre incidents of planes picking up injured Temple members in the middle of the night. "It's always, 'Accident, accident, accident, but they were beaten, man," said the assistant. He recounted one particular story about an older man who was allegedly beaten in Jonestown. He claimed that he helped hide the man, who he identified as Leon. Immediately, Tim Reiterman did a double take. The man that the assistant was speaking of was Leon Broussard, whom Reiterman had interviewed about the incident not long after. Coincidentally and unexpectedly, Leon's story was corroborated in the most unlikely of places, and by the most unlikely of sources.

With nightfall visibly approaching, a Temple tractor appeared; headed toward to group. With a Black man driving, the White woman in the passenger seat stood up and said, "Everyone who wants to out to Jonestown can come, except Gordon Lindsay. The truck is coming now." Lindsay did not put up much of a fight and kind of expected that this might happen. Apparently, a previously unpublished story written by Mr. Lindsay—while with the *National Enquirer*—was critical of Peoples Temple and had accounted for the refusal to allow him into Jonestown. Lindsay was immediately sent back to Georgetown on the plane that the group had arrived in. At 6:20 p.m., the group packed their gear up onto the Temple truck, with the plane carrying Gordon Lindsay starting down the runway. After a short detour, where McElvane was unsuccessful in retrieving logging for the group, the truck was back on route to Jonestown. The members tried to enjoy the unusual scenery, but fear and anticipation overwhelmed them. The further they went on this journey the more they realized that they were now in the control of Jim Jones. The realization soon became very clear that their only chance of getting out of Jonestown was through Jim Jones and Jim Jones only. Any thoughts to the contrary soon vanished like the setting sun.

Bumping around the marshy and muddy jungle floor, the group soon came upon a small sign nailed to a tree; "GREETINGS PEOPLES TEMPLE AGRICULTURAL PROJECT." The sun was now a distant memory; signs of civilization began to emerge. A guard shack appeared out of nowhere and by the entrance stood the same sign, only ten-times bigger than the previous one. A long chain that had been removed marked the entrance to Jonestown, where guard, James Edwards, stood watch. As the truck slowly rolled along side a fence that separated them from Jonestown residents; children on the other side ran alongside the fence in the same direction of the truck, pointing and screaming playfully as if aliens had just landed. Carefully, each member stepped off the truck onto the muddy wet ground carrying their belongings and the heavy media equipment. The first good look at this awesome encampment captured ther admiration of all who witnessed. It was immediately evident that Jonestown took a tremendous amount of work and man-power to produce.

Charles Gary and Mark Lane met the group at the gate. Lane helped carry equipment and Gary led the group towards the pavilion. Like the curtain had drawn on an extravagant Broadway Show, Jones had his cast in place and the show was under way. Marceline headed toward the stage. The band played music and the atmosphere was festive. Eyes pierced the group during their brief hundred-yard stroll down the wide wooden entrance walkway leading to the pavilion. The music slowly died down as Marceline announced their arrival. "Attention, attention, attention, Shhhh. The reporters are arriving. Some of them will want to take pictures, so anyone who doesn't want their picture taken is excused." On cue, the band began jamming-out to funk music again. Though essentially contrived, the festive atmosphere seemed contagious. The loose crowd seemed to be enjoying the music. Kids bopped up and down while clapping, women twirled as skirts opened like parachutes; and Ryan casually spoke to members who were smiling and enjoying themselves.

Gary led the reporters on a direct route to Jim Jones, who adroitly sat at a wooden table in the center of the pavilion, grimacing mildly. Jones looked in poor health and had a spaced-out look on his face. Gary introduced each reporter to Jones and announced their credentials. "Jim, the gentlemen from the press have arrived." Jones nonchalantly turned, stood only half way, and shook hands with each of them as he adjusted his dark sunglasses and returned to a seated position. Funk music blared intensely from the speakers nearby, making it somewhat hard to hear. Immediately, the reporters casually interviewed Jones, not knowing if they would get another chance to later, with Tim Reiterman taking the lead. "I've read some of your stories," Jones said. "I guess you can only print what they tell you to."

"We've tried unsuccessfully to get your side of the story," Reiterman said in defense of the media. The reporters got acquainted with Jones for about ten-fifteen minutes or so until the rare smell of meat and potatoes being served side-tracked their efforts. It was time to eat. The meal consisted of pork and gravy, homemade biscuits, greens, potatoes, and fruit-flavored punch with sweet well water. The Jonestown members had eaten before the delegation had arrived. However, Jim Jones, Karen Layton, Carolyn Layton, Jack Beam, Harriet Tropp, Dick Tropp and Patty Cartmell also joined the delegation for dinner.

Anthony Katsaris had been seated at the table with his sister Maria, but hadn't had a chance to speak with her alone. Anthony wanted desperately to speak to Maria in private. After dinner, Anthony asked Maria to show him to the bathroom and she led him to the outhouse. She waited for him to finish and when he came out he tried to engage her in conversation about the Temple and asked if she wanted to come back to the States with the group and spend some time with the rest of her family. However, Maria did not want to talk about it and got quite disturbed by the line of questioning. Anthony tried to walk with her away from the pavilion and talk more, but Maria talked little and soon made her way back to the pavilion.

When they finally got back to the pavilion, Jones was going around introducing himself to the other three relatives with a Temple photographer present. As Jones shook hands with each member, the photographer snapped pictures. The shoddy Jones was once again working every angel and using the Concerned Relatives as just another cheap PR stunt. Carolyn Layton Moore had slipped away only to return with John Victor Stoen. Jones was parading him around and calling John his child. One of the other Jonestown residents commented, "Doesn't the boy look just like Jim?"

Around this time, several Temple members had congregated on the stage and commenced to entertain the crowd with singing and dancing. The media members continued to swarm Jones and resumed their informal interview with him. Jones began to rattle off the groups objectives, switching from subject to subject at a furious pace, like he was reading off cue cards. He was clearly not his sharp, coherent self. "What have we got to lose? We don't have barbwire here. We don't have 3, let alone 300, that want to leave. We're not a violent people; we don't do violence to anyone. Ageism, sexism, racism have all been eliminated here. Elitism has almost been eliminated. We're Marxists in the sense of sharing work and in the distribution of goods and services." Suddenly, McElvane leaned over and whispered something in Jones' ear. Jones soaked in his words and replied back with a whisper. McElvane then disappeared, but was close by patrolling the pavilion.

CHAPTER 12 – THE FINAL DAYS II

Vern Makes His Move

Vern Gosney was holding his son Mark with the note sitting firmly in his pocket that signified either a potentially life-saving ticket to freedom and or a possible death sentence. Observing the media group, Vern tried to decipher which one of them was the congressman. Suddenly, he saw a handsome man in a light blue suit smoking a cigarette and standing alone. Believing that this man was the congressman, Vern decided to covertly hand him the note explaining that he and Monica Bagby wanted to leave Jonestown. What Vern did not realize was that the man he believed was the congressman was in fact NBC reporter, Don Harris. Vern knew that if his attempt was unsuccessful there was no doubt that he would be killed. Vern put his son down and grabbed his hand, and they both walked closer to Harris. Vern was extremely nervous, and his body language mirrored his emotional state; he looked awkward and suspicious. All members were on high alert and Vern knew that he had to be cautious in his approach. Vern was being a little too cautious, however, as he walked up to Harris and stood alongside him. Vern looked at Harris then took a conspicuous look around; trying to build up the nerve to make the move. Time seemed to move in slow motion. Instead of thinking about how he would approach and hand-off the note, visions of getting caught danced around his head.

Harris was standing with a cigarette in his right hand and his left arm was folded across his body while the left hand was holding his right bicep. Without saying a word, Vern hastily shoved the note into the bent arm of Harris; but before Harris could comprehend what was happening, the note bounced off of Harris' arm and helplessly floated to the ground. Quickly trying to cover-up his impulsive action; Vern bent down, picked up the note, and handed it to Harris. "You dropped this," Vern said. Vern then turned and quickly began walking away, but it was too late. A young child of about ten years of age had spotted the transaction. Pointing and calling it to public attention, the child screamed, "He passed a note; he passed a note."

McElvane, who was nearby, scurried over to Vern to assess the situation. "What was that," McElvane inquired suspiciously. Playing it cool, Vern said, "It was nothing. He dropped something and I picked it up for him, that's it." Harris was confused, but had sense enough not to open the note or bring attention to it. He simply put the note in his pocket and acted like nothing happened. The brief commotion was quickly dismissed, and McElvane and the surrounding adults dismissed the incident as a figment of the child's imagination. Moreover, the incident was overshadowed by the finally of the show occurring onstage. Vern continued to distance himself from Harris and the scene of the incident, and nothing more was made of it that night.

Ryan addresses the crowd (Q 048)

When the performers left the stage, Marceline grabbed the microphone and introduced Congressman Ryan, who was preparing to publicly address the community. "And now everyone, I'd like to introduce you to a very special guest. He comes to us from California. He has represented many of us who have lived in his district back in California, and we welcome you, and we'd like for you to say a few words to us. Thank you." At that moment Vern turned and looked at Don Harris, thinking that he was about to take the stage; but Harris was didn't move. Vern then saw another man walking toward the stage. With a shocked look on his face, it was at that moment that he realized that the man he had handed the note to was not the congressman. Carrying his son as he watched the real Congressman walk to toward the stage, Vern reached a state of panic.

The crowd gave Ryan a warm welcome with applause as Marceline handed him the microphone. "Thank you very much, Marceline. I didn't ex—I'm not used to making public speeches." Ryan said as he chuckled. The crowd received the comment warmly, and they laughed as well. "Uh—I don't know, it's—it's—I'm very—very glad to be here. Um, I already have met a former student of mine; I've already met a former classmate of one of my daughters at uh, Mills High School in Burlingame. Uh, many of you I discover are from my own area and my own congressional district. As a matter of fact, in San Mateo County; so we are at least uh, friends in that— that extent. I'm very glad to be here. This is a congressional inquiry. I think that all of you know that I'm here to find out more about uh, questions that have been raised about your operation here. But I can tell you right now that, from the few conversations I've had with some of the folks here already this evening that, uh, whatever the comments are; there are some people here who believe this is the best thing that ever happened to them in their whole life." This comment caused thunderous applause from the crowd, who gave Ryan a standing ovation that lasted for close to a minute. With an expressionless look on his face, Jones was one of the last to stand and clap.

"After that kind of a response, I feel terrible that you can't all register to vote in San Mateo County." Ryan chuckled again and the receptive crowd followed suit. Ryan's personality was contagious; even to the hostile crowd, whom he seemed to be winning over. "…I hope to be through here tomorrow some time. In the meantime uh, you're obviously having a very good time tonight; I don't want to spoil any more with the political speeches. Just let me say, thank you on behalf of my staff, on behalf of the press who are here, on behalf of the relatives who are in here now, uh, for hosting us here this evening. We really appreciate it. Thank you so much." The crowd gave Ryan one last round of applause as he exited the stage.

Things seemed to have been running smoothly. The "pre-Ryan" hostile crowd was temporarily soothed by his complimentary words and the festive atmosphere. Ryan seemed genuinely impressed with the conditions in Jonestown up to that point. But the facade would soon fade into the ever present dark cloud that existed underneath the veneer. Congressman Ryan and his aid, Jackie Speier, were busy throughout most of the night. Ryan and Speier were privately talking to Peoples Temple members whose names had been provided to them by relatives in the United States. They were interviewing them (To see if they were happy, being treated correctly, were being held as prisoners, and wanted to go back to the United States) and passing on information from their family members.

Before and after his speech, Ryan conducted these inquiries with certain members, with Jones' knowledge and approval. Before Ryan and the group had arrived Jones made a P.A. announcement to the community explaining this to them: *"Please listen: anyone that's not called by them to see them, that they don't seek out, do not talk to them."* Jones had prior knowledge of the list of people that Ryan requested to speak with, and Jones prepared these members thoroughly on what to say and how to act. Jones gave special attention to making sure that these members said exactly what he wanted them to say. For the most part, though, Jones and his top-level staff had been preparing every member throughout the week, accordingly. Consequently, not one member that Ryan and Speier interviewed expressed interest in wanting to leave. The interviews were being conducted since Ryan had arrived in the early afternoon. By all accounts, Jones' plan was working perfectly. Up to this point, the officials of the delegation and media members were beginning to believe that Jonestown was a model community of happy, healthy members.

Ryan meets Gosney

A short time after Ryan's speech, Don Harris read the note that Vern had passed him to the congressman and covertly gave it to him. Ryan read the note and—accompanied by Don Harris—approached Vern in an official and clandestine capacity. Acting very loose, even with a smile on his face, Ryan and Harris stood next to Vern. "Are you Vernon Gosney?" Ryan asked. Vern shook his head up and down. "Did you give this man a note to leave Jonestown."

"Yes, sir," Vern replied.

"Then let me tell you; you've got seats [he and Monica] on the first plane out of here tomorrow." Vern shook his head in relief, but had a sense that Ryan had no idea what he was up against in Jonestown. Vern believed that Ryan did not understand the full scope and magnitude of Jones' power in the Guyanese jungle. How could he? Vern was there for all of the speeches from Jones. He heard all of the threats and he had seen Jones' wrath first-hand. He knew that Jones was fully capable of carrying out a sinister plot against the congressman. That is of course the reason that he wanted to leave. Ryan's lack of fear and overconfidence scared Vern a little. He didn't think that Ryan was taking Jones seriously enough.

"I'm not sure we should wait until tomorrow congressman," Vern replied.

"We've got a lot of work to do here," Ryan said, alluding to others who might want to leave. McElvane was not very far away from them while they spoke, and he gazed over at them suspiciously.

"You're in danger, you have to know that," Vern explained.

"We'll be fine," Ryan said. "We're under the protection of the U.S. Congress." Ryan smiled and tried to assure Vern of his security. Vern turned, tilted his head, and squinted at Ryan with a puzzled look on his face. After talking to Ryan, Vern knew that it was apparent that Ryan could not conceive the level of danger that he was in. Before the night was over, Ryan was notified of another possible defector. That same evening another Peoples Temple member approached Dwyer saying he wanted to leave "immediately." Dwyer passed the message onto Ryan.

The interview with Jones continued throughout the night. Jones' morbid demeanor and self-pitying talk was clearly disturbing to the interviewees. Jones had a hard time speaking about his views and how they applied to Jonestown. Applying his philosophies into a working model in Jonestown seemed to be how it suited him. Jones spoke of equality of the races; yet, the Temple was 90 percent Black. Moreover, White members assumed 95 percent of the leadership roles. Jones claimed that the Temple was a church, but it was very clear that Jones was the one being worshiped, not Jesus Christ or any other divine being. Jones was actually an atheist who believed that there was no God, except for the goodness and love inside each person. Jones believed himself to posses more goodness than anyone else. Like Caligula, Jones claimed himself to be God. Jones was often heard telling people that he was the only God that they would ever see.

Jones claimed that sexism had been eliminated; yet, he was an outward sexist. He claimed that elitism was almost eliminated; yet, he was one of the greatest elitists to ever live. He claimed that people were free to leave Jonestown whenever they wanted; but this was clearly not the case. Jones claimed that he didn't have a dime or control over any money; yet, the Temple had more than $10 million in overseas banks. The list goes on and on. Jones contradicted himself on just about every subject. When he wasn't contradicting his own professed views, he spoke of his self-pity and being demonized by his enemies. Clearly incapable of putting his views into practice, Jones knew that this interview was not going to sound good to the people back in the United States.

After Anthony Katsaris's brief time alone with his sister Maria, he did not get another chance to talk with her in private. The relatives were getting a taste of what Jonestown members faced every day. They were rarely alone with just one other member. Anthony did not want to try and influence Maria to leave while other members were around, because he knew he would wind up in a verbal altercation with other members. He had a hard enough time just speaking to Maria alone about leaving. After the show Anthony finally had another chance to speak to his sister alone. As they walked outside behind the meeting hall, Anthony brought up the situation at home. He was a bit overzealous, but he knew that he would probably not get another chance that night to speak to her about leaving.

This time, however, Maria became ever angrier when Anthony began pressing her about leaving with him. "I told you it was a bad idea for you to come down here at this time," she shouted. Maria continued on, and at one point Anthony got angry at her nonsense talk and grabbed her arm. Maria immediately tensed up and yelled for help from the guards. Anthony was so stunned and frightened by her screams that he jumped back and walked away from her. He quickly gathered himself and saw that no guards had come, so he mildly resumed the conversation. "I don't want to go home! I enjoy what I am doing and I don't want a change of lifestyle at this point," Maria stated firmly. "You can't put any conditions on me whatsoever," she continued.

The time was just past 10:30 p.m., and Temple aides gathered around Jones, signaling for the media to wrap-up the interview. Sensing his time was nearly up, Reiterman chimed in with the million dollar question: "What about the threats of mass suicide, reverend?" Jones paused for a moment, turned his head away, ran his tongue around the inside of his gums, and turned his head back around.

"I only said that it would be better to commit suicide than kill." Jones really didn't have a reasonable or witty answer for this question and really didn't answer any question directly. Jones' aids then whistled, indicating the end of the interview. Reiterman pointed out that on the way from town they were unable to secure accommodations for the night. Jones, however, was not receptive and claimed that they did not have room for them. Reiterman even suggested that they would sleep on the tables at the pavilion, but Jones said, "No, no, no, we couldn't have you do that." He then turned to McElvane and Johnny Brown Jones and asked them to find the group lodging in town for the night. Only Ryan, Speier, Dwyer, Annibourne, Garry, Lane, and Charles Krause were allowed to stay in Jonestown for the night. Krause seemed to be Ryan's chosen personal reporter and it probably was because he was representing the Nation's capital as a Washington Post employee.

At 11:00 p.m., the media members and Concerned Relatives set off for Port Kaituma (approximately 15 km east of Jonestown). During the 45-minute ride the reporters talked quietly, going over what they had learned. Reiterman believed that they might not get another chance to speak to Jones and that they would be leaving the following day not knowing the answers to whether Jonestown was a *"concentration camp"* or a *"human social experiment."* Javers seemed to be the most taken aback by the seemingly wonderful conditions—and happy people—in Jonestown; he even wondered aloud if Jones was possibly being persecuted for his progress in social development. However, the rest of them all believed that Jones appeared paranoid and possibly out of his mind. Had Jones almost pulled off his greatest scam yet—to fool a congressman and experienced media members while under fire? Still they had many question yet to be answered and no clear resolution one way or the other.

The delegation stayed in a local Port Kaituma disco that night, where the owner lived next door and agreed to house them for the evening. The women went to bed, but the men went to the disco's bar and downed some drinks and talked about their encounter. They met a policeman during their stay that they had a chance to speak with. The policeman told them about "mysterious night-time flights" that occurred on two or three different occasions where flares were lit to light the runway. The flights were for injured Temple members who needed immediate attention. Moreover, they used excuses like "tractors had fallen on" these injured members who had broken arms and legs. What were people doing operating tractors during the night? It was widely speculated that these people had been beaten. There were many other myths going around town, the policeman explained; like the "the hole" they found in Jonestown that members claimed was for beans; but they believed that it was a holding cell for members that were unruly—and they were correct.

November 18, 1978 – Saturday

After a long night of drinking and socializing, media members slept on the hard wood floor of the disco. In the morning they all prepared for the venture back to Jonestown. At some point during that time, Don Harris shared with the other media members that Vernon Gosney had slipped him a note asking to leave Jonestown. This confirmed the worst for the newsmen, as not only answering the question, "did anyone want to leave," but also confirming the fact that there were people who were fearful of expressing it openly. The group was expected to be picked up at 8:30a.m., as promised by the Temple members who had dropped them off; but nearing 10:00a.m., there was no sign of them. Corporal Rudder had soon arrived and Don Harris took him aside and notified him of the note from Vern. Harris asked Rudder to provide protection for the group. They feared possible problems when Jones and the others were informed that people wanted to leave. Rudder agreed, and canceled his other plans for the day in order to provide support for the group.

The group re-entered Jonestown at about 10:30a.m., and were met by Marceline Jones. Shortly after breakfast, Marceline took the media members on a formal tour of the Jonestown. The tour consisted of the library, hospital, kitchen, wood shop, lumber mill, machine shop, the piggery, the chickery, fields, citrus orchards, and the living quarters. After a year of lobbying to get into Jonestown, they were finally granted permission to tour the grounds. However, this now became a distant second to the fact that at least two people wanted to leave Jonestown—and possibly more—and were scared to let this be known publicly. Jack Beam and Johnny Brown Jones accompanied the group on the tour. Like the night before, all of the members took their places in each location, as choreographed by Jones. Each member was on their best behavior. Marceline was particularly happy about the "Cuffy Memorial Baby Nursery." It was truly Marceline's baby, no pun intended. It was perhaps the only thing left in her life that she had complete control over. As the group came upon it during the tour, Marceline explained to them that 33 children had been born there since the inception of Jonestown.

Neither Marceline nor any other member in Jonestown knew of the note passed by Vern, and the delegation waited for the right time to spring the news on them. Moreover, no one had known yet that in the early morning hours more than a dozen Temple members had secretely escaped Jonestown in the early morning hours. The escapees included five members of the Evans family as well as Leslie Wilson and her two sons (who were the family of Jonestown's head of security, Joe Wilson). They took off on foot before anyone was awake. They headed toward Mathews Ridge, through miles and miles of unforgiving jungle. Either they knew something that they did not agree with and did not want to be around for, or they just sensed impending danger. Whatever the case, they made a silent, hasty early morning departure. Knowing that one of the escaped members was the wife of the head of Jonestown's security force; it can be assumed that she may have had prior knowledge to a possible pre-meditated coup against Congressman Ryan (or worse), and decided to pack up and leave. The conditions of their departure—leaving on foot with no passports, no money, and with kids definitely shows the desperate mind-state that they were operating under at the time they made their escape.

Word spread quickly throughout the camp that something was going on at the pavilion. One of the members frantically ran over to Marceline and whispered in her ear. Right away Tim Reiterman knew that she had just been informed that there had been pending defections. However, Marceline went on with the tour as if nothing had happened. Some commotion was coming from the pavilion that was almost impossible to ignore. "Tim," Don Harris said, as he tapped Tim on the shoulder. "Something's going on; I'm cutting out." Harris then signaled for Steve Sung and Bob Brown to follow him to the pavilion. Reiterman was left alone with Marceline, Beam, and Johnny Brown as the tour continued. He was distracted by the commotion and continually looked back at the pavilion, unable to concentrate on the tour. Finally, Reiterman politely excused himself and headed toward the action.

Back at the pavilion, Ryan was speaking to other potential defectors regarding their safe passage to the United States. In addition to Vern and Monica, two large families had approached

Ryan and wanted to leave Jonestown as well: the Parks and the Bogue families—along with Christopher O'Neal and Harold Cordell, who were partners of women in the two families. To make matters worse, the families had been with Jones for many years. In the midst of the tour, word had spread from the pavilion that there were defectors. The tour was cut short as one by one each reporter heard the commotion going on at the pavilion. Their main concern at that time was the defectors and the thought that there might be more among them. This was now the main story, the very thing that the group had come to Jonestown to find out. The media wanted to capture the unfolding drama on camera.

There were several incidents that occurred during this day that only fueled the growing tensions between the group and the members. The first occurred when a dispute broke out between newsmen and members, because the newsmen wanted to get a closer look at living conditions of the elderly, who were living in a small wooden dormitory building with the windows tightly shut. The quarters held about 60 people in what was described as very overcrowded and probably the worst living conditions in Jonestown. Only days before their arrival, an enormous amount of lumber had arrived at Port Kaituma that was going to help erect one-hundred new cottages in Jonestown. Strangely enough, arriving along with the lumber—perhaps using the lumber to conceal its delivery—was a large amount of cyanide. The cyanide was not listed on any inventory list. The newsmen thought that there might have been others inside that wanted to leave and were being locked inside. However, this was not the case. The dorm held elderly Black women who openly said that they did not want to speak to the media. The real dispute occurred between newsmen and Johnnie Brown Jones, who would not let them enter the dorm. He eventually let them see for themselves that there was no one in the dorm that was being held against their will. However, this incident only furthered the deterioration of trust between the two groups, and the situation quickly turned into an "us against them" mentality for both sides.

Jones had awoken late that morning; although he was unaware that his worst nightmare was already in progress. He stayed up until 3:00a.m., the night before talking to Charles Gary who gave Jones an ultimatum, "Either Lane goes or I go." After Jones had gotten ready—wearing the same red shirt that he wore the night before—he headed toward the pavilion where he was immediately advised of the possible defections. He seemed sickly even before he heard the news. His worst fears had now come to light. Jones believed that if these people wanted to leave that they must have a hidden agenda, which included exposing him and Jonestown to the world; hence, destroying it from the inside out. His fears were not far from the truth, and he knew that the world would not take kindly to what they were going to hear from these defectors.

As Tim Reiterman explained in his book Raven, at this point, "the cautious optimism of the previous night had faded into the past like a cloud over the horizon." The atmosphere had changed dramatically into a fevered pitch. There was too much commotion going on all around for anyone to completely comprehend, let alone document. Things really started to become chaotic at this point and during the storm more defectors had come forward. For about the next hour or so, Jones privately spoke with all of the defectors, disallowing any of the media members from eavesdropping. Jones and Marceline were desperately attempting to pressure the defectors into staying. All members stood with a hint of shame in their eyes and a look of intimidation on their faces. Jones corralled the defectors into an area under the pavilion for his interrogation. The whole camp seemed paralyzed, and split into three different groups: the defectors, potential defectors, and the die-hard members.

Along with Charles Gary, Jones approached Vern and Monica, who were standing together, and made his pitch. He stopped briefly at the Parks family and informed them that he wanted to have a word with them. Jones asked them not to go anywhere. Jones was very composed and was being very kind. Yet, he couldn't hide the disappointment relayed in his body language. He was not his normal belligerent and charismatic self. He was in victim mode. "Why are you doing this," he asked Vern and Monica. "Are you lovers?" They looked at each other puzzled, "No" Vern said. "Because you can have a relationship here," Jones pleaded. Again the two seemed confused. "We're not lovers," Vern replied more firmly.

"Don't you talk to any of the reporters, alright? They're liars, they're all liars. You don't have to say anything." Jones sounded more desperate with every word. "Even the ones who lie, they always come back," said Jones. "I want you to know, you'll always have a place hear," Jones said, almost mechanically, as he handed

Vern a paper and a pen. The paper was a document that stated that he was leaving his son, Martin, there of his own free will. Gary directed Vern where to sign and went over the document with him. Vern was caught off guard and in a bad state of mind as it was. He just wanted to get out of there. Believing that he was doing the right thing at the time, Vern signed the papers. While Jones was talking to the disenchanted followers, Ryan looked on with Mark Lane and they had a few words. Ryan was looking at Jones almost sad for the man. Ryan, like many others, believed that Jones was a walking contradiction; a blessing and a curse. "It really is a shame," said Ryan, "that Jim is both the village's best friend and its greatest enemy because of his paranoia and his thirst for absolute power." Lane was very impressed with Ryan's analysis, especially after spending only about 24-hours in Jonestown. Lane knew that Ryan's judgment was spot-on.

Jones was only a shell of his former self, as he strolled around the camp. His attempts to thwart defections had failed. He had asked the Parks and Bogue families why they wanted to leave after all the years that they had spent following him, but many of them evaded the question by saying that that wanted to leave with their family members. "How many you've got congressman," asked Reiterman. Ryan looked at him almost gloating: "I think we're gonna need another plane." They both shared a quick smirk of victory. For legal reasons, Jackie Speier went around with a small tape recorder and mini microphone and took statements from each defecting member. She worked her way around to each defector taking statement after statement until she was soon in front of Vern and Monica. "I am Jackie Speier, an attorney on the staff of Leo Ryan. What is your wish today?" The protocol was to announce your name and your wishes. "My name is Monica Bagby. I wish to leave Jonestown on my own free will and return to the United States." Jackie then moved over to Vern. "My name is Vernon Gosney," he said, and then paused, viewing his son skipping nearby. Torn over the thought of leaving his son, the reality of the situation was never clearer. He continued: "…and I wish to leave Jonestown of my own free will and return to the United States."

After the defectors provided their statements to Miss Speier, it was time for them to pack their things and get ready to board the truck. "Now what?" Vern asked Monica. "Now we pack up; trucks leaving soon," she replied. With the atmosphere sizzling with animosity and angry Temple members, the defectors paired up so that they had some type of back-up in case an incident broke out. Yet, they all knew that constant harassment for the remainder of their stay was inevitable. Monica had paired with a friend who would aid in her security while she packed her belongings. Vern was terrified and for good reason. After all, he was the one who set the defection train in motion. Monica suggested that he find someone to escort him to retrieve his belongings. Looking around frantically for some help, Vern was at a loss. Now the most notorious member of Jonestown, Vern needed help, and quick. Gerald Parks paired with attorney, Mark Lane. When they had a minute alone, Parks told Lane that a lot more people would leave with Ryan if they were not afraid. He reaffirmed that conditions in Jonestown were horrible and work hours were obtrusively too long. During this time, Jones was informed that Joe Wilson's wife and others had left on foot earlier that morning without saying goodbye to anyone. This defection was probably the most devastating blow to Jonestown, and Jones knew it. Joe Wilson [a muscular, Black man, age 25] was head of Jonestown security and his wife certainly had to have known that trouble was brewing.

A few minutes later, Vern swung the door open to his cabin. Low and behold, the cabin was filled with several Temple guards with intimidating looks on their faces. Vern stopped dead in his tracks just as he entered the cabin. The men were not just there to intimidate Vern; they were clearly there to provoke an incident. Extreme fear and terror overcame Vern as he tried to squeeze through the unmoving guards. One man had his arm up holding onto one of the bunk-beds, forming a barrier between Vern and his belongings. Vern gently pushed his arm away and proceeded forward. There, standing at Vern's bunk was big Jim McElvane, a menacing figure. Suddenly, Congressman Ryan entered the cabin and eyed the guards as if ready for a confrontation. It was a stale mate! For a few seconds, there were no movements, no talking; it was a showdown; neither side giving ground.

Like two men standing in the middle of town waiting for the clock to strike 12 to draw their guns; the men held steady. Vern knew the first move would have to be his. Scared stiff, Vern turned and looked at Ryan for his approval. Like a scene out of an old

Western, Ryan gave him "the nod" to proceed. Conflict was almost inevitable in the cramped quarters. Suddenly, Vern went for his bunk. Simultaneously, McElvane moved directly in Vern's path, blocking him from his bed. "What ya doin, Vern?" McElvane asked sarcastically. Ryan moved Vern out of the way and stood face to face with McElvane. Not backing down an inch, Ryan said, "He's packing up. What are you doing?" Diplomatically, yet matter-of-factly, Ryan moved McElvane out of the way, grabbed Vern's bag, threw it to him, and in a stern voice said, "Pack your things!" Ryan continued to stare down McElvane as Vern frantically packed his things. This was just another example of Ryan's tenacity and the way he lived his life. Ryan knew his fight was the good fight. He was not going to be intimidated by anyone or anything.

Vern was soon done packing, but was still terrified. With a look on his face like a deer in headlights, Vern tried to negotiate his way out of the cabin without incident. Almost tip-toeing through a space half his size passed McElvane, who still refused to move; Vern continued forward led by Ryan. As Ryan got to the front door of the cabin, he stopped and let Vern walk out first. The men followed closely behind Vern and stopped only inches from Ryan. After Vern had safely exited the cabin, Ryan looked at the men and said, "Thank you." Ryan put his sun glasses on, turned away from the men, and walked out the door.

Jones' Exit Interview

While the defectors were gathering their things, no less of a dramatic scene was building at the pavilion. NBC was conducting what is known in the business as a "confrontation interview;" which is exactly what it sounds like and is done at the end of most investigations. Like vultures circling their almost dead prey, all of the reporters huddled around Jones as the hot lights focused on his pale face. There would be no holding back in this interview; reporters went into attack mode. With Jones completely exposed, the media lashed him with a barrage of questions that stung like a series one-two combinations from a heavy-weight prize fighter.

Jones, however, would fight back with rhetoric and contradictions as he always had. "We want to fade out of the whole arena of public attention, but obviously we haven't because of lies," he retorted. The fact that Jones wanted to fade out of the public arena could be attributed to a host of things. Jones may have wanted to fade out because there was so much bad press about him and the Temple at that point that he may have wanted the heat to blow over. Another reason could have been that—seeing as how he incorporated so many unorthodox, disagreeable and downright heinous acts in Jonestown—he knew he could only get away with these things if he flew under the radar. To do this, he knew he had to isolate himself and his members to the point that they were completely invisible to outside eyes. Another reason could have been because Jones—with the help of the CIA—had moved to Jonestown to continue the CIA's mind control experiments.

"I never understood how people could lie with such total freedom and conviction," Jones said. The contradiction from Jones here was like many of his others; he was projecting (or rejecting his own unacceptable attributes by ascribing them to others). Jones practiced lying on a regular basis. It was as much a part of his beliefs as was the truth; and by this point, it was probably even more so. Even when Jones told the truth he lied. He would always have to tell some outlandish story along with some truth, in order to bring home his main point. Anytime someone accused him of something, he would always turn right back around on them and claim the exact same thing of them and worse. If anyone stood up against him they were liars, child-molesters, accused of working for the government to bring him down, and everything else in between.

Don Harris had the note from Vern Gosney in his possession and he was planning to spring it on Jones with the camera rolling to record his reaction. Harris was hoping that it would make Jones lose his composure. However, through the plethora of attacking questions, Jones somehow remained poised. "Last night someone passed me this," said Harris as he handed Jones the note from Vern. Jones took a few moments and read the note, obviously pondering its content as the note only contained a few words. With a slightly embarrassed look on his face he looked up and said, "Friend, people play games…People can go out of here when they want." Jones then handed the note back to Harris. As Harris began to fold the note, Jones quickly grabbed the note from Harris and causally passed it to Temple PR man, Mike Prokes, who was standing to Jones' right.

"These people-they lie, they lie, what can we do about lies? Are you people gonna…just leave us! I beg you please just leave us! Anybody who wants to get outa here can get outa here," Jones pleaded with them. He had, had enough questioning, enough criticism, and enough abuse; he was fed up. He knew by the line of questioning that the media "spin" on the story would yet again expose the inadequacies and wrong doings of the Temple. "I'm gonna go say goodbye," Jones said as he got up from his chair and walked away. Gary, who was standing behind the camera listening to the interview came to Jones' side and put his hand on Jones' shoulder as they walked over to say goodbye to defectors. By now Jones knew that he could not let the group leave. He knew the end of Jonestown was now near.

Evil Blows into Jonestown

At about 1:45p.m., the group was ready to part Jonestown with about nine defectors, when a freak storm blew in. Even Jones exclaimed that he's never seen a wind such as the one they encountered that day. The sky turned black with thunder and lightning as rain and high winds poured in. The delegation and defectors were forced to wait out the storm for nearly two hours. "Out of nowhere, out of nowhere, the sky, I'm not talking metaphorically, the sky turned almost black," Tim Carter said; recalling the storm. "It was as if evil itself blew into Jonestown. Everything changed, everything changed on that storm!" Over the course of the storm, in his compromised emotional state, Jones had time to fester and time to plot a crisis strategy. Jones' mood also changed dramatically with the storm, and he knew that he had to do something to stop the defectors from leaving. The true dark nature of Jones had surfaced.

During the course of the storm, one particular incident changed the dynamic in Jonestown within minutes. The most underrated and most impactful incident had occurred. As the drama was reaching a boiling point, a Native American man named Al Simon approached the congressman with his two small children asking to return to the United States. Al's wife, Bonnie, vehemently objected, and a fight broke out between the two. Al had taken one of the children in a tug of war from Bonnie and carried him to the truck. "I'll kill you! I'll kill you! You bring those kids back here," Bonnie screamed. Her screams reached high pitched tones, mixed with tears and anger. "Al, you bring them back! Don't you touch my kids!" The hysterical White woman was gently consoled and held back by a tall skinny Black man in a blue rain coat and a tall skinny Black woman wearing a red shirt. Both tried to calm her down, assuring her that her husband was not going anywhere with the children. But she was inconsolable. Al came back and took the final child and headed toward the truck. Becoming even more frantic and hysterical, Bonnie (a small White woman wearing red jeans, a red shirt with white stripes, and a matching red bandana on her head) lashed out violently.

Marceline came rushing over to Bonnie and huddled around her. Marceline tried to calm her, but Bonnie didn't even notice that Marceline was there. Escalating the spectacle, Jones had Bonnie called into the radio room, where she got on the P.A., with encouragement from other members, and publicly berated her husband. This single incident alone turned the mood dramatically darker and fueled the growing tensions between the group and the members. Gary soon stepped in and, with his fierce presence and expert verbal skills, secured the situation. Both attorneys agreed that Al had no right to rip the children from their mother's grasp and that if there was going to be any separation it would have to be dealt with in court. Al did not put up much of a fight after that and decided to stay in Jonestown with the kids, who were traumatized and didn't want to leave their mother. This incident also cemented Ryan's decision to stay another night in Jonestown and speak to more potential defectors and give them more time to think over the decision to stay or leave. "The emotional climate changed dramatically after this incident," said Reiterman. "The threat to kill—whether in a fit of temper or not—had changed the air." Every delegate knew that it was time to leave and leave quickly!

Time to Go!

The time was about 3:15p.m. The storm had finally cleared enough for the group to travel; so they gathered their things and loaded them onto the truck. The time had finally arrived to say goodbye. The tension only thickened as Jones made his rounds—seeming sad, sincere, and defeated. As Vern headed toward the truck, Mark's Jonestown care taker (Edith) had brought Mark over to say goodbye. Vern knew that his son was too young to understand the turbulent circumstances; so he kept it light. Vern knelt down on one knee and smiled at Mark, who sweetly smiled back. "See you soon, ok? I love you," Vern said in an optimistic voice. Vern hugged Mark and squeezed him tight. There was no thought in his mind that he would never see him again. Edith grabbed Mark's hand and led him away, as Vern took a look at his son for the last time. Like the devil himself, Jones slithered up to Mark, patting him on the head and watching Vern walk toward the truck.

"Traitors!" shouted some of the members as the group mounted the huge flatbed truck. "I hope they shoot the plane down!" one man screamed. Jones walked over to the truck for his final goodbyes. Vern had his back to Jones and was putting his bag on the truck. Jones came up behind Vern, spun him around, and held him by each arm. "Come back anytime," Jones said in a monotone and loving voice. "You'll always have a place here, ok? Come back anytime and visit your son." Jones pulled Vern closer and gave him a big hug. Vern turned and jumped onto the truck. The minute Vern turned away, the look on Jones' face changed from sad and defeated to a look of pent-up hostility. "Come back anytime, you'll always be welcomed here," Jones said again, dragging out his words as an almost apparent taunt as he walked back toward the pavilion. Knowing Jones and his facetious rhetoric, Vern was at that point even more terrified. He knew that Jones always had a motive, especially when he was faking sincerity.

Jones fixed his glasses and walked down the wooden path toward the pavilion. Directly in his path was Tim Reiterman who was on his way to the truck. As Reiterman and Jones approached each other, Reiterman turned and walked with Jones. Reiterman nervously asked, "Reverend, can I just ask you; can I just get your reaction on what's going on here today? Did you try to stop anyone from leaving?" Fed up with the whole ordeal at this point, Jones said, "No, I feel sorry that we are being destroyed from within. All we want is to be left in peace." Reiterman reported that Jones had looked somewhat crestfallen, yet still very angry at that moment. Reiterman wrote down the conversation on his note pad and headed for the truck, ready to leave Jonestown with his story. Little did he know that the story was about to take such a dark turn that it would be entrenched in the psyche of American history forever.

Reiterman had his story and he was anxious to get back to Port Kaituma to file it with the paper. Walking toward the truck, he met up with Don Harris. "If we get out now I can still make deadline," Reiterman said to Harris. Almost ignoring Reiterman's comments, Harris looked around. "Where's Ryan," he said. "He's staying back to help with the rest of the defectors," Reiterman said casually as he packed his bags on the truck. "You mean there's more," Harris asked. "Ya, only he's not saying so," Reiterman replied as the others grabbed his hand and pulled him onto the truck. Jones returned passports to each defector and gave each $5,000 in Guyanese currency. Other defectors had also stepped forward, but there was not enough room on the truck; so Ryan decided to stay behind to protect them and see if there were any others that wanted to leave.

Ryan, Gary, Lane, and Dwyer all were in the pavilion discussing the situation. Ryan was trying to persuade Jones into believing that the situation was not as bad as it seemed. However, both men—Ryan and Jones—knew that the situation was critical. "Jim: why are you so upset?" Ryan asked. "There are only fifteen people leaving out of nearly a thousand. I mean, if four-hundred were leaving I'd be worried." He knew that he had Jones beat and he knew at that moment that all of his skeptics, especially the ones that were critical of his trip to Jonestown—saying that he was doing it for publicity—were proven wrong with his current findings. Jones knew this also. Jones looked around, appearing to be ignoring Ryan's comments. His body language showed genuine anger, disgust, and disappointment for what was transpiring. Jones was in a desperate state of mind.

Jones had lost control for the first time in years and certainly for the first time in Jonestown. This time, however, he had lost control for good. Ryan's choice to stay another night in Jonestown and speak to more families about leaving cemented the fact that Jones had not only lost control, but that Ryan, who represented his enemies, had assumed that control. Moreover, Ryan's impending stay threatened to reveal even more defectors. Charles Gary stood by with a worried look on his face as well. He knew that he was partly to blame for pressing Jones to let the congressman in. Gary sensed the end of Jonestown was near as well. Jones still remained uncommonly silent. Ryan and everyone near sensed Jones' frustration. "It's only fifteen people," Ryan pleaded with Jones as if he was trying to persuade Jones to look on the positive side of things. Still, Jones did not respond. "When I get back I'm going to report to congress that of the sixty people cited by the concerned relatives, none of them wanted to leave. They were completely happy." Jones could not even look at Ryan. His mind was made up and he knew what he had to do.

By now, Jones had already summoned the help of Larry Layton to pose as a defector. Jones believed that it was his duty to carry out the task as it was his sister, Debbie Layton, who had been partly the cause of Ryan's visit, and Jones used this reasoning to manipulate Larry into taking on the task. Larry had just lost his mother, Lisa, to cancer some ten-days prior. Larry was in a very fragile state of mind and was even more vulnerable than usual to the misguided thoughts of an angry tyrannical madman. The two men together, at this particular time, were a dangerous mix, and disaster could be the only outcome of this dubious coalition. Larry grabbed a poncho and headed for truck. The secret defection was only known at that time by the devilish tag-team of Layton and Jones.

Jones watched as Larry Layton ran down the wooden walkway to the truck of defectors. A small sense of happiness came over Jones as he felt a bit of control coming back to him. "Hey," Layton called out. "You got room for one more?" James Cobb Jr., leaned over and whispered in Reiterman's ear, "No way he's a defector." Weary, Reiterman opened the truck gate and helped Larry aboard. "Why ya leaving?" Reiterman asked suspiciously. "I'll tell ya later," Larry oddly replied. Suddenly, Larry's wife Karen came bolting over to the truck totally freaking-out. "I don't understand this, what's this all about?" she bellowed. It was a clear demonstration that Larry's wife—a woman in almost the highest position in Jonestown—had no idea that Jones had sent Larry on a top-secret Temple mission: a mission to kill.

This was also further evidence that if anyone knew about Larry's orders, it was only one or two of the highest level members. Karen was not a very good actress; and from all accounts, she was sincere in her tantrum. Larry ignored Karen. He didn't even look at her. Every defector knew Layton was planted by Jones, but Congressman Ryan would not listen to them, and he allowed Layton to board. Dale Parks announced that he heard Layton ask Jones earlier: "Is there anything that I can do?" Every defector voiced their disapproval, including Dale Parks and Jerry Parks, both of whom informed Reiterman to keep an eye on him.

Fifteen Defectors in total had piled onto the truck along with all nine media members and the four representatives of the concerned relatives. The defectors were as follows:

VERNON DEAN GOSNEY
MONICA BAGBY
TOMMY BOGUE
JIMMY BOGUE
EDITH BOGUE
JUANITA BOGUE
TIMMY BOGUE
HAROLD BOGUE
CHRIS O'NEIL
EDITH PARKS
PATTY PARKS
DALE PARKS
TERRY PARKS
BRENDA PARKS
…and at the very last minute, LARRY LAYTON

The truck was packed solid. Just before the truck was about to pull off, Maria Katsaris approached. With all of the people on the truck, she could not find her brother, who was stationed on the other side. Instead, she looked up at Reiterman. "Here," she said angrily as she threw the cross that Anthony [her brother] had given her at Reiterman. "Tell Steve [her father] I don't believe in god!" Reiterman caught the chain and Maria stormed back to the camp.

Anthony was traumatized after Reiterman gave him the chain and the message; so much so that he collapsed in tears on the truck.

Cobb looked over at Layton, who looked crazed, and he knew that it was some type of set-up. "We won't get out alive," said Vern. Hearing this, Cobb's mind raced. The defectors had a secret bond, an intuition. They knew that the media members and officials were not truly aware of the danger they were facing. Cobb was ready for anything and he believed that trouble was just around the corner. Seeing Larry Layton cemented the fact that trouble was near, and this made him alert and responsive to any impending danger. During the first few minutes of the bumpy ride, Cobb intentionally fell into Layton a few times in an effort to see if he had a gun. He was satisfied that Layton was unarmed after several brush-up attempts. Layton was the only defector without luggage or additional clothing. Everyone was suspicious of him. Where others might freeze-up in shock, hoping that trouble would pass them by; Cobb was alert and focused that trouble was imminent and that they were going to meet trouble head-on at some point during their escape.

The truck did not start moving for some time. All of the defectors were anxious and wanted to leave the camp immediately. Vern sensed imminent danger and kept insisting that they get out of there at once. After about a fifteen minute delay, for reasons unknown to all on the truck, Vern began to get angry and his murmurs built to a crescendo. "Let's get going! We should get going!" Vern shouted. Other defectors chimed-in as well. "Let's go! Let's get going!" they shouted. The truck finally started moving, but after only a few feet the truck stalled in a ditch. A collective sigh rang out and many defectors' voiced that this was a planned stall. "It's a set up," said Vern. "We're never gonna make it out of here alive!" Had Jones ordered the truck driver, Ed Crenshaw, to stall their departure so that he could get Ryan on the truck in order to have him set up at the airstrip? Their departure was even more delayed as they awaited a Temple bull dozer to come and pull them out of the ditch.

Meanwhile, Ryan continued his talks with Jones at the back end of the pavilion. Still silent and looking more displaced than ever, Jones looked as though he was in a trance. "Jim, this is a wonderful thing you've got going here," Ryan said as a man approached him from behind. The man was Don Sly, nicknamed "Ujara" by Jones.

Suddenly, Sly grabbed Ryan by the head with his left hand and put a homemade knife to his throat with his right hand. "I'm gonna cut your throat, you motherfucker!" he screamed. Ryan, who wasn't sure if this was a joke or not, clutched Sly's arm in a natural defensive posture.

Acting quickly were Lane and Gary. Lane immediately went for the weapon and Garry grabbed Sly around his neck. Gary tried furiously to pull Sly backward, away from the congressman. Sly did not release his grip on Ryan, and the three men went crashing to the ground. Tim Carter dove onto the ground to help Ryan and Gary, and eventually they wrestled the knife away from Sly. Everyone rushed toward the back of the pavilion in what sounded like a roar of cheers. The truck carrying the group suddenly halted, and Don Harris ran to see what the commotion was. A few minutes later, Harris waved his arms in a fury, signaling the group to come quickly. Frantically running through the mud, they reached Harris, who tried to compose himself. "Some guy tried to kill Leo. Leo's alright," he said. The group was stunned and angry. Out-numbered, they quickly took the "Us against them" stance and rushed toward the pavilion to back up the congressman.

As quickly as it began it was over; but everything changed in an instant. After the scuffle, Ryan brought himself to his feet and looked down at his safari jacket, which was stained with blood. In shock and shaken up, Ryan frantically checked himself for cuts or the source of the blood. Also shaken up, Jackie Speier checked Ryan as well, but he did not appear to have any open wounds. However, Don Sly did have a cut between his thumb and index finger, which had occurred during the scuffle and accounted for the blood on Ryan's jacket. Throughout the whole ordeal, Jones did not move a muscle, and remained indifferent, even after the incident.

Ryan's mood changed dramatically after the incident and for once his tough veneer had turned to a nervous twitch of looking over his shoulder. Possibly the most shocking thing about the incident was that Jones had not said one word in protest of the incident, nor did he apologize to Ryan. Ryan's shock quickly turned to anger "I guess this changes things, doesn't it?" Jones asked, seeming as though he was disappointed that Sly had not completed the act. Too shaken to correctly assess the situation and Jones' possible role in the incident, Ryan assured Jones that his report would not change provided that Sly was arrested by local authorities and brought to justice. It appeared as though Jones was not going to agree to even calling the police regarding the attack, but he agreed to after further persuasion from his lawyers.

As the group rushed toward the pavilion, they were met by Johnny Brown and a group of Temple men. The stand-off was temporary, as Johnny advised them that the situation was under control and that their presence would only add to the tension and possibly set-off another incident. The group looked behind the men and saw the glaring faces coming from Temple members and agreed that it would be best for them to go back to the truck. After the incident, the tough-minded Ryan still was set on staying the night to negotiate more possible releases. However, Dwyer and Ryan had a discussion where Dwyer virtually ordered Ryan to leave Jonestown. Dwyer volunteered to take Ryan's place and stay the night in Jonestown and continue to interview potential defectors.

At 3:45p.m., the truck started on its way only to be stopped again just a few yards later. They were stopped by a young man who was running at them from the pavilion screaming at the top of his lungs. Out of breath; the young man informed the group that Ryan would be accompanying them on their journey. Suddenly, through a hail of dirt and dust, Ryan, Dwyer, and Speier appeared, followed by the lawyers; all headed for the truck. Dwyer had agreed to accompany the group to Port Kaituma and then travel back to Jonestown. Lane was not leaving Jonestown; he was just seeing off Ryan and the group.

Gary stayed back with Jones and reflected on the incident. "That God damned fool," Jones said, speaking of Ryan. "Why did he come here without security?" Gary was stunned and told Jones that if Ryan did come with security it would have offended him and the members. Agreeing with the sensible logic, Jones tried to play off the attack as simply the response of an angry crowd. Gary did not know what to make of Jones' indifference toward the incident; and because of this indifference, Gary believed that Jones was responsible for the act. The odd thing was that Sly was a big man and caught Ryan and everyone by surprise. He literally had five-six seconds with the knife to Ryan's throat while people stood in shock. Realistically, he could have easily killed Ryan if he really wanted to, and in retrospect, many of the witnesses wondered the same.

The group's mood had also changed dramatically. Seeing Ryan with blood spattered on his shirt and looking disheveled; it was a very depressing site. Up to that point, Ryan had been their shield, their protector; but now he was looking like he had been through a war and was himself fearful. Literally and figuratively, Ryan had been their protector; but he now needed protection himself. The psychological effect of this sudden change was devastating to all involved. Vern knew that the congressman was tough. He had witnessed the cabin incident where Ryan stood his ground. Looking at Ryan now, Vern could finally see that Ryan was coming to the realization that the danger of the situation was quite real and his congressional position was no longer something that he could hide behind. Ryan was now just like everyone else; it was like he was stripped of his position. At no point did Vern believe that any of them were going to make it out of that jungle alive. Many of the defectors shared the same sentiment, sensing that there would be an ambush at some point during the ride to Port Kaituma.

CHAPTER 13 – THE FINAL DAYS III

Sherwin, Liane, and Sharon

Back in Georgetown, Sherwin Harris arrived by cab at Peoples Temple house at about 2:00p.m., as scheduled. He was greeted outside by his daughter Liane, who hugged and kissed him and seemed very happy to see her father. Sherwin lit up like a Christmas tree when he saw his lovely daughter for the first time in over a year. After sharing pleasantries, the two headed into the house. Because of the storm that had already begun, Sharon had decided to prepared lunch, instead of going out and facing the fury of the weather. The three sat down in the living room and got reacquainted with small talk. "I wish you could see the wonderful, the great work we do. You'd see there's nothing to be concerned about," Liane said, boasting about the Temple's good deeds. Sherwin was happy to see his daughter so passionate about something and he thought nothing of the horrible rumors of Jonestown. "How long are you thinking of staying," Liane asked.

Sharon sat mostly silent, but was being somewhat pleasant and cordial, not interfering in the bonding. Sherwin was not sure how long that he was going to remain in Guyana. He estimated from two-weeks to a month. Sherwin was hoping that Liane would show him around. He suggested that Liane even be his tour guide. Sharon didn't seem very upset by the news. "Why don't you two sit down to dinner," Sharon said pleasantly as she went into the kitchen to finish preparing their meal. Sherwin and Liane moved into the kitchen and continued their conversation. Sherwin was on top of the world, and the twenty-one year old Liane seemed very happy that her father was in her presence.

As Sherwin and Liane were conversing, in walked Stephan Jones and the basketball team. It was an awkward situation, and Sherwin thought they were there to intimidate him. Stephan had awoken early that morning, took team pictures, played basketball, and was now at the Lamaha Gardens Peoples Temple facility. Georgetown had not yet been informed about the growing tension in Jonestown or of any defectors. As far as they knew, things were going great in Jonestown. They had received the update from the night before and they had heard of the congressman's kind words about the camp. Hopes were high in Georgetown and in the United States. Sensing his presence was overbearing, Stephan suggested that the team take in a movie in Georgetown (the John Saxon movie, *The Deadly Thief*).

Sherwin and Liane had a moment alone in the living room sometime before 3:00p.m. Alone for the first time, they stared at each other for a moment in silence with emotions building. "It is so good to see you again," Sherwin said, bursting into tears. Liane began to cry as well. "I just want to get to know you again," Sherwin said. It was a cleansing moment for the miles that had separated the two for so long. Even though Liane had made comments months earlier to the effect that Sherwin was a "dead-beat-dad," all that pent up anxiety had peaked as the two shared tears of their long awaited reunion. The mood lightened considerably just before dinner, though Sharon was not so fortunate. She was trying to act as though nothing was wrong after hearing news from Jonestown of the defectors. Sherwin was telling jokes and laughing with Liane and the two children, Christen [age 7] and her younger step-brother, Martin [age 6].

The light hearted atmosphere in Georgetown would soon not only change, but it would change into a critical situation with just one radio transmission from Jonestown. Sharon was periodically checking the radio room for any messages from Jonestown. After all, it was seen by all members as one of the most important days in the history of Jonestown. Everyone was on high alert, including the San Francisco Temple. Sharon had been previously concerned that Sherwin might try to persuade Liane to leave Guyana with him or at least try to poison her mind against the mission. At this point, she was not concerned at all. She knew that a critical time was upon them and all her focus was on Jonestown; she became very passive to Sherwin's visit. Moreover, Liane was conditioned very well to the idea of Jonestown and she had the routine of being cordial and hospitable to the enemy down to a science. In reality, Sherwin just wanted to see his daughter, spend some time with her, and rebuild their previously estranged relationship. Sherwin could not see far past the trip; he was all about the moment. Sharon also had bigger fish to fry. She knew that she could not stray too far from the radio room.

Though Sharon was on guard, she never expected the message that would be sent in from Jonestown. Tim Carter's brother, Mike Carter—who was the Jonestown operator at the time—made a critical call to Sharon at about 3:00p.m. Mike was in the room with the deputy chief of United States mission in Georgetown, Richard Dwyer, who informed her to contact the U.S. Embassy and order another plane. When Sharon asked why, Dwyer advised that they needed another plane because they had too many defectors for the plane that was already waiting for them. Sharon was in shock. Sharon stuck to the radio even closer after this, leaving Sherwin and Liane to converse without her. Sherwin and Liane were not aware what was transpiring all around them. Sharon was patiently waiting for more information from Jonestown. Mike Carter could not speak freely while Ryan and others were still there. It wasn't until they left that the messages became more bizarre. Mike Carter finally answered one of her transmissions at about 4:15p.m., and Sharon asked him if it was a joke. Mike advised her that it was very serious and went as far as naming all of the defectors. Sharon was even more in shock to find out who the defectors were. Not only were there several defectors, but they were long time members, people who no one thought would have left Jones at this stage of their membership.

A little earlier, Sharon had notified Stephan's brother, Tim, who in turn immediately went over to the theatre and informed the team. Cutting the movie short, Stephan and the basketball team raced in a fury to get to the house to find out more. Skidding into the driveway, Stephan hopped out of the vehicle and raced inside, leaving the rest of the team to wait in the car. Stephan hurried into the radio room in just enough time to hear Jones tell Sharon, in a coded message, that they were to take revenge. That's all they knew, but they knew exactly what that meant. It meant to kill relatives and possibly defectors and media—but definitely relatives. The message was also coded for them to use knives to kill, as there were no guns in Georgetown. Though only 19-yrs-old at the time, Stephan Jones was still a very intelligent and relatively rational young man. He knew that his father was nuts and he was not going to just follow orders without a legitimate reason. Stephan tried to slow things down and talk the incident through.

The first order at hand for Stephan, however, was to assess the situation with the team and his brother, Tim. He ran out to the van to break the news to the team and figure out what they were going to do. The team took much the same stance as Stephan. None of them were buying into Jim's madness. Mike Touchette had stumbled into the PT House with Debbie Touchette. Mike Touchette was also devastated about all of the defectors and stormed out of the house screaming, "Bullshit!" Sherwin witnessed the incident and wondered what was going on. Tim Jones and Johnny Cobb decided to go over to the Pegasus Hotel to speak with the Concerned Relatives and see if they could extract anymore information out of them.

S.F. members huddle around radio

The San Francisco Temple was also on high alert all day. Buzzing from the good news the previous night, they were expecting more good news on this day. At about 4:30p.m., they were sent a message via Morse code from Mike Carter stating that Carolyn Layton wanted to speak to Sandy Bradshaw. They were instructed to switch frequencies for the transmission. They waited for almost a half-hour, but still there was no answer. They had good reason to be worried, as it was bizarre for Jonestown not to respond.

The calm before the storm

Meanwhile, the departing congressman and his group neared the Temple gate, which was about three-miles from the actual Jonestown camp site. Even though weather conditions were not very good, many noticed that driver Ed Crenshaw had been driving unusually slowly. When they arrived at the main gate they noticed that the chain had been secured, stopping them from leaving yet again. They also noticed several Temple guards waiting up ahead. Vern at no time believed that they were going to make it out alive, and he felt that this was the end for the group as they approached the guards. The head of Jonestown security, Joe Wilson, was one of the men who greeted them at the gate and he was not in a good mood. His head was still swimming with thoughts of his wife and children's escape. Thinking that his wife and children may have been on the truck, Wilson shouted angrily, "Let me see who you've got there?" Wilson had everyone spread out so that he could see who was on the truck and it appeared as though he was trying to get a head count.

The truck was stopped for what seemed like an eternity. Wilson began counting to see how many members were on the truck. No one is really sure what the purpose of Wilson's head-count. It is possible Wilson knew there were going to be problems in Jonestown and sent his wife, children, and some of his friends packing to save them from sure doom. It is also possible that he was counting to see how many people they needed to kill and account for. No one will ever know. One thing that is known is that the security men were armed and many in the group envisioned the men opening fire on them right then and there. Surely, they could have killed them all right there in a bloody massacre if they truly wanted. Maybe Wilson wanted to wait until he found his wife and children first? Joe Wilson, James Edwards, Bob Kize, Tom Kize and Ed Crenshaw all jumped on the back of the truck and took the ride with the group back to Port Kaituma.

Finally, the truck resumed bumping down the unforgiving dirt path. Upon arrival at the airstrip, at about 4:30p.m., everyone loaded their luggage into a small metal shack that served as a waiting area on the edge of the runway. The reporters and Ryan stayed in the small shack to wait for the planes to arrive. The others waited outside. Ryan graphically described the attack on his life while Greg Robinson snapped several pictures of him. Spatters of Don Sly's blood were clearly visible on Ryan's shirt. Large spatters of blood on the right side of Ryan's chest and on his upper left arm were evidence of the horrifying ordeal. They hung around the shack for about fifteen-minutes and then Ryan did an airstrip interview with Don Harris. He summed up his Jonestown visit by saying, "It was very different from what I thought I'd find, in both positive and negative ways." That sentence itself truly tells the story of what was to come next. Though he said that he was more impressed in ways than he thought he'd be, he also said that the negative aspects that he found were worse than expected.

At the conclusion of the interview, the two planes arrived and were ready for boarding. The six seat *Cessna* had flown in first, followed by the slightly larger twin-engine *Otter*. Unfortunately, it was determined that there were still not enough seats for the whole group. Stubborn yet selfless, Ryan had decided to stay behind and possibly return to Jonestown to see if there were any other defectors. It was decided that the defectors should be let out first then the rest of the group. Some of the media members were going to have to stay behind and wait for another flight out. Layton was the most vocal of the defectors, insisting to be placed on the first plane (the six-seat Cessna). Layton went on and on about how he believed that Joe Wilson was going to shoot down the big plane and that he had to get on the small plane. Layton's wish was granted and he stood in line to board the Cessna. Amidst a rumor that someone might have a gun on their person and bring down the plane, a few media members took the liberty of searching each defector as they boarded the plane. Reiterman deliberately stood behind Larry Layton in order to keep an eye on him in case he tried something. Suddenly, Layton broke from the line and scurried around the other side of the plane, entering and sitting behind the pilot's seat.

Seeing Layton's shifty move, Jim Cobb shouted, "Layton has not been searched!" The situation became very hectic and Jackie Speier became visibly nervous. Congressman Ryan quickly confronted Layton who claimed that he was frisked already. Reiterman called Layton on his bluff and the men frisked him. Reiterman then went and checked the inside of the plane to see if Layton had stashed a gun, but found nothing. Reiterman's search efforts were, however, distracted by the confusion of the situation; but he did search briefly and found no gun in the plane. Shortly after Layton was searched and exited the plane, he was seen shaking hands with Joe Wilson at the airstrip. At least two eye-witnesses claimed that it was at that time they saw Wilson hand something to Layton, though they did not see if it was a gun or not; but it was speculated by many that it was.

During the confusion, a Temple dump truck and a tractor-trailer had appeared. It appeared to many of the defectors as though Ed Crenshaw was driving the truck and Stanley Gieg was driving the tractor. The tractor was pulling a trailer with a group of Black and White men. The mysterious thing about this was that they appeared from the 'Jonestown road.' This was the only road leading in and out of Jonestown and there were no roads intersecting or merging with this road. Dramatically, another truck rolled in carrying Dwyer in the front seat along with the constable and a few other armed men. Relief poured over some, impending doom over others. Media members felt secure with the presence of such authority; the defectors still believed that it was a trap. Ryan was particularly happy to see Dwyer, and he quickly embraced him and they began walking together toward the entrance of the plane. But, Dwyer veered off to the left, suddenly, to talk to the pilot.

The time was approximately 5:15p.m., and the Cessna had boarded all six passengers. Among them was Vernon Gosney, Monica Bagby, Dale Parks, Tracey Parks, the pilot, and Larry Layton. Most of the defectors had boarded the second plane—the Otter—when the Cessna started down the runway. An unknown Guyanese official had strangely boarded the Otter and was just sitting in one of the seats. Jackie Speier boarded and told the man that he had to leave. The man then got up without saying a word and exited the aircraft. The group sensed trouble and was in a rush to board the plane and leave the premises. Almost as soon as the Cessna started rolling, the tractor, carrying a trailer of about nine men, pulled onto the runway right in the path of the Cessna. The Cessna was forced to swerve to the left, causing it to stall out on the left bank of the airstrip. The tractor continued on a direct route across the runway until it was directly in front of the Otter. The truck had moved from about 200 yards away from the nose of the Otter on its North East side, to about 30 yards away, North West—crossing from the back of the plane all the way to the loading side of the Otter. Immediately the grouped scurried to board the Otter, as they sensed danger. Once the vehicle came to a stop, one of the men began waiving. Some members of the departing group were sort of hypnotized by the waving, enough not to notice the Guyanese people heading for cover at the instruction of the trucks passengers.

Massacre at the Airstrip

Suddenly, the nine men ducked down and each came up with a firearm. Each of the men held one of the following weapons: a bolt-action .30 caliber rifles (mounted with black telescope sights), a shotgun, and an automatic hand gun. They jumped down from the trailer with firearms in hand—in an aggressive and strategic manner—and methodically headed toward the Otter. "Everybody spread out," screamed Don Harris. Terrifying screams reverberated as the first popping of gunfire sounded off. "Get down," someone screamed; "Hit the dirt," screamed another. Shock quickly made way to sheer panic and terror. The defectors in the Otter instantly became sitting ducks when some of the shots fired hit the wheels and the base of the plane and shattered the glass on the windows while the engine was running. Some ran in circles, dazed. Most ran for immediate cover; some fled into the jungle. Guns close by erupted. The airstrip had become a war zone. Ron Javers was hit first, with a slug to his left shoulder. The blast knocked him clear off his feet and onto the ground right next to Bob Brown (camera man); who had somehow managed to continue filming. Brown held the camera steady—draped over his right shoulder—on the gunmen as they diligently fired shots and moved in army-style formation.

Congressman Ryan ran and hid behind the big wheel of the plane. Camera man Bob Brown was hit in the leg and fell down right next to Javers, with his camera still shooting the footage, now tilted on its side. Reiterman crouched down and ran for the far side of the plane and tried to hide behind the right wheel. Steve Sung, who was the NBC soundman, was standing next to Brown when he saw him fall. Sung was holding the sound equipment and the cord only reached about two-feet from Brown's camera. Sung hit the deck next to Brown and played dead, making believe he was hit. Bullets sprayed the landscape as confused American's were being mowed down like cattle. Greg Robinson was in the immediate line of fire and was quickly bombarded with shots that slammed him to the hard tarmac.

The Otter was taking several shots, and Jackie Speier had been hit by two bullets while sitting in the plane. It had appeared that two shots had struck her, one in each leg. Inside the Otter Don Harris had told everyone to stay down and stay very quiet, and then he quickly disappeared. Harris ran out of the Otter and directly into the line of fire of the gunmen. Harris was immediately struck in the mid section and fell backwards onto the ground. Ryan was hit next with a shot to the right side of his chest. Ryan fell forward and was hit with another shot on the left side of his back. Suddenly a shot came whizzing through the plane door striking defector Patricia Parks in the head, blowing her brains all over Jerry Parks and the inside of the plane. Patty fell to the floor, dead on impact. Stunned and mortified, Jerry Parks screamed, "My God! Look what you've done to Patty!" Beverly Oliver was waiting to board the Otter when the shots began. She was struck by a bullet in the leg. Jacky Speier climbed into the cargo compartment, crawled up into a ball and prayed for dear life. The tractor then drove around to the right side of the plane where the gunmen had repositioned themselves. Suddenly, the shooting resumed. More shots were fired, with the gunmen deliberately targeting the plane. They shot out the engine and fired into the cargo compartment, where Jackie Speier had crawled into for safety. Speier suffered three more devastating shots. Tina Bogue and Tommy Bogue rushed to the door of the Otter and somehow managed to get it closed during the hail of gun fire.

Tim Reiterman had managed to stay low, tucking his head behind the wheel of the airplane. Instinct had taken over. He was terrified, but not hit. Everything was happening so fast. At first, Tim thought the shooters might just have been trying to disable the plane; but it was soon apparent to him that their intent was to kill. He could hear the screams from people getting shot all around him; some getting hit numerous times. Anthony Katsaris had been standing right next to him, trying to duck underneath the right wheel of the plan when he was blown clear off his feet from a slug to his chest. Suddenly, Reiterman saw an explosion of red mist shoot from his upper left forearm. The bullet had ripped right through and out of his arm. The shot had been so forceful that it pushed his body forward into a four point stance, where he caught himself. No sooner did his fists hit the ground when he'd been struck in his wrist with another shot, blowing his watch clean off his arm and passing underneath him while he was still in mid air. He was now in the cross-hairs of a rifle. The rifleman tried to steady on Reiterman as he shuffled for position. Survival instincts took over. All in one motion, Reiterman sprung to his feet, turned, and took off toward the jungle: he put his head down and ran for his life.

James Cobb Jr., was probably the member that was most ready for this ambush. Cobb was the first to notice local Guyanese natives being pushed aside by Peoples Temple representatives. At that point he knew imminent danger was inevitable. He tried to warn others, but the commotion and the loud noise of the plane's engine was debilitating to his cries. Once the shots broke out, Cobb immediately ducked for cover behind the plane. Cobb looked and saw Ryan and Harris fall to the ground at nearly the same time. Getting his bearings, he picked the right moment, turned, and ran toward the jungle. While others stood in shock and amazement, Cobb had already had a premonition that a gunfight would ensue. Bullets whizzed by his head as he legged out the fifty-yard sprint for the bush.

Upon arriving at the edge of the clearing, Cobb looked back and saw Tom Kice [carrying a .45 caliber automatic pistol] put a gun to Don Harris's head and fire a shot at point blank range. He also saw Bob Kice, Albert Touchette [carrying rifles] and Joe Wilson [carrying a shotgun] simultaneously shooting victims in the head. His heart raced and his stomach sank as he hurled himself head first into the brush, quickly picked himself back up and ran through the dense jungle for all he was worth. He pushed and hopped furiously through the tall weeds. He stopped about 50-yards into the jungle and looked behind to see if anyone had followed. He believed that the gunmen were not far behind. Looking around for a safe place to hide, he remembered the warnings that Jones had told him and the others about the hungry jungle cats that would attack humans upon smell or site. Believing that he would be shot or eaten, Cobb ran for approximately two-hours through the swamp, at which time he climbed up a tree, where he would remain until 9:30a.m., the following morning.

The six passengers in the Cessna had turned in horror to watch the slaughter, stunned and motionless, as a firing squad was taking out Americans. Some of those being gunned down were their own family members. "They're killing everyone," screamed Vern. Distracted enough by the overwhelming scene, Larry Layton seized the opportunity among the confusion. He pulled out a .38 caliber Smith and Wesson revolver and opened fire in the small plane.

Gosney was shot first (twice in the abdomen and once in the leg). Next, Layton turned the gun on Monica Bagby, pumping two shots into her back. Quickly, he turned the gun on Dale Parks and fired a shot. In shock, Dale's mind was in denial. He had not fully grasping the situation. BANG! The gun sounded as it was pointed at Dale, but no bullet had come out. Finally his motor skills caught up with his racing mind. Dale Parks grabbed the gun from the weaker Layton and they wrestled for position. Somehow, a petrified Vern had managed to gather himself and scramble out of the plane. Monica was not far behind. They had a clear path into the jungle and they hobbled and limped frantically toward the brush. Dale Parks and Larry Layton had wrestled themselves out of the plane and onto the tarmac. Finally, Parks was able to wrestle the gun away from Layton. Furious, Parks pointed the gun at Layton and tried to fire a shot into him, but the gun was jammed.

Sung had been lucky; so far he had not been hit. He tried desperately to remain completely still, with his right arm over his head, resting his head on his left arm and playing dead. The next thing he knew the firing had ceased and the men had started walking directly toward the wounded and the dead. Sung began thinking of his daughter and wondered if he would ever see her again, when he heard a brief explosion. Suddenly he felt tremendous pressure in his right arm: he'd been shot! Though the pain was excruciating he remained motionless. The shot had struck his right arm, the one that was covering his head. His blood poured out onto the pavement in front of him. Not only did his arm block the bullet from hitting him is the head, but it also gave the gunmen the appearance that the bullet had struck Sung's head. Sung had fully committed to not moving at that point. His chance to run had come and gone. His only chance now to live was by luck and by remaining completely still.

One man walked up close to him. Sung still had Bob Brown in his site as did Javers, but it appeared that he was dead already. Their hearts were beating faster than ever and time had slowed to almost a stand-still. Their lives flashed before their eyes and everyone they loved were lingering through their minds. The man stood over Brown and with one close range shot—that Sung and Javers witnessed and will never forget—blew his brains out of his head. A large chunk of flesh that was Bob Brown's face now resided about five-feet from his body. Then, the same gunman fired another shot into the back shoulder of Sung. The bullet was partially deflected by his thick leather shoulder strap, but still hit enough to blow part of his shoulder off. Luckily for Sung, though, it had appeared to the gunman as though Sung was fatally wounded.

Reiterman's arms and legs never stopped pumping as he reached the apron of the airstrip. Continuing on, he dove head first into the brush, and furiously crawled deeper into the jungle. He took a look at his wounds as he continued crawling, trying to assess the damage. Regardless of his injuries, he was moving on pure adrenalin and instinct, never looking back. He was also sure that the gunmen were resolved on finishing off the whole group. Ron Javers was not too far behind Reiterman, but Javers had run about 150 yards into the jungle. By the time he gained his composure, Javers was waist-high in water. After several minutes, Reiterman stopped and remembered that he had been shot twice. Close enough to hear the Otter's engine humming; he tore his belt off and tied it around his forearm to cover the wound. Breathing heavily and still fearing for his life, he again began crawling further away. After crawling about forty-yards with two bullet wounds, Reiterman crawled into a small tunnel of weeds—which was probably the home of a jungle animal—and remained completely still. He waited for any signs of the shooters, trying the whole time to remain quiet. He listened, but heard nothing. The shots had died down, but only because the gunmen had been methodically advancing on the grounded group. Suddenly, he heard several deliberate shots over the time of about a half-minute, which were the sounds of the shooters firing close range shots into the faces of their victims.

Greg Robinson was closest to the tractor. Appearing dead already, the men fired a quick shot into him to see if he would move. Next was the primary target, Congressman Ryan, who was face down on the tarmac. One close range shot blew more than half of his face in different directions. Anthony Katsaris was lying face down next to Greg, but received more merciful treatment than some. Trying to play dead, one gunman fired a shot into his back. Bob Brown's brains had been blown all over the ground and were caked on his camera. Reiterman had described that "if not for his clothes and camera he would have been unrecognizable." The whole Parks family, except for Dale, was in the Otter during the shooting and was unfortunate enough to witness the brutal killing of their mother

Patricia, whose skull was blown wide open. Patty was later dragged from the plane and placed behind the left wing.

The Outsiders

At the same time back in Jonestown, the members were back in their quarters resting, after an order from Marceline over the loud-speaker. Charles Gary was worried and desperately looking for an ally. He turned to Lane, his once fierce rival, and asked him to take a walk to discuss the downward-spiraling circumstances. Both knew that the situation had spun out of control. As they neared the basketball court and cottages, Jim McElvane and Jack Beam approached the lawyers on orders to bring them to the school building. It was the right two men to send for the job: Beam and McElvane were two, big, ominous figures. The men talked casually as they walked; perhaps Beam and McElvane were feeling out the mood of the lawyers. Just before they arrived at the school, an announcement came over the loud-speakers. "Everyone report to the pavilion immediately." The see-sawed crowd—who had just been ordered back to their cabins—now found themselves rushing back to the main area. Once in the School building, the men stood in front of Jones, who had by now regained total control over Jonestown.

Jones began by telling the lawyers that all had been lost and that he knew something bad was going to happen to the congressmen and delegates. Both lawyers tried to reason with Jones, but it was too late; Jones had gone fully over the edge and his plan had already been set in motion. "Mark, we have proof that they're going to shoot up that plane," said Jones. He alluded to Larry Layton as the main culprit to the impending doom. Jones claimed that he had lost control and that some of the members had taken all the guns out of the camp and headed to the airstrip. Jones tried to lay his premonitions upon his gifted psychic-intuition, but Lane and Gary believed that it was Jones' way of telling them what he had ordered. In fact, Jones had been angered with the Lawyers for persuading him to allow the delegation in and attributed some of the blame to them, though he did not directly admit it.

The lawyers were no longer consultants to Jones; they were now expendable commodities who had worn out their welcome. After being temporarily interrupted by a secretly whispered message from Maria Katsaris, Jones told the lawyers that they were in danger and must leave immediately. Jones ordered the lawyers to the East House under the armed guard of none other than Don Sly (Ujara)— Ryan's attacker. Not only did Jones not report Sly, but it had appeared as though he was rewarding him for his earlier actions. For several reasons Jones did not want the lawyers to witness the mayhem that was to come. The two would have been obvious dissenting voices; and though they were the Temple's lawyers, they were still seen as outsiders; they were not allowed to partake in such rituals.

Airstrip Shooting Aftermath

The shooting took only about six or seven minutes, but had seemed like a lifetime. The gunmen began a two-minute shooting spree from a stationary position then in military style formation they circled the plane, firing shots for an additional two-minutes. Finally, they spent the remaining minute finishing them off by firing close range shots to the skulls of their victims.

Slowly, people emerged from out of their fox holes and crept back to the blood spattered war grounds. Bodies lined the airstrip as a grim and eerie reminder of the horrifying incident they had just endured. Everyone was cautiously looking around to see if the gunmen had left the scene as the survivors attempted to regroup, assess the damage, and tend to the wounded. With about a half-dozen people still missing, the rest of the survivors cautiously walked about the Otter looking for signs of life. The Otter was slumped over on its side due to one of the wheels being shot out. Reiterman crept back to the apron of the airstrip and recognized Bob Flick and Neville Annibourne, who were both surveying the field. Immediately recognizable were Steve Sung and Jackie Speier, both severely wounded on the ground next to each other. Sung was in bad condition, but Jackie Speier was even worse. Speier and Sung were carried from the plane and placed in the small shed near the Otter. A humongous chunk of flesh had been ripped out of Speier's thigh and the muscles were dangling. A total of five bullets had ripped through her flesh, including shots to her arm and pelvic area.

The survivors who were in better shape carried the critically wounded to the small shed—where Ryan had just recently done his final interview—in an effort to stay out of site in case the gunmen were to return. Most feared that the gunmen would in fact return to finish the job. Grouped together as they were, they were actually in a bad position if this was to occur. The ambulatory, such as Anthony Katsaris, were taken to the edge of the airstrip and laid out on the tall grass. Out of nowhere someone screamed, "They're coming back!" Everyone scampered into the weeds. It was again, every man and woman for themselves. Reiterman paired with Carolyn Boyd and together they fled deep into the jungle. After about an hour, they realized that if they had gone any further they would no doubt be lost out in the boundless jungle. Frustrated, after what seemed like an unwinnable feets, Reiterman said, "I don't know about you, but I'd rather take my chances getting shot!" Carolyn smirked and agreed, and they headed back to airstrip.

On their way back, they heard a burst of engines churning. Back on the airstrip, some members had, had enough and decided to get out while they could. The crew of the Otter dashed into the plane and started the engines. Bob Flick followed the crew into the plane and they quickly loaded—severely wounded—Monica Bagby on board and started down the airstrip. Many in the group were furious at the men for leaving them, particularly with Flick; especially because they only took one of the critically wounded with them. In shock and still very terrified, (but physically unharmed), Flick recounted the horrifying events. Flick had no doubt in his mind that all the shooters were Americans. He saw the killers attack as "carefully planned and mercilessly executed." The attackers moved "calmly, silently, brutally, methodically" and in *zombie-like* fashion.

Four Guyanese soldiers witnessed the whole incident, but did nothing. They were stationed by a Guyanese Air Force plane, which they were guarding, located at the north-west corner of the airstrip in the direction that the planes were facing. When later asked why they did not intervene they informed Javers and others that that they "had not been able to shoot at the attackers during the assault because they were afraid that they would kill still more people" if they did so. They also told other survivors that they didn't offer help because it was "Americans shooting Americans." Obviously the first reasoning given by the soldiers was very speculative if not just plain idiotic! First of all, they were soldiers, trained to defend. Secondly, wouldn't it be more likely that the shooters would retreat faster with gunfire being sent back at them instead of unabated to their victims? The second excuse was more reasonable, though inexcusable. They did not want to get involved, plain and simple. The soldiers did, however, provide first aid kits and a few stretchers to the severely wounded who were placed in the shed.

Howard Oliver was not in good health, but he was flying high with hopes of seeing his wife and possibly his two sons. Along with James Schollaert, Oliver took a cab over to the Timehri Airport to meet Ryan and the rest of his congregation, who were due to arrive shortly. They arrived at about 5:00p.m., they waited and waited for about an hour, but there was still no sign of the Ryan party. Schollaert took it upon himself to enter the control room and found out quickly the terrifying news. Knowing Oliver's condition, Schollaert put him in a cab and sent him back to the hotel to wait with the others as he gathered more information about the incident. Word spread quickly soon after that, as airport officials notified U.S. Ambassador John Burke and Prime Minister Forbes Burnham. Ambassador Burke informed the US State Department at 8:30p.m., by cable.

Mrs. Frazier: *Nightmare in Georgetown*

Arriving at the East House at about 5:10p.m., the lawyers talked small-talk with Don Sly; who was not willing to give up any information as to why he attacked Ryan. Sly sat on the steps of the East House while Lane and Gary pondered the situation from inside. Looking out the window, the lawyers suddenly saw a number of men running past the building with several guns and boxes of ammunition. Their fear grew even more when moments later two shirtless armed men relieved Sly of his guard duty. Gary had recognized both men from the *San Quentin Six Trial*, related to the attempt to free George Jackson and other prisoners from San Quentin following the *Soledad Brothers case*. "We are going to commit revolutionary suicide," one of the guards told the lawyers. Lane and Gary tried briefly to reason with them, but they knew that they had no real say in what was occurring. "We will die to expose this racist and fascist society," the man said.

Both lawyers feared that they would not be allowed to leave and that they would be killed. They were right! One of the guards was Marceline's personal body guard, "Pancho." Jones had personally sent Pancho with special instructions to take Lane and Gary out to the bush and put a bullet in each of their heads. Thinking quickly Lane bargained with Pancho. "Charles and I will write your story," exclaimed Lane. "I will be able to tell the world about the last moments of Jonestown," Lane said, masking his terror. The men warmed to the idea and were soon giving the lawyers directions out of Jonestown. The lawyers could not just walk directly out the front door, per se, they had to work their way around the perimeter and make their escape covertly. The whole time, they heard Jones' voice talking to his congregation. They heard the voice of Christine Miller disputing Jones and the voices of the crowd opposing her. They ran and chugged frantically and stealthily toward the jungle. Suddenly, they heard Jones say, "Mother, mother, mother," followed by several shots of gunfire. Lane claims that he heard 80–90 shots, but the older Gary—who was dragging and struggling to keep up—claims that he only heard about three shots. Lane saw several members running toward the jungle after the shots. Both lawyers did not slow down; instead they continued along at top speed.

Meanwhile, Sharon Amos prepared to pass on the most important message of her life. She did not want to make the call over the radio, so she went upstairs and used the landline phone in Peoples Temple House. It was about 6:00p.m., and the call was to the Geary Street Temple in San Francisco to inform them of the critical situation in Georgetown and in Jonestown, and to relay the message that the White Night was for real this time. It was 1:00p.m., S.F. time when Sandy Bradshaw answered the phone. "There has been an incident," said Sharon. "Some people have gone to see Mrs. Frazier [Temple code for *death*] and others will be going to see Mrs. Frazier." Sharon passed on the message from Jones that the existing members in the United States were to get revenge on all of the defectors and all Temple opposition; by revenge, Jones meant killing them all.

It was very hard, however, for any of the members outside of Jonestown—with the exception of the die-hard zealot, Sharon Amos—to conceive Jones' orders, let alone carry out his sinister plot. In Jonestown, Jones had been able to steadily manipulate his members by consistently instilling fear into them. This was not possible for Jones to accomplish with members who were not in his immediate range of control. Moreover, no member outside of Jonestown knew the details of what was actually happening there; and any members outside of Jonestown knew that Blacks were not being put into concentration camps in the United States, for instance. Confusion was the primary emotion accompanying the news. The members in the United States were reluctant to do anything without a reasonable explanation as to what had transpired in Jonestown that warranted death and vengeance.

Sandy relayed the grim message to the rest of the S.F. members, but none of them were convinced as to what actually was supposed to happen. By the time that Sandy had relayed the message to the members, she had little or no details, and certainly no reasons to go ahead with murder and suicide. Jones' chaotic mind was to drugged-up to truly plan the situation out thoroughly and contact the S.F. members himself. By now, Jones had too many loose ends to tie up in Jonestown. Furthermore, they were well aware of Jones' scare tactics and they did not want to make a move, thinking and hoping that Jones would call it off as he had done every other time in the past. Their only recourse was to sit by the radio and hope and pray.

Sherwin, Liane, and the two children (Christa and Martin) were still sitting at the table, having just finished dinner. It was about 6:30p.m., and Sherwin was telling jokes and they were all having a genuinely good time. Suddenly the laughter was abruptly cut short by a somber announcement from Sharon: "Liane, there's a call for you." Sherwin did not hear the phone ring, so he assumed that it was a private Temple radio call. Liane excused herself and left the room. Sherwin looked on suspiciously as an outsider. As Liane walked into the room and closed the door, Sharon looked at her with a serious face. Stephan could barely look at the two. He paced back and forth nervously, trying to contemplate the surreal circumstances.

"Liane, the order has just come through: we have to die," said Sharon. It was as if they all had suspected this would someday come. Without batting an eye, Liane paused for a moment then very calmly said, "Ok." Acting like it was nothing, Liane asked, "Should I go back to dinner?" Sharon sighed and shook her head up and down (yes). "You'd better have him leave," she replied, speaking of Sherwin. Liane returned to the kitchen. Stephan was flabbergasted and could not believe the bizarre conversation that he had just witnessed. Stephan was overwhelmed. He had just witnessed a mother tell her 21yr-old daughter to go end the dinner with her father, because they were going to kill themselves.

Stephan tried to slow his racing mind from attacking thoughts. What was happening in Jonestown, he thought? What would happen to his mother? What would become of his siblings? What would happen to his girlfriend? What would happen to all his friends? Too many questions, and it was all happening so fast. He couldn't help but wonder just what the scene was like in Jonestown. Liane returned to the table and finished her dinner. She played it cool and humored Sherwin when he made plans with her for the following day. At about 7:00p.m., Liane said that she was tired and was going to go to bed. Sherwin did not sense that anything was wrong. He was just buzzing that things were working out so well. He didn't even find it odd that Sharon was being very cooperative and even said that he could visit Jonestown with them in the next few days. Sharon had been very combative with Sherwin, and her normally intense nature had permutated into a compromising and laid back one.

Sherwin called a cab to take him back to the Pegasus Hotel. He enjoyed his last few minutes with his daughter. The cab arrived at about 7:30p.m., and Liane walked Sherwin out to the curb. "When should I pick you up tomorrow," Sherwin asked. "Tomorrow?" asked Liane. "Ya, tomorrow," Sherwin said. Sherwin had planned on spending a nice, quiet day fishing with his daughter. "Whenever you'd like," she replied. She knew it didn't matter. She had to make sure that Sherwin did not catch on. They both smiled. Liane looked at her father with a sweet, daddy's girl look on her face. It would take a mind reader to see just what she had planned. "I like seven in the morning," Sherwin proclaimed. Liane graciously agreed and the two shared another admiring glance.

Suddenly, Stephan Jones, Mike Touchette, and Harold Cordell came storming out. "This is bullshit," said Touchette, as the three young men hopped into the van and sped off. They were headed for the Pegasus Hotel to get some more information. Stephan was more than anxious to find out what was going on and he figured that he would go to the Pegasus to find out what his brother (Tim Jones) and Johnny Cobb had found out.

Sharon came down the stairs from the radio room. "Sharon, I just want to say thank you," Sherwin said. Sharon looked at him with a sincere, yet grim smile and kissed him on his cheek. Sherwin turned and hugged and kissed Liane and got in the cab. Sherwin was riding high, like a naive school boy who had just finished a first date. He was feeling like they had really gotten his message and felt his sincerity. He believed that he was making certain progress with not only his daughter, but with Sharon as well, which was a huge breakthrough for him. "See ya tomorrow, 7:00a.m.," Sherwin said, through the open window of the cab, with a smile. He grabbed Liane's hand for a moment just before the cab drove off.

Several other members were still in the PT House at the time, including Lee Ingram, Paula Adams, Debbie Touchette, Calvin Douglas [forward for the JT basketball team], Charles Beikman, and nine-year-old Stephanie Jones. Before leaving, Stephan asked Lee Ingram to keep an eye on Sharon. Stephan needed to buy some time to see what was happening and to see if this could all be avoided. The problem was that Sharon was a Jones-like figure when Jim was not around. Sharon was about as high a level member as there was. There wouldn't be much that could stop her if she set her mind to something; especially with specific orders from Jim Jones, himself.

At approximately 6:00p.m., the Concerned Relatives had all gathered in Steven Katsaris's room in the Pegasus Hotel awaiting news from the Congressman's crew. They had already heard that Ryan was staying overnight in Jonestown and, knowing Jones and his hold over the members; they were worried that things would go awry. Gordon Lindsay commingled in the room with them and he was the best source of information for the group. With periodic calls to the United States, he was able to get vital updates on the situation. The problem was that every piece of information that they had gathered was getting worse with each update. Authorities and officials all had been well aware of the Port Kaituma shootings by about 6:30p.m., but none of them had the presence of mind to warn the Relatives. This was the beginning of a plethora of mishaps and faulty executions that the authorities would commit.

If Jim Jones had his way, this would have been an even bigger massacre. The Concerned Relatives were easy-pickings; but thankfully, there were some cool heads among some of the Temple members. Stephan Jones, being one of them, arrived at the Pegasus Hotel at approximately 8:00p.m., and immediately saw his brother Tim and Johnny Cobb speaking with some of the Relatives. Stephan was frantic, but tried to keep his cool—that was until he saw Tim Stoen. Suddenly, his blood boiled. Any number of other Temple members would have already made this scene a blood bath. Timothy Oliver Stoen was the Temple's greatest enemy. In Jim Jones' eyes he was the main cause of all of their problems.

Stephan immediately confronted him and the conversation quickly got heated. Seated around Tim were Grace Stoen and Steven Katsaris. Stephan asked Tim why he was doing this and indirectly blamed him for what was happening. In an effort to defend himself, Tim stood his ground and tried to dispel the rumors of his involvement in the CIA, and so on. He also said that he was doing this for his son and reiterated to Stephan that he would give his own life for his son's. Tim warned that he was not going anywhere without his son. In the heat of conversation, Stephan alluded to the bizarre radio conversation with his father and a possible mass suicide. "Do you mean he'll kill everyone?" Tim asked. Stephan inverted his thoughts and looked into space. "He's a mad man!" Tim exclaimed. When Stephan angrily agreed with him, Tim was shocked. Realizing that there was nothing he could find out there, Stephan quickly rushed off, bumping Lindsay on the way out, and hurried back to the PT-House.

The Guyana police had heard about the Ryan shooting and were informed that Peoples Temple members were involved. At about 8:30pm, they arrived at the Lamaha Gardens Peoples Temple house to investigate the allegations. Observing their arrival, Sharon Amos panicked! She thought that they were there to take the kids and may have been called by Sherwin. She knew now that the time had come for her to execute the murder-suicide, quickly. Even though completely out of her mind, Sharon was nervous and scared; yet, she was even more committed to the cause than anything else. Stephan described Sharon as a woman who actually really loved her children, believe it or not. In her mind, he believed that she thought she was saving them. Sharon went into the kitchen, grabbed a huge butcher knife, put it to her chest (as if hugging it) and took a deep breath.

The kids were playing the card game "War" in the living room and having a good time. Liane played the game as if everything was normal. She was smiling and playing girlishly. Sharon walked into the living room with the knife on her right hip, out of site of the kids. She stood in the arch of the door and summoned the children with a gesture. With Sharon's three children—Liane, 21, Christa, 11, and Martin, 8,—along with nine-year-old Stephanie Jones, Sharon stopped at the stairs and let them walk up in front of her. She had also called upon Charles Beikman to help her with the daunting task. Chuck, however, was reluctant to partake in the incident, but Sharon was an imposing figure and certainly the de facto leader in Georgetown in the absence of Jones.

Once in the bathroom, she gathered the children into the bathtub. With ruthless determination, she grabbed Christa by the face, put the knife to her throat, and slid the knife deep across her throat from ear to ear. Falling to the ground screaming, Christa hit the floor kicking her legs and squirmed to her death, with blood gushing from the devilish thrust. Martin tried to get away, but there was nowhere to run. The door was shut and three over-powering adults guaranteed death; he was trapped. Martin had the sense enough in Jonestown at such a young age to refuse to take the poison at one particular suicide drill. Sharon had looked down on him for that, thinking that he was weak and uncommitted to the cause, when in fact he was a strong, free thinker.

Sharon quickly grabbed Martin by his nose and mouth and cut his throat from ear to ear. Martin fell to the floor landing in the blood of his sister and suffered the same convulsive and spastic somatic innervations. Both had fought futilely for air—for one last breath. Sharon then ordered Chuck to kill Stephanie, but as he began to cut her throat his hand went limp. He cut her only enough for her to fall to the ground, but not enough to kill her. Sharon then handed Liane the knife and said, "Here, you've got to do me;" an enormous and gruesome task for a twenty-one year old daughter to conceive! Sharon helped her, guiding her hand as she slid the knife across her own mother's neck. "Harder, harder," Sharon ordered. With her throat cut and her eyes rolling to the back of her head, Sharon fell to the floor. On the way down, Sharon uttered her final words: "Thank you father!"

Liane had it the worst! She was left to cut her own throat and had a hard time of it. Putting the knife to her own throat meant a slow death and a slower time to bleed out. She choked and gagged on the way down, falling into the co-mingling pool of her own family's blood. Liane twitched and convulsed on the floor with the knife still in her hand, barely alive; it was a blood-bath! Stunned and horrified, a traumatized Chuck fled the room and found Calvin Douglas rushing toward the bathroom, after he had hearing the terrifying screams of the children. Nothing could save them now, but little Stephanie was still alive! Calvin knew there was still hope for her!

The Relatives were patiently waiting at the hotel trying to keep their spirits high. Yet, things were about to drastically change the already somber mood. The hotel manager began calling the Relatives into his office one-by-one. Two police inspectors accompanied him with news of the tragic shootings at the Port Kaituma Airstrip. Spastically, each reacted with shock, fear, disappointment, and an "I-told-ya-so." The Relatives had been warning people for years about the volatility and dangerous nature of the group, but all their talk had always fell on deaf ears. Sadly when they were finally realized, it was too late. Sherwin Harris had been en route from the PT-House. Riding high he sat in the cab thinking fondly about the previous events of his day.

Arriving at the Pegasus Hotel at 8:30p.m., however, Sherwin was hit with news that equated to being hit by a runaway train. Your twenty one year old daughter and ex-wife—whom you were just with less than an hour ago—have just brutally murdered the children and slit their own throats in the bathroom. He was completely devastated; like an air balloon violently shot out of the air. Grief had made a new home, overwhelming Sherwin to the point of a nervous break-down. Sherwin also was not sure what to think; no one did actually. The police were so awestruck by the event, that Charles Beikman was the prime suspect at that time and in the days that followed. On November 26, 1978, the Guyanese Police told The New York Times that Beikman cut the throats of Sharon and her children. Nothing was certain at that stage and certainly no one thought that they could have actually cut their own throats. It just wasn't an option to authorities.

The Geary Street S.F. Temple had begun a complete panic and had called for an emergency meeting. They had been trying to contact Jonestown and Georgetown for several hours by 9:00p.m., with no response. Like Stephan they tried to remain hopeful, but they had even less information than the members in Georgetown. However, they were aware of the volatility of the situation and of the mental condition of those in Jonestown. Yet, their minds could not let them conceive of this being the end. Each member in the S.F Temple had relatives in Jonestown. Shortly after the deaths in the PT-House, Lee Ingram used the Georgetown radio one last time to notify the S.F. Temple of what she knew and to call off the previous orders of the now dead, Sharon Amos.

Stephan returned to the Lamaha Gardens house at 9:00p.m., clinging to hope that things at the house had not spun too far out of control. A young Black female Temple member met Stephan on the stairs leading up the front door. "Sharon killed herself and killed her children," she said, with the frightened voice of finality. Stephan was horrified! On the way up the stairs to view the carnage, he imagined their last moments. He knew what Sharon's state of mind was and he knew it was the same state of mind of the inner circle in Jonestown. His hope faded quickly; he knew that since Sharon had executed the plan that this time was for real. Stephan rushed up the stairs and opened the bathroom door hoping for a survivor; but hope only led to horror. Opening the door, the first thing that he saw were the two small children in a pool of blood; clearly dead; clearly gone. Sharon was curled in behind the door and Liane lay still holding the murder weapon—elucidating the fact that true darkness had come to Guyana.

Will to Survive

The sun had set at 6:33p.m., and the moon didn't rise until 9:54p.m., on the night of November 18, 1978. The moon's illumination factor was as high as 88.4 percent: lighting up the night sky like a humongous street light. Vern had been slipping in and out of consciousness for several hours, laying about 100 yards into the jungle. Vern awoke from an unconscious state, amidst jungle weeds and a group of Guyanese citizens who had been walking through the brush searching for any survivors of the airstrip shooting. Vern thought it was all a dream until he was soon reminded that three bullets had torn through his body. Because the daylight had long faded to a pitch black sky, Vern realized that he had been unconscious for hours. Suddenly, he heard footsteps crackling on branches nearby. He looked up and saw what might as well have been a group of angels gathered around him (a group of dark-faced men). Lucky to be found alive at all after so much time had passed, the men took Vern to a tent where other survivors had been gathered. The Guyanese people were very generous, going as far as vowing to fight for the wounded if the perpetrators had returned. The Black, Amerindian men banded together with survivors. They even loaned the Americans a few shotguns for protection. The severely wounded were tended to by the less severely wounded and uninjured survivors.

The night was surreal and sleepless, and there was nothing left for anyone to do but wait for more information and hope for the best. Nothing was clear and nothing was final. The long, arduous night seemed like it would go on forever. In his weakened condition—and not knowing whether his wife or two sons were alive—Howard Oliver suffered a nervous breakdown during the night. For the Airstrip shooting victims it was the longest night of their lives! Not only did they have to wait until morning, many waiting with several bullet wounds; but they also waited with their guards held high—in fear that the attackers would soon return. Every sound from outside rattled those who stayed up to guard the house. Just before sunrise, Dwyer informed them that Guyanese troops were taking a train in from Mathews Ridge, which was about thirty miles north of their current location.

Even the Guyanese Government had a healthy fear of Peoples Temple. They did not want to put their own troops in jeopardy by having them fly an airplane to the yet unsecured airstrip at Port Kaituma for fear that an ambush might be waiting for them. A few hours later, when the train had arrived, they were again informed that the troops had gotten off the train several miles back and were cautiously marching toward them on foot. The survivors were split into two different groups, and each group knew nothing of the fate of the other at the time. Reiterman and other reporters made a pact to hold off on interviews for the time being out of respect for the situation. Moreover, they were all still traumatized and spent. In the morning eight wounded persons were treated and airlifted by a United States C-141 Military transport plane back to the Naval Hospital at Roosevelt Roads, Puerto Rico, and Charleston. Steven Katsaris had accompanied his wounded son, Anthony, who had suffered a gunshot wound to the chest.

CHAPTER 14 – NEWS & INVESTIGATION

Sunday, November 19, 1978 – "The Day After"

Within one hour (presumably 6:00pm) of the airstrip shooting, Ambassador Burke was notified. At 8:30pm, Burke informed the US State Department by cable. Stanley Clayton and Odell Rhodes reached Port Kaituma at about 2:00a.m., Sunday morning. They were the first eye witnesses to officially report the Jonestown incident to authorities.

The official "Joint Chiefs of Staff communications log" shows that one of the entries made on Sunday, November 19th was that of *the Jonestown suicides; reported at 3:29 a.m., on a C.I.A. radio channel, NOIWON* seen in the picture below. The only functioning radio in the area belonged to Richard Dwyer.

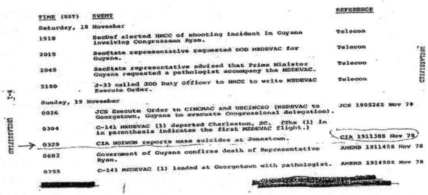

At dawn, the first contingent of the Guyanese Army Rescue Forces arrived in Port Kaituma. Within one-hour more soldiers arrived to secure the runway. Officially, there was about a twenty-four-hour period before troops arrived in Jonestown to confirm the deaths. By the time they arrived in Jonestown there had been wide-spread looting, allegedly the doing of some Guyanese natives. At about 10:00a.m., the first Guyanese Rescue Aircraft landed at Port Kaituma, but without medical supplies or personnel. As reported on the above Joint Chiefs of Staff communications log, a C-141 transport plane had left from Maguire Air force Base in New Jersey carrying a medical evacuation team. It was reported that the plane was unable to land or approach the airstrip until dawn because the airstrip "lacked landing lights." United States news papers reported the "possibility" that Congressman Ryan had been killed, as a *NY Times* headline read, "Coast Congressman Believed to be shot dead" (November 19, 1978). Neither the American media nor the public was aware of the enormity of the situation. Most of the reports on the 19th were just introducing Ryan to the public, the reason for his visit, and his political background. Not much else was known.

It wasn't long before the FBI notified California State Authorities about a "hit-list" that Jones had allegedly prepared in case of his death. This had been well documented by the FBI, even before November 18, 1978. The FBI had good reason to believe—as they noted in their files—that there was a "suicidal" group of individuals that were to carry out contingency plans in case Jones was ever arrested or killed. On this hit list were dissident members and top United States Government Officials. Immediately after the United States was notified of Ryan's death, the San Francisco Police Department and the Berkeley Police Department set up command posts—patrolled by SWAT teams—due to what they called, "the threat of retaliation against dissident members of Peoples Temple." Authorities estimated that there were fifteen to seventeen dissident members in Berkeley and in the East Bay area. Police notified the potential victims accordingly, explaining to them that they were potential backlash victims. Most of these members were staying at the Human Freedom Center Located at 3028 Geary St. Berkeley, CA, which was set up and run by Jeannie and Al Mills. Local California authorities also located and made arrangements to move other dissident members from Ukiah and Mendocino County to safe houses. The SFPD had also placed the S.F. Temple under surveillance.

Note: *News paper articles are always from the prior day [i.e. Monday, November 20th articles would be from the 19th's events—even though the articles were written in the late night hours of the 19the and early morning hours of the 20th].*

Monday, November 20, 1978

The first truly *mysterious* occurrence in this story (publicly) happened on Monday, November 20, 1978, with the less-than adequate body count. The *NY Times* headline on the 20th read, *"Guyana official Reports 300 dead at Religious Sect's Jungle Temple."* Looking back now, the world was taken by storm and it was impossible for an outsider to realize the enormity of the situation. Most of the reports were familiarizing the general public of who the Temple was and what they were about. Guyana Information Minister, Shirley Field Ridley, announced that 300-400 bodies had been found dead at the Jonestown site. Get used to the word "mysterious," because it will be used throughout this reporting process. Ridley mysteriously said, "There were no marks of violence on the bodies and no living persons had been found in the camp so far." This was the first of many lies to come in this story; but it obviously started with this heavy dose of misinformation.

For one, Hyacinth Thrash and other older seniors survived in the camp. Thrash was 76 years-old at the time. When she realized that the whole camp was being exterminated she crawled under her bed and stayed there all night. Seventy-nine-year-old Grover Davis missed the White Night announcement on the loudspeaker because he was hearing impaired. When he realized what was happening he hid in a ditch and pretended to be dead. A five-year-old boy escaped by hiding in the jungle. He was rescued by Guyanese government officials. Thrash and Davis never left the camp until they were rescued, long before Ridley made her announcement. However, the biggest piece of misinformation was the body count, which was yet to be contested, and was accepted as factual information at the time. As the American public was being distracted by the much deserved memorializing of the terminated Congressman and media members, the story tantamount to that was being down-played by officials through the media. Two days after one of the biggest tragedies in American history the details of Jonestown were being casually reported. Ryan's administrative assistant, Joe Holsinger, spoke from Washington on November 19, 1978, and stated that the congressman had initially asked the State Department to investigate allegations of abuse, poor treatment, and enslavement of Jonestown members. As

Holsinger explained, "They told us that everything was fine. They said it was a private matter between private citizens."

Tuesday, November 21, 1978

It wasn't until Tuesday, November 21, 1978, that Jonestown finally took over the headlines, as the first pictures of the dead were displayed on front pages all over the nation. The *NY Times* headline read, "*400 are Found Dead In Mass Suicide by Cult; Hundreds More Missing From Guyana Camp.*" In this article it was again mysteriously reported that "all but three dead from drinking a concoction made of kool-aid and cyanide." Somehow it was confirmed that all but three died of ingesting the poison; yet, no mention of how the other three had died. With the only coroner/pathologist on scene up to that point being Dr. C. Leslie Mootoo (Guyana's top pathologist) and his team, how could this statement have been made? Was it based on surviving witness accounts? There were several accounts given by survivors at this point and no mention of any violence (although many of these survivors would later publicly claim that violence occurred). Was this an oversight of some sort or an obvious cover-up attempt? Furthermore, Dr, Mootoo's findings were "allegedly" not communicated to the proper U.S. Officials on site, and later U.S. Officials would claim to never have even received Mootoo's conclusions. Dr. Mootoo and American Forensic Pathologist, Dr. Lynn Crook, performed brief post-mortems on Ryan and the others killed at the airstrip.

The headlines all across the nation are very important pieces of information in this story that really help build the case for conspiracy apologists. It was reported and assumed that there were 400 found dead in Jonestown and 400-500 members missing. They were thought to have fled into the jungle on foot. This was assumed, because it was known and reported that there were about 1100-1200 members living at the camp at the time. Successfully diverted by scene officials, the media now shifted to evoking the imagination of the American public with thoughts of 400-500 Americans running around amongst flesh-eating piranha's, swarming insects, electric eels, and the mid-day heat.

Jim Jones and Peoples Temple weren't truly known by the American public at this point, and this further clouded the on-going details of this story. The Temple and Jones were very new to the American public and their back-stories needed to be introduced by the media. This meant going back and explaining who the Reverend James Warren Jones was and how he had gotten to this point. It was also time to interview several S.F members and survivors and tell their stories. Anyone involved with Jones or the Temple became a sought after commodity, and Jones became both instantly famous and infamous. Shock took hold of the public and they were more intrigued by stories of the "transcendental" Jim Jones, his mentality, and the ongoing search for the "missing" survivors.

Two police photographers and two fingerprint specialists arrived on the scene on Monday, almost two full days after the incident. The crime scene was heavily contaminated by the time the police had arrived on scene. The gun believed to have killed Jim Jones was laying some 25-feet away from his body. It was speculated by police that the recoil of the gun after the shot was possibly the reason for the gun being so far away from Jones' body. According to U.S. Embassy Officials, the scene was heavily looted and the camp was rumpled with clothes and papers everywhere. It was also speculated that the looters could have tampered with the gun.

On Jones' body lay a suicide note, which the FBI attributed to a woman, but did not rule out that Jones had written it himself. The note was handwritten on lined notebook paper that had been torn and folded. The note said:

> *"Dad—I see no way out—I agree with your decision—I fear only that without you the world may not make it to communism. For my part—I am more than tired of this wretched, merciless planet & the hell it holds for so many masses of beautiful people— thank you for the only life I've known."*

The FBI said that the signature was not the full name of Marceline, and that it appeared to be a short nickname or endearment for a female. The word "Dad" had been written on one side of the folded paper as though it were being addressed.

An Emergency task force was set up by U.S. Ambassador, John Burke, which included Guyana's Minister of Health, Housing, and Labor (Hamilton Green) and other officials from the two governments to handle the tragedy. On Monday morning, they had an emergency meeting and considered autopsies. Ambassador Burke cabled the State Department after the meeting:

"Government of Guyana has in mind to separate poison victims from gunshot victims and perform spot autopsies on randomly selected bodies in each group for purposes of their investigation. Obviously there is no intention to perform autopsies on all bodies."

This, at least, proves that there was full government knowledge of several shooting victims at the time. Burke claimed they would be separating the shooting victims and poison victims for the purpose of doing random autopsies in each "GROUP." If there were only three gunshot victims, as earlier reported, Burke would not have referred to them as "different groups" and he would not have had to do "random" autopsies on the gunshot "group." Moreover, it was later found out that Burke had served in the CIA with Richard Dwyer in Thailand. But this official statement to the State Department alone makes his tactics very questionable, in the fact that not all 400-pplus bodies would receive autopsies.

Wednesday, November 22, 1978

More survivor accounts and other stories of the cult's beginnings emerged on Wednesday, November 22, 1978. Pictures of the dead and bloated, decaying carcasses filled the covers of newspapers and magazines all over the nation. Jonestown mania had now swept the nation! The first picture of Jim Jones' lifeless body surfaced and instantly became national media. Jones was allegedly photographed where he died; lying on his back; his arms stretched out over his head as if he were stretching. His eerie stair looked like he was sleeping with his eyes wide open staring off into space. His shirt was pulled up almost to his chest, showing his bloated stomach, and blood visibly appeared around his head. His autopsy showed that the bullet had entered the left side of his head (the left temple area) moving front to back and slighty upward, eventually exiting his head through the right temple area. This is consistent with a suicide of a left handed person. However, Jones was right handed. The pictures of the bodies were atrocious, to say the least! The visual imagery was horrifying and revolting. The surreal scene of body's laid-out as far as the eye could see was worse than any horror movie. Bodies were everywhere; some were face down in the mud; some were holding hands; and some were hugging others to death, literally. The famous shot of the poison-filled vat sitting on the wooden walkway to the pavilion with medical supplies and dead bodies everywhere still provokes feelings of dismay, to this very day.

The Guyanese authorities were holding Tim Carter, Michael Prokes, Mike Carter, and Larry Layton for questioning in connection with the airstrip ambush. Larry Layton was suspected of starting the shooting right from the start, but was not mentioned as a suspect for killing anyone. It was known immediately what happened at the airstrip. The *NY Times* had a step-by-step account of the airstrip ambush, equip with pictures and diagrams of exactly how it occurred. Guyanese police investigators also said that they found "hundreds of rounds of ammunition" in Jonestown. An estimated 1200 residents were in Jonestown and 800 passports were found on site. The number of survivors was uncertain at the time, but estimates varied from as high as 800 to as low as 200. Stephan Jones, Jim's biological son, and 45 other commune members were being detained at Peoples Temple House in Georgetown, virtually under house arrest. Stephan told reporters and police that he estimated about 500 members had fled into the jungle. About 200 Guyanese troops were reported searching for survivors in the jungle surrounding Jonestown. Foreign journalists were restricted from entering Jonestown with the exception of a few. One official said the "the government feared that newsmen wandering around the edge of the jungle might be mistaken for members of the commune."

Ambassador Burke was very adamant about calling the deaths suicides, reaffirming several times that the people committed suicide without much physical coercion. He had basically no evidence to back up his claims, what so ever. Furthermore, they didn't even have the correct body count, how could they possibly know that there was not much physical coercion? In late afternoon, helicopters were carried in a C-141 Star-lifter Jet from Panama. Some speculate that is was these helicopters that found and brutally murdered survivors, and then brought them back to Jonestown. Burke said that some of the helicopters would be equip with loud speakers so that the crewmen could reassure the survivors and lead them to clearings in the jungle. Earlier that day, C-Rations, tents, cots, and rubber body bags were flown in as well. An American military command center was set up at the Timehri Airport in Georgetown. The H.Q. was set up in a remote section of the airport field, some ways away from the main terminal. The control center held American transport planes, but by nightfall three C-130 transports, two C-141's, and a small six-passenger twin-engine plane had also arrived.

American Officials reported that 10-12 more helicopters were expected as well as 30 members of the *Grave Registration Unit*. No ground troops were expected to participate in the search. One of the soldiers helping with the cargo planes said that "he and others had been instructed to keep as low a profile as possible." Why was secrecy so important in this situation? Ambassador Burke stressed the difficulty of a ground search in the thick jungle with limited visibility. However, many officials had also said that an aerial search was virtually impossible and visibility was far worse from the air. The bodies had been in the tropical heat now for 72-hours. Identification of the bodies was becoming almost impossible. The body count was officially reported at the mysterious number of 409! From the way it was reported this number (409) appeared to be an exact count and not rounded-off or estimated. The very bizarre thing here is that several helicopters were flown in and a lot of work, effort, and money was being put into finding survivors that later would be confirmed as being dead already back at the camp—all because of a "miscount" that was off by several hundred.

The United States believed that there were 409 bodies found dead and around 500 missing in the jungle. A *NY Times* headline on Nov 22nd read, "*U.S. Copters Reach Guyana to aid Jungle hunt for Cult Survivors; up to 500 may be lost in Wild Area.*" Later, it was reported that there were no survivors and no one got fired or publicly reprimanded for incompetence! It wasn't an impossibility that members had fled into the jungle. Temple lawyer, Mark lane, claimed to witness people fleeing into the jungle in mass, and 20-30 adult members and 5 children had emerged from the jungle in relatively good condition on Nov. 22nd. Some of the adult members even helped police identify some of the dead bodies from Jonestown.

Friday, November 24, 1978

The search continued all day on Thursday, November 23, 1978, but yielded no positive results. Doubts about hundreds fleeing into the jungle had come to a swell by the next reporting day (November 24th). Still, after six long days and nights, the body count remained at 409. Still, the media continued to speculate what might have happened to the fleeing members, which continued to divert attention away from what was really happening. Reports that the rain may have washed away footprints; Aborigines families living in the jungle may have housed some of the members; the food that was available and edible in the jungle and the water—which was drinkable—all continued to be the main topics of discussion. Media reports tried to sound hopeful and vigilant. Guyanese horticulturist, D. Thompson, was called on by the *NY Times* to discuss the ramifications of being out in the jungle for this long. Thomson explained that the piranhas do not harm people; that the local Indians would actually feed and shelter people rather than harm them; and in 30-years of experience in similar settings, he has only seen two Jaguars.

Optimism was still lingering, but it seemed as though continued shock and confusion was the primary reaction. Hope seemed to be masking the true feeling of pessimism. Ten light planes and other communications equipment—generators for lights and radios, sleeping bags, c-rations, and a four-man army communications team—was supplied on November 23rd. U.S. Lt. Col. Alfred Keys, who was in charge of the Army Graves Registration Unit, said that it was his hope to have all the bodies on their way to the U.S. by Saturday or Sunday. Two Air Force cargo planes landed at *Dover Air Force base* in Delaware, Maryland, carrying the bodies of the Congressman and the other airstrip victims—along with some of the Jonestown diseased. The first shipment of 40-bodies in aluminum coffins, were dropped off in a C-141 just before dawn. The second shipment of 81-bodies arrived in Dover late that night.

The second shipment included an aluminum coffin that had "*Rev. Jimmie Jones 13B*" written on it, that carried the body of the late Jim Jones. The bodies were taken to a large, one-story white cement building that housed the base's mortuary. Dozens of forensic pathologists and morticians embalmed the bodies before any autopsies were performed, and they were allegedly completely unaware of Dr. Mootoo's conclusions. Using dental and medical charts, they sifted through the 121-bodies in an effort to identify them. After unloading the bodies, the aluminum coffins were disinfected and sent back to Guyana to pick up more victims.

At the Timheri Airport, bodies were lifted by hand from H-53-helicopters and carried to trucks that were waiting nearby. The men who had this taxing task spent hours carrying bodies in the harsh Guyana heat for a total of eight days. The men tried to block the horrific smell from their minds, holding the bags away from their own persons as the bags dripped putrid bodily fluids. The first few days weren't as bad, relatively speaking. Each body bag was filled with a single man and carried by two-men, who conversed to pass the time. Two-men working together had the opportunity to not only pass the time, but talk through the nightmare of their experiences. Soon, however, body-bags held the bodies of women—many of whom had killed their own children. Next came the teens, adolescents, and then the preadolescents. And to make matters worse; the last day-and-a-half consisted of carrying the bodies of babies, infants, and toddlers. These bodies were so small that many of them had several babies stuffed into each one. The job that was previously done by two men now became a solo endeavor. Men who were already at their "breaking points" were now forced to work solo. While the previous days were passed by conversations with others they were now spent with their own wandering imaginations of the horrific events that took place that lead to this. Many soldiers recounted their own childhoods and their own children; the unimaginable events of this tragedy were all too real.

The second shipment of bodies was also met by ten FBI Fingerprint Specialists as it landed on the base. The agents compared their records to the corpse positively identified as Jim Jones. It was a known fact that Jones was known for doubling himself in an effort to fool his potential assassins. Allegedly, the FBI did positively identify the body as that of James Warren Jones. Though most of the bodies were barely recognizable, the American Red Cross set up an information center on the base where family and friends could get information.

The families of the diseased victims were baffled over the choice to bring the bodies to the Dover Air Force Base, which was about 3,000 miles away from their homes. Many families were unable to make the trip for monetary reasons. Many pondered why the bodies weren't taken to Oakland Army Base in California, site of a large military mortuary that had processed bodies during the Vietnam War, and was where most of the families lived. Furthermore, it would have been easier to request and obtain medical records (especially from San Francisco), and the bodies would not have had to be shipped across country for burial, which was a monetary impossibility for a majority of the families.

According to *Last Rights*, by Rebecca Moore, Officials gave two reasons for taking the bodies to Dover: (1) it was closer to Guyana; transporting them to Oakland or to Travis Air Force Base fifty miles north, would have required the planes to stop en route for refueling; (2) the Dover mortuary was supposed to be better equipped to handle a large number of dead people.

Volunteers from the air base enhanced the small mortuary staff. 35 pathologists and specialists from Walter Reed Hospital in Washington, D.C., 29 graves registration experts from Fort Lee, Virginia, and FBI some fingerprint technicians joined the crew. A local funeral director who had an annual contract with the mortuary also received approximately $25 million for his participation in the processing.

In her article, Rebecca Morre goes on to say:

"The government's stated reasons for choosing Delaware are totally fabricated, since most of the people working on the Jonestown bodies did not normally work at the Dover mortuary. The volunteers and specialists could have worked anywhere. We believe the bodies went to Dover simply because they would be close to government bureaucrats in Washington, D.C. who might have to travel there. We also believe the Air Force flew the victims to Delaware rather than California because the government didn't want to be hassled by relatives. NBC Nightly News reported that Dover was selected because of its 'distance from California, thus reducing chances of families crowding the scene.'"

Saturday, November 25, 1978

Just when things couldn't seem any worse, the nightmare took a dramatic turn! On November 25, 1978, the *NY Times* front page headline read, *"U.S. Says Guyana Toll Has Nearly Doubled; Deaths In Jungle Commune Could Reach 780."* It was terrible. The death toll had nearly doubled; and to make matters even worse, there was no reasonable explanation as to why. The American public was getting hit with an aftershock that almost equaled the earthquake. The U.S. State Department was frantic and under intense pressure to deliver a reasonable narrative for the extreme spike of dead bodies. The American Government then side-stepped the responsibility, blaming it on the Guyanese—basically announcing that they "couldn't count."

The State Department said that the counting mistake was a "rough preliminary estimate by the Guyanese troops and police." Yet, there was no explanation given as to why the rough estimate ended in a nine (409)? John A Bushnell, Deputy Assistant Secretary of State for Inter-American Affairs, offered another less than believable explanation at a news briefing on Friday morning. Bushnell said that the "United States Army Graves had given priority not to counting, but to identifying bodies and preparing them for evacuation." Bushnell also claimed that the highest priority for American personnel was searching for survivors; which as we now know didn't exist. Perhaps the most absurd excuse provided by American Officials, in regard to the miscount, was that many of the bodies were piled on top of other bodies. All of the pictures taken clearly show absolutely no evidence of any bodies lying on top of other bodies. Moreover, logically speaking, 400 bodies could not have covered 500 bodies.

By this time, the stench in the air was putrid and almost unbearable! All of the soldiers and officials were required to wear face guards to protect them against possible disease and aid in warding off the smell. Two men—one, navigator and the other, a pilot of a UH-1 Army Ambulance Helicopter—both agreed to be interviewed by the *NY Times* on the condition that they remain anonymous. One of the men said, "I expected it to be bad, but I've been in Vietnam for two years and I've never seen anything like this; and I hope I never do again." When the Major was asked if it is likely that additional bodies could have been found underneath others, the major said, "No." He claimed that he did not see all of the bodies, but the ones he saw, could be counted.

Sunday, November 26, 1978

Eight days after one of the most horrific tragedies in American history, the death toll was raised again; this time to 900! The American public felt like the incident was ongoing at this point. Post Traumatic Stress Syndrome was not even a classified term at that time, but it was certainly setting in across the nation. Everyday more and more dead were being discovered. It was as if the tragedy was still occurring. Furthermore, most American's were "Jonestown-ed-out" by this point. It was basically water-cooler talk now for nearly eight-days. The American public was numb and needed a break from the constant drama. It is not as if the people didn't care, one source revealed; but the ongoing coverage and constant new, and quite frankly, daily errors being reported was just too much to contend with for the average working Joe.

Not only were no autopsies done, but American Officials claimed to be unaware of any examinations or autopsies done by Guyanese Doctors. Major Robert W. Groom, a Dover Air Force Base spokesman, confirmed this; adding that he had no knowledge as to whether any autopsies were performed by Guyanese doctors. Groom was asked how U.S. Officials knew whether the victims had died of cyanide or were murdered; he replied, "I don't know." Groom went on to say, "Due to the enormity of the project, the bodies would be embalmed before autopsies could be performed."

Pathologists interviewed by the *NY Times* stated "detection of cyanide and other drugs, such as alcohol, is severely impaired by the embalming process." Evidence of trauma can also be found by performing an autopsy; even though the cause of death could have been due to cyanide poisoning. This could very well have proved if the victims were forced to drink the deadly concoction, changing the circumstances from suicide to murder. An autopsy is also important in determining gunshot wounds and fractures. It is not always easy to determine these things just by looking at the bodies, especially in these circumstances where the bodies were so badly decomposed. Even an x-ray is not a foolproof way of detecting a bullet wound, as the bullet may have gone in and out of the body.

In any case, the U.S. Government made every attempt to thwart autopsies from occurring even though they were under heavy public criticism from the medical community. Dr. Sidney B. Weinberg, then Suffolk County, NY's Medical Examiner, said, "Of the several ways the situation should have been handled, certainly the one chosen was the most unsatisfactory." Dover Air Force Base Medical Examiners described the governments conduct toward autopsies as "incompetent," "embarrassing," and "doing it backwards," among other things. They also contended that the government failed to meet the basic social responsibilities to determine the manner and cause of deaths.

The examiners were agast over the embalming of the bodies before the standard collecting of samples for toxicology tests. The examiners all agreed that the government should have sent a team of forensic specialists to Guyana to perform these tests immediately. One of the examiners, Dr. Leslie Lukash, who was at the time the Medical Examiner for Nassau County, said that the Justice Department's plan—as was indicated to him—was to do autopsies on four randomly selected bodies to confirm cyanide poisoning as the cause of death of the entire group. Dr. Lukash criticized the Justice Department by saying, "No court will accept that as evidence of how all members of the group died." After this ridiculous idea failed, Justice Department Officials said, "No Federal Legislation authorizes autopsies on the bodies of people who are murdered or die in foreign countries." This was the worst and most suspicious excuse of them all, and reeked of a cover-up attempt. After this statement it was clear the the U.S. government was searching for any legal excuse not to perform autopsies.

What makes matters worse is that American Officials claimed on November 20, 1978, that 50 American mortuary experts were scheduled to be flown into the interior of Guyana to conduct autopsies. Clearly they were not sending 50 specialists to do 4 random autopsies. Yet, when later pressured about the subject, they used legal rhetoric in an effort to walk-back this statement. It was as if they thought that the American public and the media would have just forgotten about autopsies all together and they weren't even making a concerted effort to lie. Conversely, this wasn't far from the truth.

The Dover medical examiners said that it is "standard policy" to perform autopsies for medical and legal reasons. The chief medical examiner for New York City at the time, Dr. Milton Helpern, wrote, "When anyone dies by violence, or suspicion of violence, regardless of whether violence is suicidal, accidental, or undetermined, it is an ancient responsibility of government to officially inquire into the death. This is of paramount importance to the administration of justice." Famous HBO personality and at the time a New York City Medical Examiner, Dr. Michael Baden, said in an interview with the *NY Times* on November 25, 1978, "The catastrophe requires better authentication than we've heard and requires documentation of each death for the sake of the families and for history. The distinction between homicide and suicide can have great consequences in future legal actions." It's evidently clear beyond a shadow of a doubt that the medical community unanimously agreed that this incident was handled in the worst possible way by the United States Government. The question remains: why?

The last of the bodies were brought in on the afternoon of Saturday, November 25, 1978. Soldiers cheered and clapped their bright orange rubber gloves. "They cheered because they finally finished the job," said one young soldier. Lieut. Col. Alfred Keyes, the man heading the operation said, "It was the worst job I've ever done in my life." Keyes went on to say that he "still didn't know how the initial count of bodies had been so far off." Keyes and his troops arrived in Jonestown on Wednesday morning. By then, estimates of the truly vital cover-ups came prior to Wednesday. Keyes claimed that they were under strict orders not to count bodies, but to recover them as quickly as possible, and even he was stunned by the miscount.

"We accepted somebody else's count," said Keyes. The question is who and what department of government did they occupy? It's clear that Keyes gave the most honest account of the situation, and that Keyes and his soldiers were not involved in any type of foul play. Even Keyes was baffled by the miscount and made no hint of bodies lying on top of one another. Keyes claimed that he and his team began to think that there was a mistake in the body-count on Thursday morning; only 24-hours after their arrival. On Friday morning, he said that there was "No Doubt!"

Eye Witness Accounts

Among the mayhem of the situation, it seemed as though there was an absence of reliable and credible witnesses. One U.S. Embassy Official said that he asked some of the survivors for details of the incident, but that it had been "very difficult to get a coherent sense of what had happened from the varying reports that were given by the individuals." Certain eye witness accounts seemed to contradict themselves and many stories from survivors contradict accounts by other survivors. Stanley Clayton told the *NY Times* on November 25th that he "had seen only one woman struggle to get away from the men who led her to the poison." He also claimed that he escaped when only 100 or so remained alive. This story is dramatically different in the pages of Tim Reiterman's book, Raven. Reiterman interviewed Clayton and in chapter 54, pg. 561, Clayton claims in regards to this that he "saw adults being forcibly injected with poison—murdered." Clayton went on to say, "It seemed there were about 60 of them" who died in this way.

Odell Rhodes was the only one to add any type of credible testimony to the final moments and remained quite consistent in his account. Yet, even the most credible accounts in this story raise other questions that don't necessarily add up. Rhodes laid out Jones' exact plan of Congressman Ryan's assassination for the *NY Times* on November 20th, 1978, not even 48-hours later. Rhodes went into great detail, explaining "the plan was to send one of his loyal lieutenants with the Ryan party as a feigned defector." He claimed that when the plane was in the air, the accomplice would kill the pilot and the plane would crash. Rhodes also said that Jones had told the whole congregation of his plan to kill the Congressman and his outrage, which completely contradicts the death tape and every other survivor's story. Rhodes then says that when the guards came back from the airstrip where Congressman Ryan was shot and told Jones that some had escaped; it was at that point that Jones had first ordered the "mass suicide." Clearly, Jones had instructed suicide long before word came back from the airstrip.

Somehow Rhodes clearly missed the first 30 minutes of banter between Jones, Christine Miller, and the others. Jones began his speech with "we must die." How could he have possibly mistaken this, even in the sensitive state that he was in? Simply explained, Rhodes had to have known that the suicide was well underway before the guards returned. The banter between Jones and Christine Miller was not something that could be overlooked for any reason. Even the lawyers, who were on the perimeter at the time and trying to escape, recall the incident between Miller and Jones. Moreover, the poison was already being mixed and Jones acknowledges this at least an hour before the guards returned. It is true that Jones believed that if the plane went down with no survivors that it would take some time for authorities to figure out that it was foul play and head to Jonestown. At least, it would have taken long enough for Jones to complete his murderous objective. When the guards returned, Jones knew that many witnesses were left alive and were going to relay the incident quicker than if there were no survivors. This in turn, forced Jones to speed up the process that was clearly already under way.

The only question here is how did Odell Rhodes get his information? He knew way too much at that time to be an innocent bystander. There is no way he could have known Jones' plan unless Jones told him individually, which would raise a whole host of other questions. Rhodes was not even a high level member in relation to what he claimed to know. Even Karen Layton, who was part of the elite, was surprised of her husband Larry Layton's fraudulent defection, according to Tim Reiterman. Karen supposedly pitched a fit when Larry got on the truck with Congressman Ryan to leave the camp. Unfortunately, contradicting eyewitness accounts and lack of credible witnesses lead to more speculation as to what truly occurred during the final moments in Jonestown.

It was also reported that Rhodes helped assistant Police Commissioner, Skip Roberts, identify (by name) and tag 183 of the diseased. Tim Carter and Mike Prokes were also reported to have been accompanied by authorities back to Jonestown to help, but were too horrified to do so. Later they were arrested in connection with Congressman Ryan's murder, but no charges were announced.

Another huge discrepancy with the testimony of Odell Rhodes is his claim that "After the first few adults took the poison, they stood around calm, talking and waiting for the poison to take effect." Rhodes then claimed that "panic began to sweep the assembly hall when people started going into convulsions." However, he also claimed that "the children were given the poison and died first." My question is do children die from cyanide poison any differently than adults? Of course not! So, adults would have witnessed their children convulsing, foaming at the mouth, bleeding from their nostrils and dying first; the same fate as the adults endured later on.

It had to take time to kill 270 children and not only did adults watch, but some gave up their children and some had them ripped from their grasps! The unforgiving tape of the incident, known as the "death tape" is proof of this. It's on that tape that the unforgettable and undeniable screams of children and adults can be heard. Moreover, only the most loyal members were heard on the death tape, as they were closest to the stage. The tape did not catch what was going on throughout the camp. Solidarity did not reign supreme and, at times, Jones can be heard trying to calm down those as they screamed and begged for their lives.

On December 12, 1978, the *NY Times* reported that sources said that it appeared to the authorities that many of the adults were sitting when the injections were administered. To me, this is in alignment with the death tape, as Head of Security for the Peoples Temple, Jim McElvane, can be heard authoritatively saying; "Everybody ... hold it! Sit down right here ... (loud background noises, agitated)... Stay seated ... sit down, sit down, sit down." No doubt with guns pointed at them, they had no choice but to comply. The same sources also said that Christine Miller was among the persons found injected. Again, these injections were positioned on the upper outside portion of the arms and the government ruled out the possibility that the victims had administered the shots themselves. Guyana's top pathologist Dr. Mootoo was also quoted as saying "those who were injecting them knew what they were doing."

On Monday, November 27, 1978, just eight days removed from the unprecedented tragedy, U.S. authorities set the final death toll at 909. The last of the bodies were shipped to Dover Air Force Base and the soldiers packed up their gear and took a collective sigh of relief; although all of the men and women who were involved in the clean up were instantly changed forever. The death toll would fluctuate in the ensuing weeks until it was finally set at **918**, which included the Congressman and the rest of the airstrip victims. The survivors were still being held by Guyanese authorities for the ongoing investigation. As the soldiers spent their last day working in the extreme heat of Guyana loading the last few bodies, dismantling helicopters, and stacking equipment, they all breathed a sigh of relief. It was finally over. But there was one more thing for them to do before the job could be complete. The boots, uniforms, and rubber gloves of the soldiers were stacked up high and torched, symbolic of a cleansing ritual. The grim physical reminders of the harrowing event went up into a curl of black smoke, as soldiers with dazed expressions looked on.

On the final day of the mission, when the soldiers finally finished the longest eight days of their lives, they had been notified that the State Department had arranged the biggest after-mission party in history. One hundred and forty cases of Guyana's finest brew (Banks Beer) and more than 200 fifths of DM Gold Label Rum awaited a couple-hundred soldiers in the Timheri Airport terminal for a much needed stress reliever. The men spent their last night drinking and eating mixed nuts and Frito Corn Chips as they tried to relax and talk-out their unnerving ordeal. Each man had his own story, his own point of view of the tragedy, and his own way of dealing with his individual experience. All would be forever tainted from the experience. Some would never look at their own children in the same way, holding them even closer to their hearts. One thing was certain: none of them would ever look at life in quite the same way.

CHAPTER 15 – CIA/MKULTRA
(*BRAINWASHED ASSASSINS*)

"Man does not have the right to develop his own mind. This kind of liberal orientation has great appeal. We must electrically control the brain. Someday armies and generals will be controlled by electric stimulation of the brain."
- *U.S. government mind manipulator, Dr. Jose Delgado, Congressional Record, No. 262E, Vol. 118, 1974.*

The story originated in Europe in the middle ages with a disturbing phenomenon called, *St. Anthony's fire*. This phenomenon started when people consumed bread made from diseased crops of rye. Upon consuming this bread people were mysteriously driven mad by hallucinations. Flash forward to Nazi Germany in the 1940s. During WWII, the Germans were testing mescaline on prisoners at Dachau—a city in SE Germany, near Munich, site of a major Nazi concentration camp—as a way of controlling their minds. After the war, several men were convicted of "Medical" crimes against humanity. This is most commonly known as the *Nuremberg Trials*. During these trials, U.S. investigative teams got their hands on records of the experiments, which have never been made public. Soon after, the Office of Strategic Services (OSS, America's WWII Intelligence Agency) created a truth drug committee. This committee created an odorless and tasteless extract of marijuana. Through these experiments they found that the extract puts one in a "state of irresponsibility, causing the subject to be loquacious and free in his or her impartation of the information."

In 1943, during that time, Chemist, Albert Hoffman, conducted separate experiments studying and analyzing specimens of the diseased rye that caused *St. Anthony's fire* and made a startling discovery. He found that the fungus on the rye contained a chemical identified as *Lysergic Acid Diethylamide* (LSD). On April 19, 1943, Dr. Hoffman synthesized and took the first taste of pure LSD to experiment its affects. Hoffman determined that the drug could serve as an important tool on how the mind works. Dr. Hoffman informed his colleague, Dr. Humphrey Osmond, of his findings. At the time Dr. Osmond was studying mental illnesses, such as schizophrenia, doing so by inducing temporary madness.

Enter Author, Aldus Huxley, who was considered by most European intellectuals as the brightest young literary minds of his generation. Osmond and Huxley soon found themselves working together. This unlikely duo teamed up as "doctor and subject" for ground breaking mescaline experiments. In 1954, at the conclusion of their experiments, Huxley wrote a book about his experience called, *The Doors of Perception*. The book proposed that everyone should experiment with mind altering drugs. This idea resonated like wild fire and ushered in the age of true mind-altering drugs; spawning a radical new way of thinking that included psychologists, poets, movie stars, musicians, and the CIA. Famous musician, Jim Morrison, named his band "The Doors" after Huxley's book.

When the CIA first entered the mind control field, their research started primarily with hypnosis. In 1950, Project BLUEBIRD—which later became ARTICHOKE, then MKULTRA, and variations from there ranging from MKSEARCH to MKDELTA—attempted to discover if hypnosis could help a subject beat a lie detector test. These programs started as defense programs against the growing concerns of Soviet achievements in this field. However, in the 1950's the U.S. took an offensive stance when they knew that they had advanced far past the Soviets in this area.

In a memo dated January 25, 1952, the CIA described project ARTICHOKE as:

"The evaluation and development of any method by which we can get information from a person against his will and without his knowledge, to find out if it is possible to get control of an individual to the point where he will do our bidding against his will and even against such fundamental laws of nature as SELF-PRESERVATION."

BLUEBIRD and ARTICHOKE were run by the CIA's Office of Scientific Intelligence. The money was channeled through the Office of Naval Research. In some instances, the doctors who conducted the research would report their findings to CIA agents who used code names, so as not to reveal their true identities. These were highly sensitive and very secretive operations. MKULTRA hypnosis began in 1953. In this project, agents were given sensitive information which they would not remember unless a certain cue was given for it to be recalled. So if the agent was captured by the enemy, he would not be able to pass on any sensitive information.

The CIA has a long history of experiments that aimed to create programmed assassins. After being programmed, the assassins were given a specific cue that would snap him or her into a "zombie-like state" that allowed the person to carry out the specific mission. CIA agent Morse Allen proved in a series of experiments that through hypnosis people could be forced to do things that they would later have no recollection of. This would aid in blackmailing the subjects later. During one of Allen's experiments he hypnotized a CIA secretary, gave her an unloaded gun, and ordered her to shoot another secretary, which she did. When she came to, she had no recollection of the incident. In 1951, a Denmark hypnotist, Bjorn Nielsen, hypnotized one of his patients and ordered him to rob a bank. The patient did so, killing a guard in the process. Nielsen was put on trial for his crimes. The jury refused to believe that anyone could be turned into a "lethal robot" against his or her will until Dr. Paul Rieter, chief of the psychiatric department of Copenhagen City Hospital at the time, performed an unnerving experiment with a woman sitting right in front of them." Nielsen was sentenced to life. This incident is popularly known as the *Palle Hardrup Affair of 1951*.

Soon, hypnosis coupled with LSD became the standard. To test the affects of the colorless, odorless, and tasteless LSD, government researchers secretly slipped it to one another. Experiments were also done on doctors and nurses, such as LSD testing done by Dr. Hyde and his associates on doctors and nurses at the Boston Psychiatric Hospital. This was not a normal procedure, as the goal was to experiment on the "spare change" of society, or those who would "not be missed." However, the CIA did get sloppy, brining unwanted attention to their programs after a few incidents that turned out to be major mishaps on high profile subjects.

Dr. Sidney Gottlieb, a CIA pharmacologist (known as the father of MKULTRA), and Richard Helms, CIA Deputy Director, were in charge of several of the MK programs. Gottlieb's signature can be found on several MKULTRA documents; especially the ones that there are deletions on. In 1959, Gottlieb trained children at *Deer*

Creek Camp in Maryland to be child prostitutes for blackmail operations. Gottlieb went under the alias *Mr. Sheiber*. One of the alleged children, Claudia Mullens, testified at the Advisory Committee Hearing about these experiments, claiming that she was only seven-years-old when she was "taught different ways to please men and at the same time ask them questions to get them to talk about themselves." Richard Helms later inadvertently admitted that the CIA did practice some type of behavioral modifications (BeMod) on children. Helms stated, "Cybernetics can be used in the molding of a child's character...the amassing of experience, and the establishment of social behavior patterns..."

On November 19, 1953, during a work retreat with CIA technicians and Army Biological Warfare Scientists at a hunting lodge in the backwoods of Maryland called Deep Creek Lake, two of the CIA agents decided to administer LSD in the "after dinner drink" of the others. Dr. Frank Olson, an Army Biochemist who was working on top secret germ warfare, was unwittingly given approximately 70 micrograms of LSD in a glass of Cointreau that he was drinking. It was administered by CIA officer Dr. Robert Lashbrook as part of an experiment that he and Dr. Sidney Gottlieb performed. According to the CIA, Olson went into a deep depression and exhibited symptoms of paranoia and schizophrenia. Others say that Olson was enraged over the fact that he was unwittingly dosed with LSD and that this was the final straw for Olson in a long string of occurrences that made him believe that the work being done by him and his colleagues was immoral.

Upon returning from Deep Creek Lake, Olson expressed his overwhelming desire to leave the CIA, and he did so days after, tendering his resignation to Ft. Detrick Special Operations Chief, Vincent Ruwet. Whether from this or other occurrences, Dr. Lashbrook had concluded Dr. Olson to be a "security risk," according to a classified CIA memo. Dr. Olson was taken to a New York City treatment center where he was treated by CIA Psychiatrist, Dr. Harold Abramson. He was scheduled to be put into a sanitarium on November 28, but the night before he was admitted, he mysteriously "leaped" from a ten-story window in the *Statler Hotel* in Manhattan. Dr. Lashbrook was in the room that night when Dr. Olson plunged to his death.

Earlier that same year, the army was conducting psychochemical experiments at a civilian facility when Doctors decided to give Harold Blauer, professional tennis player, an injection of *methyl di-amphetamine* (MDA). A few hours later Blauer was found dead from the injection. The CIA knew that they had made a big mistake experimenting on such high profile subjects when media reports spawned *Congressional Hearings* on the incidents. During the first set of hearings, then president, Jerald Ford, apologized to the Olson family. Dr. Abramson sent a telegram to the Senate Health Subcommittee in 1975, in which he admitted that he worked with the CIA doing LSD testing at Mount Sinai Hospital in New York. In 1976, congress passed a bill to pay $750,000 in compensation to Mrs. Olson and her three children. The Olson family voluntarily dropped their federal lawsuit after the bill was passed, but many still believed that Frank Olson was murdered because he posed a security risk. The family independently continued their investigation and in 1994, they had Frank Olson's body exhumed. The examining forensic pathologist found a large bruise over his left eye. The Doctor determined that the bruise occurred prior to his 10-story leap. He also determined that the bruise occurred by a possible striking of some sort to the head. Obviously the CIA's ideal subjects were those that were insignificant or unimportant to society.

Immorality Refined

In 1960, another MKULTRA program was started. This time, its goals were to quickly hypnotize an unwitting subject; creating long-lasting amnesia and implanting a lasting PHS (post hypnotic stress). However, hypnosis only worked on about 20-percent of its subjects. In most instances, hypnosis needed to be combined with certain drugs for more affective results. The CIA was trying to maintain their lead on their Russian counterparts, staying one-step ahead in regard to mind control. However, even though they were ahead of the Russians in this field, it did not mean that they could not still learn from their findings. Dr. Wolf was approached by the CIA at the Cornell University Medical School and asked to prepare a report on brain-washing based on Soviet and Chinese methods. The Russians did not use drugs in their experiments. Instead, they used isolation, humiliation, and discomfort, until the subject was ready to be re-educated and confess to an alleged crime. The MKULTRA project proved to be far ahead of that of the Russians' according to the CIA deputy director, Richard Helms at the time.

MKULTRA was a large umbrella, covering about 150 subprojects. These projects were conducted all over the world and in hundreds of secret facilities. In a declassified CIA document, there is some explanation as to why the programs were being kept so secret. Not very shocking information by any stretch of the imagination, the document basically details that when you're doing bad or immoral things you don't want anyone to know about them. In the document was an internal memo in which the secretary of the project explained, "Precautions must be taken, not only to protect the operation from exposure to enemy forces, but also to conceal these activities from the American public in general. The knowledge that the agency is engaging in unethical and illicit activities would have serious repercussions in political and diplomatic circles…"

MKULTRA subproject 58 featured Dr. Harris Isbell conducting LSD testing on volunteering inmates at Lexington Federal drug hospital in exchange for heroin. Some of the inmates were left on LSD for 77 days straight. LSD was given to volunteers and also to people who were not aware that they were being drugged. Dr. Sidney Gottlieb determined that the best MKULTRA test subjects were *"the borderline underworld or the drug addicts, prostitutes, and other small-timers who would be powerless to seek any sort of revenge if they ever found out what the CIA had done to them."* The CIA built three top-secret research facilities called "safe houses" set up in both New York and San Francisco. Established by Sidney Gottlieb and placed under the direction of Narcotics Bureau officer, George White, the project was titled OPERATION MIDNGHT CLIMAX.

These safe houses were so secret that even the agency's Inspector General, John Earman, was not aware of their existence. Prostitutes on the CIA's payroll lured clients back to these safe-houses and covertly slipped them LSD then monitored these subjects behind one-way mirrors. The Inspector General and others finally found out about these underhanded experiments in 1963. Pressure from the Warren Commission and other government agencies finally had the S.F. safe-houses closed down in 1965, and the New York safe-house closed in 1966.

By 1963, the CIA's MKULTRA umbrella included 44 universities and colleges, 15 private research facilities and companies, 12 hospitals or clinics, and 3 penitentiaries—which, in total, were estimated to cost about $10 million tax payer dollars. CIA officials claimed publicly that the MKULTRA programs ended in 1963; but in reality, they had just become MKSEARCH. Only 7 of the 149 subprojects survived and were transferred into MKSEARCH:

1. **Subproject # 1** – Sex and unwitting drug testing in safe-houses by George White, agent for the Federal Bureau of Narcotics.

2. **Subproject # 2** – Production of biological weapons on a large scale.

3. **Subproject # 3** – Custom-made chemical weapons for attack by the CIA.

4. **Subproject # 4** – CIA document stating, "Clinical testing of behavioral control methods" on inmates at California Medical facility at Vacaville.

5. **Subproject # 5** – Collecting data on the creation, use and effects of drugs.

6. **Subproject # 6** – Lobotomy experiments involving sensory deprivation, radio energy waves, etc. (for instance, experimented on cutting off heads of monkeys and transplanting the heads on top of other decapitated monkeys: headed by Dr. Maitland Baldwin).

7. **Subproject # 7** – Knocking subjects [monkeys] out with radio waves.

These programs went on until 1973, when the CIA claimed that they were discontinued, which again was another diversion. The mission of its last phase, code named CHICKWIT, was to "acquire and evaluate compounds believed to have effects on the behavior of humans." Sound familiar? Coincidentally, Jonestown was categorized as just this. Moreover, it was the most popular. And in a classified CIA document one of the goals of CHICKWIT is eerily similar to the mass murder/suicides in Jonestown: *"...to find out if it is possible to get control of an individual to the point where he will do our bidding against his will and even against such fundamental laws of nature as self-preservation."*

In 1973, the CIA reported that this program was discontinued before any testing was done on humans. But was their greatest achievement yet to take place? Two senate committees were formed in 1977 to investigate the CIA's drug testing in the years of 1975 and 1976. However, the senators reported that many of the records of these experiments were destroyed and or deleted in regard to any behavior control research. These same senators reported that "only a fragmentary picture emerged of the extent to which the agency was engaging in behavior control research."

Dr. Ewen Cameron conducted experiments on behavior control through isolation and sensory deprivation on humans at the *Allan Memorial Institute of Psychiatry* at McGill University in Montreal between 1955 and 1960. He died in 1967, but an associate in his told the NY Times that Dr. Cameron was unaware that the research was funded by the CIA. However, Dr. Cameron's "horrific experiments" were in fact funded by the CIA. Judging from the type of experiments that he conducted it's very hard to believe that he wasn't aware that he was doing work for them. His treatment of 53 patients started with "sleep therapy." He had patients knocked out for months in an attempt to "de-pattern" their thinking through electric shock and LSD. His goal was to wipe out old behavior patterns and reinstitute them with new ones.

Another experiment that Dr. Cameron performed was called "psychic driving." During these driving sessions subjects were heavily drugged and placed into "sleep rooms" where stereo speakers were placed under the individuals' pillow as a tape recorded message played over and over for 16 to 24 hours a day straight (which equals about 250,000 times a day). His experiments succeeded only in destroying his subjects for the rest of their lives. Dr. Cameron became known worldwide as the first chairman of the *World Psychiatric Association* as well as president of the American and Canadian psychiatric associations. Coincidentally, Dr. Cameron had also been a member of the Nuremberg medical tribunal only a decade earlier.

Dr. Carl Pfeiffer, a pharmacologist, conducted LSD experiments on prisoners at the Federal Penitentiary in Atlanta and at the Bordentown Reformatory in New Jersey between 1955 and 1964. In a telephone interview with the NY Times, Dr. Pfeiffer claimed that he was paid $25,000 a year by the Geschickter Foundation. The Geschickter Foundation later contributed $375,000 to Georgetown University Hospital to aid in the construction of a $3 million Medical Building in Washington D.C. In return, the agency would receive one-sixth of the hospital's beds. According to CIA documents, the CIA wanted to "establish at an appropriate university so that agency needs could thus be served with complete control, legal performance, and appropriate cover." A Georgetown University spokesman claimed that there was no indication, via their records, that the money came from the CIA.

Dr. Gottlieb was adamant about leaving little trace of the testing. In 1973, when Gottlieb retired, he ordered the Technical Services Division personnel to destroy and delete the most damning documents of their programs, making an investigation almost impossible. Gottlieb testified that he was working on direct verbal orders from Helms, which Helms later confirmed. Dr. Gottlieb was a major concern of the Subcommittee at the hearings. Because he did not work with the CIA any longer he was not included in the hearing at first, but the Subcommittee was determined to have him contacted. Eventually Dr. Gottlieb agreed to testify at the hearing, but only after receiving immunity from criminal prosecution. Gottlieb testified that "the purpose of the MKULTRA program, and related programs, was to see if and how a person's behavior could be altered by covert means." Aside from the paper-trail left after the Olson death, Gottlieb and his colleagues blamed everything on George White, who was dead at the time of the hearings. It should also be noted that White reported to Gottlieb.

Stansfield Turner, Director of Central Intelligence from 1977 to 1981, under the administration of his Naval Academy classmate,

President Jimmy Carter, had the daunting task of accepting this high profile position at a time of great MKULTRA scrutiny. Turner took the stance that he was going to put a stop to any secret experiments if they were still occurring. It should be noted that this was around the same time that Jim Jones had moved to Guyana. Turner announced that seven cases of records containing about 5,000 pages of documents pertaining to these projects were disclosed in agency archives. Turner and others testified before a joint hearing of the Senate Select Committee on Intelligence and Senator Edward Kennedy's Subcommittee on Health and Science Research. However, the hearings did not yield any new information.

The CIA did make available the newly discovered documents, but senate investigators said that the agency had deleted the names of medical researchers and institutions that performed the experiments. Without this information it's impossible to determine the extent of the testing, whether the tests had resulted in death or permanent impairment, or whether the rights of physical and mental health of the subjects were considered. One part of the hearing that should be noted was the part when Turner took full responsibility for any further mind-control experiments that take place. This was very noble, but came back to him later as he was taken to court in a lawsuit by surviving members of Peoples Temple in a suit alleging mind control testing on the Jonestown compound.

Senator INOUYE. What would you do if you criticized officials of the technical services staff and they continued to carry on experimentation for a number of years?

Admiral TURNER. I would do two things, sir. One is, I would be sure at the beginning that I was explicit enough that they knew that I didn't want that to be continued anywhere else; and two, if I found it being continued, I would roll some heads.

Senator INOUYE. As you know, Senator Huddleston and his subcommittee are deeply involved in the drafting of charters and guidelines for the intelligence community. We will be meeting with the

President tomorrow. Our concern is, I think, a basic one. Can anything like this occur again?

Admiral TURNER. I think it would be very, very unlikely, first, because we are all much more conscious of these issues than we were back in the fifties; second, because we have such thorough oversight procedures. I cannot imagine that this kind of activity could take place today without some member of the CIA itself bypassing me, if I were authorizing this, and writing to the Intelligence Oversight Board, and blowing the whistle on this kind of activity.

I am also doing my very best, sir, to encourage an openness with myself and a free communication in the Agency, so that I am the one who finds these things if they should happen. The fact is that we must keep you and your committee and now the new committee in the House informed of our sensitive activities. I think all of these add up to a degree of scrutiny such that this kind of extensive and flagrant activity could not happen today without it coming to the attention of the proper authorities to stop it.

To speak of the validity of his statements, in regard to his encouragement of whistle blowing, Turner later became outraged when former agent Frank Snepp published a book called *Decent Interval,* which detailed incompetence among senior American government personnel during the fall of Saigon. Turner accused Snepp of breaking the secrecy agreement required of all CIA agents. This may or may not answer the question whether he would be willing to blow the whistle on any of his colleagues if he did find some type of secret experiments occurring under his leadership, but it certainly alluded to the long-standing tradition of secrecy that the CIA has operated under.

Not every doctor accepted the CIA's dubious offers. Dr. Robert Heath, a Bio-psychiatrist and Chairman of the Tulane University Department of Psychiatry and Neurology, had pioneered the implanting "depth electrodes" in brain procedures. He identified these electrodes as the pleasure and pain centers of the brain. The goal of his experiments aimed to find different ways to treat schizophrenia. In November of 1962, after a symposium in New Orleans, he was approached by the Chief of the CIA's Medical Service Division, Dr. E Mansfield Gunn. Dr. Gunn attempted to persuade Dr. Heath to experiment on the pain center of the brain for the CIA. Dr. Gunn acknowledged that Dr. Heath would be paid by legitimate medical research foundations. Dr. Gunn declared that the Russians were investigating the same areas and that the U.S. needed to keep up with them. Dr. Heath said that he found the offer "abhorrent." Dr. Heath added that he believed that "the offer violated the physician's Hippocratic oath because it promised no benefit to the patient or to mankind."

In a similar attempt by the CIA, the world famous Clinical Psychologist, Dr. Carl Rogers, was also approached by the CIA in the 1970s. Apparently, while he was working at the University of Wisconsin, Rogers said that a man named Mr. Monroe told him that "they wanted to fund some straight projects to lend credibility to the foundation." The foundation that Mr. Monroe spoke of was the CIA front, "the Geschickter Foundation." Rogers declined the offer. Nonetheless, not all doctors were as admirable as Dr. Heath or Dr. Rogers. Many did accept the offers and actually prided themselves on the grounds of serving their country. The same experiments that they would be jailed for otherwise were now being protected under the law.

Dr. Isbell was part of a network of contractors covertly working on LSD experiments for the CIA from 1952 to 1963. Dr. Isbell testified in 1976, before the Senate Health Subcommittee that he was using LSD to develop a mild pain killer. He was not questioned by the subcommittee as to why he conducted these experiments for about a decade. Several professional researchers said that LSD would never have been considered for this purpose. The NY Times asked Dr. Isbell for an interview regarding these experiments, but he declined. Dr. Louis "Jolly" West, Chief of Psychiatry at the University of California, Los Angeles, and Director of the Neuro-Psychiatric Institute, was a well known and admitted CIA/LSD contractor. Dr. West told the NY Times in a telephone interview that he was offered a job to study and experiment with LSD. The offer came from Dr. Gottlieb, he said. Dr. West had previously treated Jack Ruby, Oswald's assassin. West did not live or practice in Dallas, yet was assigned to psychiatrically treat Ruby.

Timothy McVeigh, the Oklahoma City Bomber, was once assigned to a Pentagon contractor that conducted classified research in electronic warfare. McVeigh alleged that Federal Agents had implanted a microchip inside of him. As if that wasn't strange enough, Dr. West led the psychological trauma team that treated victims, families, and survivors of the explosion. Coincidentally, *Freedom Magazine* reported that "In the 1960s West could be found in the Haight-Ashbury section of San Francisco doing more LSD experiments, this time within the nascent hippie community." Note: this is the community directly related to the members of Peoples Temple; which from CIA documents would be prime candidates for such testing. It seems that we are far past the days of the use of LSD in MK-testing and lord only knows the extent and new methods that the CIA is using, if any, in this advanced day and age.

CHAPTER 16 –
MKULTRA/JONESTOWN CONNECTION

I had the opportunity to speak with *Freedom Magazines* senior editor, Tom Whittle regarding the piece he did on the Jonestown conspiracy. For those of you unaware, Freedom Magazine is published by *The Church of Scientology*, and Whittle was anxious and eager to share his information, speaking very candidly about what he had learned. He informed me that his main objective is to get the real story out there. He was adamant about this story being one of the most under-reported stories in our history and he believes that the media and American public would be interested again if they heard the real story.

It was a well known fact, for anyone who closely followed the career of Congressman Ryan, that he was very active and vocal about exposing covert CIA operations. Ryan believed that the public, and especially the people's governing body, had a right to know of any underhanded and immoral experiments that the CIA was conducting. Frankly speaking, Ryan was fearless, aggressive, and uncompromising in his campaign against the CIA's underhanded experiments. Ryan did things like making surprise visits to CIA headquarters in Langley, Virginia to do some interrogation of his own. A source who once accompanied Ryan on one of his visits to Langley told Whittle that Ryan was a "Pain in their [CIA's] ass." Ryan was known as a man who fought for those who could not fight for themselves and was a patriot in the true sense of the word. In 1974, Ryan helped institute the *Hughes-Ryan Amendment*, which required the CIA to notify eight separate committees of Congress prior to conducting covert experiments or operations. Under the Hughes-Ryan Amendment, the CIA was also banned from covert paramilitary operations without direct approval from the President and Congress.

Ryan continued to push and meddle in the CIA's involvement in "mind-control" experiments in 1977 and 1978. Ryan was investigating the possibility that Donald David DeFreeze, known as "cinque"—named after the leader of the slave rebellion who took over the slave ship Amistad in 1839—was a central figure in the 1974, kidnapping of Patty Hearst. DeFreeze was a subject of MKULTRA testing while he was in prison. Ryan was trying to expose the MKULTRA tests that were performed in the early 1970s on inmates at a State hospital in Vacaville, California, which may have included DeFreeze as one of their subjects. To show his commitment to this case, Ryan submitted a petition to then President Jimmy Carter on *September 25, 1978*, seeking to have Patricia Hearst's seven-year prison term commuted to the 18 months she had already served.

On *October 5, 1978*, Jack Anderson, a reporter out of Washington, D.C, published an article called, *"The Hearst Kidnapping: Did CIA Inspire It?,"* which Whittle claims was probably leaked from Ryan or someone from his camp. In the article, Anderson spoke with a convict named Clifford Jefferson (a.k.a. "Death Row Jeff") who shared a cell with DeFreeze. Jefferson claimed that Defreeze told him that "These tests were conducted on the third-floor of the facility in B3." Defreeze said it was there that he "met two CIA men who were giving these tests." They proceeded to give him drugs, including mescaline, Quaalude, and Artane." Whittle's article goes on to detail what Jefferson claims Defreeze told him about the incident:

> "…stress tests that were given to prisoners in which they were kept in solitary, harassed and annoyed until they would do anything asked of them to get out; then they were given these drugs and would become like robots. He [DeFreeze] said that when he got out, he would get a revolutionary group to kidnap some rich person. They would hold that person tied up in a dark place, keep him frightened and in fear of his life, then give him mescaline and other drugs and the person would become a robot and do anything he was asked to do—including killing others."

DeFreeze went on to kidnap Patty Hearst in 1974, and he kept her blindfolded and tied-up in a closet for 54 days. Corroborating this are CIA documents confirming that MKULTRA testing was done at Vacaville, California in 1974. Considering the close proximity of these two actions by Congressman Ryan to his Jonestown trip, it's easy to see why the CIA may have felt it necessary to take this opportunity to get Ryan out of the way as soon as possible. The opportunity to kill Ryan in Guyana was their best option. Two different scenarios appear here as well: (1) either the CIA took this opportunity to frame Jim Jones and kill two birds with one stone; (2) or Jim Jones was a part of the CIA and the CIA took this opportunity to Kill Ryan & Jones, and to terminate the experiment all at the same time, getting rid of the loose ends.

We know that Congressman Ryan's interest in Jonestown grew mainly out of reports from Timothy Stoen, Debbie Layton, and other defectors regarding alleged abuses in the community; but according to Mr. Whittle's evidence, it was that mixed with the broader subject of government-sponsored "mind-control" experiments that finally induced Ryan to lead a delegation to Guyana on November 14, 1978. After arriving in Jonestown and making a positive speech, Ryan told Jones that he intended to report to congress that rumors of abuse were not based on fact. However, that may have been Ryan just telling Jones what he wanted to hear, albeit to revoke that statement later in place of confirming mind-control testing in Jonestown. Alternatively, Ryan may have witnessed evidence of CIA experimentation after making this statement to Jones.

Mr. Whittle writes briefly of the attack on Congressman Ryan while he was in Jonestown. The attack was perpetrated by Don Sly (who Jones had nicknamed Ujara). Whittle makes reference to the incident as a possible CIA triggered attack. His theory is right in line with the 1954, released CIA document that stated, "As a trigger mechanism for a bigger project, it was proposed that an individual...be induced under ARTICKOKE to perform an act, involuntarily, of attempted assassination against a prominent [deleted] politician if necessary, against an American Official." However, Whittle never makes reference to who might have triggered Sly's attacked on Ryan. Could it have been Richard Dwyer, Deputy Chief of Mission for the U.S. Embassy in Guyana, who was one of the men that accompanied Ryan and his delegation into Jonestown? It was not known at the time, but later found out that Dwyer was a CIA agent. Or maybe it was a member of the PT who was planter their by the CIA? Still, it could have very well been

Sly acting out on his own, as Jones says later in his death tape monologue: "I can't control these people." However, the popular (common sense) theory is that Jim Jones himself ordered Sly to attack Ryan. If Jim Jones could do one thing, it was control "his people."

During the "death tape" Jones clearly sticks up for Ujara [Sly] several times during his speech and says that he will not separate himself from any acts of his people. He also said that he would not let them take Sly away. Moreover, Jones had made several threatening statements on tape in the days leading up to Ryan's arrival about what he would do to Ryan if he dared enter into Jonestown. One example of this occurred two days before the tragedy, when Jones told his congregation, "I can assure you that if [Ryan] stays long enough for tea, he's gonna regret it."

Whittle and others claim that the attack on Ryan at the airstrip was perpetrated by a CIA "hit squad." Whittle said in regard to the shooting that a source told him that "the actual killers had been planted in Peoples Temple." This is very unlikely unless you factor in Jim Jones as being part of the plot to kill Ryan; then I would say that the probability is extremely high. Jones clearly knew about the plan to kill Ryan; plus, the hit squad would have had to have been planted several years before and played a key role in the Temple's hierarchy, or they would not have been in Jonestown to begin with. The fact is that once again on the death tape, Jones claimed that he had a vision that Larry Layton was going to shoot the pilot because he was upset that his sister Debbie had defected and that his mother had recently passed away, dying about 10 days prior. Clearly Jones knew that Larry was a prime candidate to use in this situation, and Jones was again playing God, pretending to prophesize about an incident that had yet to occur. Jones knew that Larry was grieving the loss of his mother and Jones also used Debbie's defection as ammo for Larry to make things right again. Witnesses of the shooting describe the murderers as "zombies, walking mechanically, without emotion, and looking through you, not at you, as they murdered." The most chilling evidence that Whittle provides is the lawsuit filed by the two sons and three daughters of Congressman Ryan; the testimony of former Green Beret, Charles Huff; and the testimony of U.S. Colonel, L. Fletcher Prouty. This part of Whittle's investigation yields chilling results!

The Lawsuits

On July 30, 1980, Congressman Ryan's family—his five adult children (two sons and three daughters) filed a lawsuit in the United States District Court, Northern District of California. In it, the plaintiffs asked for $3 million in general damages, plus costs for Ryan's funeral and bringing the action. The suit charged that "the Jonestown colony was infiltrated with agent(s) of the Central Intelligence Agency of the United States." One said-agent named in the lawsuit was "Phillip Blakey," a trusted aid of Jim Jones. It alleged that agents of the Department of State and the CIA used Jonestown as part of their MKULTRA program. They referenced the massive assortment of drugs found in Jonestown, post incident—drugs also known to be used in MKULTRA experiments. Some experts have estimated that the amount of drugs recovered from Jonestown could have drugged over 200,000 people for more than a year.

John Judge, author of the article, *The Black Hole of Guyana*, documents that one foot locker contained 11,000 doses of thorazine, a dangerous tranquilizer. There were also a plethora of other drugs found in Jonestown that were also commonly used in MKULTRA experiments: these include, sodium pentothal (truth serum), chloral hydrate (a hypnotic), Demerol and thallium (confuses thinking), haliopareal and largatil (two major tranquilizers), and many others.

Judge writes that, these drugs combined with all of the other strict daily tasks that members of Jonestown had to participate in, Jonestown was "that of a tightly-run concentration camp, complete with medical and psychiatric experimentation." These drugs were all shipped from an outside source and the only known drugs to be produced in Jonestown were herbal drugs. The residents of Jonestown endured isolation, sophisticated brainwashing-techniques, and drugs—not to mention specialized torture techniques. Judge also makes a very good point when he writes, "It also suggests an additional motive for frustrating any chemical autopsies, since these drugs would have been found in the system's of the dead." According to FBI document BQ 89-495, a witness informed the FBI that Jones had stated at a meeting that a "wealthy benefactor" donated thousands of dollars worth of drugs to Peoples Temple in Guyana. However, this "wealthy benefactor" has never been confirmed or identified. The witness who informed the FBI was also crossed out on the FBI document, making it is impossible to follow up on this story—yet another loose end.

The lawsuit also made the dubious and legendary connection between Richard Dwyer, the CIA, and Jonestown. Dwyer was identified in the 1968, edition of *Who's Who in the CI,* a book written by the East German journalist, Julius Mader. The book had access to some information on CIA officers that was not publicly available. It named some 3,000 active agents of the CIA, Dwyer being one of them. When asked if he was a CIA agent, Dwyer said, "no comment." The lawsuit alleged that Dwyer doubled as a CIA agent and "arranged for the transportation of descendent [Ryan] and his party once in Guyana; briefed descendent and his party on the events and conditions at Jonestown upon their arrival; and escorted descendent and his party to Jonestown in November 1978."

In a NY Times article dated December 4, 1978, Jackie Speier, Congressman Ryan's legislative Counsel, said from a hospital bed just a day earlier; "The State Department at no time made it even remotely clear to the Congressman or to myself that there would be danger encountered of the nature that we found." Miss Speier claims that when they met Richard Dwyer in Georgetown on November 14, 1978, Dwyer started reading them the "riot act." She went on to say about Dwyer, "He said we hadn't done half enough staff work for this CODEL [acronym for a congressional delegation carrying out an investigation abroad]. He was also very upset that the press had come down with us, although the State Department was well aware that we would have press representatives along." Dwyer could have been so upset because the presence of the press made it harder for him to dispose of Ryan with fewer witnesses, particularly media witnesses.

Speier claimed that prior to the Guyana trip, she made out her will just a few hours before she left. A friend of Jackie's told the NY Times, in an article published on November 20, 1978, that she [Jackie] had "grave reservations" about the trip. She went on to say that Jackie had a case of "bad vibes" that something bad was going to happen. Jackie had drawn-up Congressman Ryan's will just two years earlier; and right before she left for Guyana she made out her own will and filed it next to the Ryan's.

Just minutes before the gunmen opened fire on Ryan and his crew at the airstrip, Dwyer is seen walking next to Ryan—on the Congressman's right hand side, while the Congressman and the others were on their way to boarding the plane. Dwyer quickly and mysteriously breaks away from the group with a sudden *back-step* and walks toward the cockpit and shakes hands with the pilot, who's sitting in the cockpit at the time. It looks very much like a premeditated act when seen on video, but of course could also have be seen as a mere coincidence. Many believe that Jones and Dwyer had a special relationship; and Jones is heard numerous times on the "death tape" yelling for someone to take Dwyer to the east house to keep him safe. Not only was this odd under the circumstances—and the fact that Dwyer denies ever going back into Jonestown after the shootings at the Port Kaituma airstrip—but Jones sounded manic about it, asking for Dwyer numerous times in the midst of his infamous his suicide speech.

In a television interview, Kit Nascimento, Minister of Information in Guyana in 1978, said that Richard Dwyer was "the head of the CIA," and that "the CIA had a presence here [in Guyana]. It was an unrevealed presence at the time." Despite the horrific incidents in Jonestown, Dwyer and other U.S. Embassy Officials would receive medals and promotions. Only certain people were killed at the airstrip. Those who were killed were methodically walked-up-on while wounded and shot directly in the head at point-blank range, execution style. Though wounded by a shot in the buttock, Dwyer never fled the scene as the reports say, and he was apparently not a target of the killers. The lawsuit further charged that Dwyer "knowingly, intentionally and maliciously led [Ryan] into a trap at the Port Kaituma Air Strip, which cost descendent his life." It also alleged that Jones, himself, was an agent or operative of the CIA.

Joe Holsinger, Congressman Ryan's Legislative Assistant, testified before the House of Foreign Affairs Subcommittee on International Operations in 1980. In his testimony he stated that the CIA had a covert operation in Guyana. Also, at a Colloquium of Psychologists in San Francisco on "Psychosocial Implications of the Jonestown Phenomenon," Holsinger stated that the CIA worked with Jones to perform medical and mind-control experiments at Peoples Temple. Moreover, Holsinger claimed to get several threats in the days following the murders. This is a significant claim by Holsinger, because he was virtually a new employee of Ryan's and it was unlikely that Jones or his staff knew of him.

At the Colloquium, Holsinger cited an essay that he had received days prior, which was written by a Berkeley Psychologist entitled, "The Penal Colony." The essay claims that "rather than terminating MKULTRA, the CIA shifted its programs from public institutions to private cult-groups, including Peoples Temple."

In October of 1981, Jonestown survivors filed a $63 million lawsuit against the then Secretary of State, Cyrus Vance, and former Director of the CIA, Stansfiled Turner. The suit stated that the State Department and CIA conspired to "enhance the economic and political powers of James Warren Jones," conducting "mind control and drug experimentation" in Jonestown. Back on August 3, 1977, then President, Jimmy Carter, decided to give Turner unprecedented authority for a CIA director, granting him definitive control over the entire National Intelligence budget—including funding of the Defense Department's National Security Agency and the National Reconnaissance Office. In response, Turner told a Senate Hearing Committee that "under a project that was most active between 1953 and 1963, the CIA secretly supported research into human behavior control at 80 institutions."

Basically, he gave the committee information that they pretty much had already confirmed. His statement or confession to the committee was seen as conciliatory in nature, by both Turner and the committee. For the record of course, Turned claimed that the tests were "abhorrent" and that he was cooperating with Senate investigators to uncover the various institutions, even though the vast majority of these institutions have never been made public. President Carter's main objective of the appointment was to centralize managerial control over the sprawling intelligence community, with fundamental direction of the intelligence effort coming from the President and his National Security Council. Coincidentally enough, Jones apparently had contact with the Carter's. In FBI tape labeled "Q 799," Jones had this nice leisurely chat with the first lady, Rosalynn Carter, on September 13, 1976. It is believed that the call below is from Mrs. Carter to Jim Jones:

Jones: (cuts in) – District Attorney here, he was highly impressed with your husband, and your commitment, in more ways than one. We appreciate your– your Christian, ethical background, and also the, the broad liberality in which you respect other people's religious perspective. I can't uh, I can't say how moved I am, I– by uh– I usually don't lack– being a, a preacher, I don't lack for words, but I'm deeply touched.

Rosalynn: Well, I–

Jones: Is there anything particular that we could do for you?

Rosalynn: No, I– not uh– I don't have anything in mind, I just wanted to call because um– Jimmy had gotten his (unintelligible words) think about it, so he told me to call you, and just try and get some, so uh–

Jones: I'd also sent a letter– uh, there'd been some negative press about uh, uh, your son uh, participating in, uh, raising funds for a gay bar, and I wanted you to know that we– uh, we're a hundred percent behind you in that, I don't know how far it has gone. There's no end to the degree that some people will– will attempt to malign good people, but I– I don't know whether you've received my letter, but I sent a letter–

Rosalynn: Well–

Jones: –of encouragement, not that you need it. We're going to win.

Rosalynn: Well–

Jones: We're going to win.

Rosalynn: We appreciate that, we–we get the mail eventually but it's stacked up so much, uh, between the time we won the Ohio primary and the, uh– you know, the last primary, and the convention (unintelligible) so much that it takes us a while to get it organized and get it open, but we're about to do that now–

Jones: Well, you call us– We have many many thousands of members, and I have considerable influence in the Disciples of Christ denomination, in which I am an official. Anything we can do, you call. We're one hundred percent behind you.

Rosalynn: Do you know Jimmy's sister, Ruth Stapleton?

Jones: I've– I've read of her, with a great deal of admiration.

Rosalynn: I didn't know. She'd been in um, California so much, and she has a, um– (Pause) Well, she just– she just travels and not campaigning, but she does so much good in the whole country, and I knew that she had been in California a lot, I thought you might know her.

Jones: Well, if she's ever on another speaking itinerant, uh, itinerary, we would be more than honored for her to come our way. Uh, I like her approach. She has such a sane emphasis on spiritual healing, and yet with a, a deep commitment to ecumenicity–

Rosalynn: Thank you–

Jones: –and, and–

End of tape.

Some of the Jonestown survivors also filed a similar lawsuit against the U.S government. Both the Ryan family lawsuit and the survivors' lawsuit, however, were dismissed. The survivors' lawsuit was dismissed for "failure to prosecute timely" just four months after it was initiated, and all requests for appeals have been denied. The Ryan family lawsuit, according to *Freedom*, was dismissed for "reasons that have to date never been fully disclosed." Tom Whittle of Freedom Magazine also claims to have spoken to a source close to the Ryan family that said that the family had received numerous threats after filing the lawsuit that he attributed to the CIA. The source said that "Every time they made a move a letter would show up on his door step saying for example, were 'watching you.'" This sounds very familiar to several Peoples Temple members who left the church prior to the mass exodus to Jonestown, accounts hitherto documented.

Now Testify

Another testimony that invokes suspicions of conspiracy is that of a man named, Charles Huff. This story begins when the *Cult Awareness Network* ran a special story dubbed, "*Jonestown: The Big Lie*," featuring a Freedom Magazine piece on a potential conspiracy in Jonestown. The piece was controversial and attracted much viewer feedback. Among the responses was a man claiming to be a former Green Beret, Charles Huff, who wrote a letter and sent it to the network. In the letter he explains.

U.S. Army Green Beret, Charles Huff was assigned to the 3rd Battalion, 7th Special Forces Group, 1st Special Forces stationed in Panama at the time of the Jonestown incident. In an interview with Freedom, Huff claimed that on November 18, 1978, they were alerted by the State Department to "rescue" American citizens in Guyana. The only information they knew was that Congressman Ryan and his staff were either killed or wounded. Within "five hours" Huff and his battalion, consisting of seven Green Berets, were "on site" in Jonestown. Huff said that while in Jonestown, his group "found more than 30 people killed by bullets and crossbow arrows; and they all appeared to be running towards the jungle." Huff also stated that the "adults who had not been shot, had been killed by injections between their shoulder blades."

Perhaps the most extraordinary findings came from the first pathologist on the scene. The Chief Medical examiner, and Guyana's top Pathologist, Dr. C. Leslie Mootoo, was on the scene within a few hours, according to the *Miami Herald*, 12/17/78, and the *NY Times*, 12/12/78. Whittle told me that he had the opportunity to speak to Mootoo before his death about 10 years ago and confirmed his testimony. Mootoo told whittle the he and his crew worked for 32 straight hours in the extreme heat of the jungle, among the grotesqueness of decaying bodies before giving up. When Mootoo and his examination team were done, they yielded startling results! Mootoo claimed that he and his team...

"examined 187 bodies and concluded that 80-90 percent of the victims that he examined had needle marks from a hypodermic syringe in the upper shoulder, as if administered from behind. Others had been shot or strangled. Many exhibited ligature marks or other signs of having been restrained just prior to their deaths."

It is important to note that human beings are incapable of injecting themselves in the way Mootoo describes, which Mootoo also acknowledges. Mootoo told Whittle that "those who injected them knew what they were doing." After analysis of the contents of the infamous Jonestown metal-vat, Dr. Mootoo along with American Forensic Pathologist, Dr. Lynn Crook, concluded that the vat was mixed with several tranquilizers and two strong poisons; potassium cyanide and potassium chloride.

On December 22, 1978 in Guyana, under the direction of magistrate, Haroon Bacchus, a Coroner's Jury declared that *"Jim Jones and some person or person's unknown, murdered all but three of the more than 900 persons who died at Jonestown."* The jury also determined that Jones, like the others, was murdered by "some person(s) unknown." The biggest problem with the story was the "timing of its release." The story was reported in the NY Times and several other papers over one month after the Jonestown incident and was basically ignored by the American public and the American media by and large, who at that point had already moved on.

Emanuel Romano, the Chief Prosecutor, claimed that some of Jones' followers had "flown the coup" and murdered Jones and Annie Moore. Romano believed that Moore was going to leave with Jones. This makes great sense, and many believe that Jones was headed on an exodus to Russia—but with only a few choice members. Debbie Layton wrote that Annie Moore shot Jones at his request at the pavilion then made her way to their cottage and shot herself in the head; the gun was found in her hand with a suicide note next to her body. However, as reported in the NY Times on December 12, 1978, Guyanese police said that Miss Moore was killed by a dum-dum bullet (a round projectile made to expand on contact). The force of the impact "blew half her face off."

Sources said that she was shot with the same kind of bullet as those that killed Congressman Ryan, and that it could have been the same gun. The gun was believed to be a bolt-action .30 caliber rifle mounted with a black telescope sight. The rifle was found in Jonestown as reported by the Guyanese police. The only weapon found at the airstrip was Larry Layton's pistol. Annie Moore was found dead in Jim Jones' cabin, which was several hundred yards from the pavilion. Police at the time claimed that she was shot from behind by someone who she was turning to speak to. "She had partially turned to speak when the gun was fired," said police. Her body was found near a file cabinet that had one drawer section fitted with a "combination-type safe." Police claimed that they were investigating whether she may have been shot while removing money or valuables. Or maybe someone shot her and took the money? Was she part of a plan to flee to Russia and was mysteriously sabotaged? If this is the case, a likely scenario is that, at Jones' request, she went to Jones' cottage to gather money and other things of Jones' for their escape when she and Jones were simultaneously executed by CIA members.

A dum-dum bullet is a hollow-nosed bullet that explodes in tiny fragments when it enters the body. It's commonly known as the "below-the-belt" bullet of war. For this reason, the bullet is forbidden to be used by the Geneva Treaty. This type of bullet was issued by the CIA for use in anti-Castro-exile raids on Cuba and has been used in several controversial assassinations throughout history. The Warren Commission's official report says that President John F. Kennedy was shot and killed by dum-dum bullets. Many experts say that these bullets could never have come from Oswald's gun. This has fueled other expert's claims that there were two types of bullets used in the assassination, corroborating the "two gun-men" theory. Dum-dum bullets also killed John Lennon. Yet, the most dubious connection is certainly Jeannie Mills, former Temple member killed in California after the mass murder/suicides in Jonestown. She was also killed by dum-dum bullets. If the gun found in Annie's hand did not use dum-dum bullets it would then be a clear indication of murder made to look like a suicide.

Obviously this was the evidence that Chief Prosecutor Emanuel Romano used to make his determination. Yet, the lead Guyanese investigator testified that it was a "mass suicide." Did someone coerce the lead Guyanese investigator into making these statements? Even Roberts, the assistant police commissioner, argued that at least the 270-plus children should be considered murdered. Romano argued that they "had no choice...You either drank it or you got a bullet." Dr. Mootoo also testified that he believed that most of the members were murdered, but he did not tell jurors what he told an American reporter: that "he believed that more than 700 of the cultists had been murdered."

Guyanese authorities reported that it took approximately five-hours for the "revolutionary suicide" to be carried out by Jones and those assisting him. Authorities found several small bottles bearing labels for a liquid valium solution that actually contained cyanide, which suggested that there were at least some who drank the poison thought they were drinking liquid tranquilizer—indicating that some, or many, may have thought that it was just another one of Jones' "white night" suicide drills. Other Guyanese government officials, who asked to remain nameless, stated that "many adults" found dead in Jonestown had "fresh injection marks high on their upper arms, just below the shoulder." They also indicated that these victims were all seated during the time of injection. Because of the location of these injections (on the upper outside portion of the arms), these government sources stated that it would have been impossible for these victims to have administered the shots themselves.

Freedom Magazine also had another piece of evidence that was very straight to the point, yet nonetheless effective. Whittle had the opportunity to speak to U.S. Air Force Col. Prouty who had spent 9 of his 23 year military career in the Pentagon (1955-1964): 2 years with the Secretary of Defense, 2 years with the Joint Chiefs of Staff, and 5 years with Headquarters, U.S. Air Force. In 1955, he was appointed the first "Focal Point" officer between the CIA and the Air Force for Clandestine Operations per National Security Council Directive 5412. He was the Briefing Officer for the Secretary of Defense (1960-1961), and for the Chairman of the Joint Chiefs of Staff. In a special interview with Freedom, Prouty claimed that "Leo Ryan had moved in too close to certain skeletons that could never be safely disturbed." Prouty notes his evidence by saying,

> *"The Joint Chiefs of Staff had prepared air shipments of hundreds of body bags. They didn't normally keep that many in any one place. Within hours, they began to shuttle them down to Georgetown. They couldn't possibly have done that without prior knowledge that it was going to happen. It shows that there was prior planning."*

During the immediate aftermath of the tragedy, Jeff Brailey spent nine days in Jonestown as senior medic of the Joint Humanitarian Task Force sent to Guyana to recover the remains of the victims of the Jonestown Massacre. While in Jonestown Brailey was approached by a man in civilian clothes who asked him to guard a large box of documents. The man told Brailey that he was from the U.S. Embassy and said to him, "If anyone tries to take this box away from you shoot them!" The man told Brailey that the box was filled with sensitive documents and that he needed to get those documents to the U.S. Embassy. Brailey claimed that he believed the man was from the CIA. Those documents have disappeared and have never been revealed.

A Wise Choice

Dave Wise joined Peoples Temple in 1971, in San Francisco at the Benjamin Franklin School auditorium. Wise was a young idealist who opposed the war, and he believed that Jim Jones was a good man who loved helping people and that the church was as genuine as it gets. Wise had aspirations of becoming a lawyer for the church; so he entered college and bunked above Larry Schacht (who later became the Jonestown doctor) in the church dormitories. Jim Jones, however, had other plans for young Wise. Jones soon asked him to leave school and become the resident minister for the Los Angeles Peoples Temple on Alvarado and Hoover. Jones once announced to his congregation that he had surveyed the whole world for a pastor and Wise was the best man for the job. Wise became so prominent in the church that he was the only pastor other than Jones whose name was ever on Peoples Temple letterhead and business cards. Wise left the Temple, however, in late 1976, in protest of power trips, humiliation tactics, and sexual improprieties.

I had a chance to interview Dave Wise a few times, and he had some pretty interesting things to say. One of the first things that he explained to me was his fear of reprisal, which is why he had changed his name to Dave Wise. His fear stemmed from the FBI, he claimed. Wise explained that he has been in hiding for many years, only resurfacing recently. He was planning on writing a book about his experiences in the church, and he would also offer some theories of his own as to what happened in Jonestown. Wise was fortunate enough to interview one of the green berets who landed in Jonestown shortly after the suicides. The soldier asked Wise to call him Scott Hooker, for the sake of anonymity. Hooker claimed that he was one of the soldiers sent to Jonestown hours after the deaths. Hooker told Wise that their mission was to kill any remaining survivors and inject all the bodies with cyanide. This scenario corroborates Jones' death tape when Jones says, "They're gonna rappel down out of the sky and kill our babies any minute now."

Hooker later explained to Wise that he pulled Jones' dead body out of his throne-like chair at the pavilion. Jones was later officially found lying on his back with a pillow neatly tucked under his head. Hooker told Wise that his helicopter hovered over fleeing survivors, waiving for them to be rescued. When survivors approached, however, Hooker says they shot and killed them. As Hooker described, "…blood misting into a red cloud" as he fired his automatic weapon at the innocent victims. The mission of Hooker and his Green Berets colleagues was to turn over the dead bodies in search of explosives before the CIA medical team took over. It is important to note that Wise does not believe that Jones was involved in the CIA; rather, he believes that the CIA had been monitoring Jones and his movement and that it was "the CIA's job to represent the Radical Right in the destruction of the Radical Left." According to Wise, Jonestown was not a CIA mind-control experiment; the CIA was an adversary of Jones and his people. The CIA wanted to "stop Jones from making a social statement on behalf of Liberation Theology and the left," he says. In other words, the CIA wanted to stop Jones from becoming a martyr and turn him into a killer.

Kiss My Gritz

Lt. Col. James "Bo" Gritz tells a similar story, yet corroborates Jones' involvement in the CIA. Commander in charge of all green berets in Latin and South America at the time—under strict CIA orders—Gritz says that he didn't know much beyond the fact that their mission was to kill Jonestown survivors. Gritz said that the man he sent into Jonestown returned with the report, "The niggers are all dead." In a special interview with *New Dawn's* Adam Parfrey, Gritz said that he doesn't know precisely what the nature of the operation was in Jonestown, because it was a compartmentalized CIA operation. Gritz said, "I think the Jonestown incident was an extension of 'In search of the Manchurian Candidate.' You look at Jim Jones' background carefully; he had a lot of intelligence contacts there for doing exactly what he did."

Gritz believes that Jones was involved in the CIA experiment and he claims that "It escalated once they killed Congressman Ryan. Basically, they had no other way to go, so they just tried to self-destruct the whole mission, and that meant death to hundreds of people." Gritz goes onto say, "The medical examiner there [Dr. Leslie Mootoo] made some startling statements, and we wouldn't even allow the bodies to be properly examined when they were brought back to the East Coast and turned in. So obviously it was a cover-up. Jonestown, I think, was an extension of MKULTRA from the CIA."

Certainly, these are shocking statements for someone who is confirmed as being a part of the operation! Gritz is also a well known man and a highly decorated soldier. Even more shocking is that Gritz kind of stuck up for the African American community when he has known racist ties. Gritz is known as the most decorated Vietnam veteran in history and became famous as the Vice Presidential Candidate on the ticket with Ku Klux Klanner, David Duke. Gritz has also been seen publicly giving the "Hail Hitler" salute to skinheads. Yet, Gritz still felt that he must point out, what to him, seems like an obvious truth.

Gritz cited his claims by stating that Special Forces units, like the ones seen in Jonestown, were often put together as an "exterminator" to destroy evidence. He claims that these units were trained to drop into these areas by helicopter, rappel, or parachute if need be, and work their way back and make surveys. In this case, however, Gritz says that "instead of surveying for nature's damage, they were surveying for human presence to mop up any that might have escaped." This also corroborates what conspiracy theorists believe. Many believe that the survivors who escaped in to the jungle were hunted down and killed and dragged back to the "official site" and put into nice, neat rows. Many claim to see marks in certain pictures that appear to be "drag marks" leading to their final resting places. Gritz acknowledges that the then CIA director, Allen W. Dulles, was the driving force behind many CIA mind-control experiments; and though Dulles is dead, Gritz believes that MKULTRA still exists today.

Although Wise references Gritz and Huff in his theory, he does not believe that Jones was connected to the CIA nor does he think that that the CIA conspired to kill Congressman Ryan and infiltrate Jonestown during the suicides. Rather, Wise believes that the CIA ordered the green berets to "Kill survivors" after the suicides and inject the bodies. Wise says in doing so, they tied up loose ends such as, the death tape, eyewitness accounts, and Dr. Mootoo's findings. Mootoo was the biggest concern for the CIA, says Wise. "They made him alter his report to say that only a few people were injected; thus, making the information fit the death tape and eyewitness accounts—which then became the 'official report' for the press and for history." However, Mootoo's findings—to a certain extent—did find their way to the press on a few occasions 12/17/78, 12/12/78 and 12/23/78 (NY Times).

More Questions

Would it be so unlikely to draw out the picture of how things played out in Jonestown, that this was a CIA Mind-Control Camp? The camp would have been in jeopardy because of Ryan's visit. Ryan, a known CIA oppressor, was hot on the trail of the CIA. Ryan had been investigating certain MKULTRA testing within the United States on prisoners in the Vacaville Medical Facility that had ties to the Patty Hurst case. Ryan had also helped institute the Hughes/Ryan Amendment, which called for the CIA to notify Congress and get authorization before conducting any secret experiments. The Amendment was eliminated soon after Ryan's death. Jones was obviously conditioning his followers toward a mass suicide for months, even for several years. This was just the date on which it was fired off. Surely, the agency wanted to get rid of Ryan, and in turn would have to exterminate the community, leaving little trace of its existence.

According to FBI document: SF 89-250 DRH: jmr, The FBI had a "large volume of records, interviews and information" in their possession that they have excluded from their report. No further explanation was given as to why the information was being withheld. In 1980, the House Select Committee on Intelligence determined that "the CIA had no advanced knowledge of the mass murder-suicide." The House Foreign Affairs Committee—now known as international relations—released a 782-page report regarding Jim Jones and Jonestown, but kept more than 5,000 pages secret.

U.S. Ambassador to Guyana at the time, John Burke—who served in the CIA with Dwyer in Thailand—was described by Phillip Agee as working for the CIA since 1963. Agee was a CIA case officer and later a writer best known for his book, *Inside the Company*, which detailed his experiences as a CIA operative. A key factor of the investigation was the fact that the Senior Police Investigator testified that it was a "mass suicide." This is a major contributing factor as to why the investigation was so poorly conducted. Was he coerced? If there was a cover-up, he certainly would be the low man in the food chain and the public-pawn for the sharks that were feeding off of the incident.

Others, like Judge, raise the question of Dwyer having a hand in Jim Jones' death. Did Dwyer head back to Jonestown after the airstrip shooting, terminate Jones, and make the mass suicide report from a CIA channel? On November 23, 1978, Dwyer was contacted by the FBI concerning the details of the airstrip shooting of Congressman Ryan and others. Dwyer advised the FBI that he was preparing an official report that he would momentarily make available to the FBI. Dwyer wrote a twenty-four page report that he submitted to the FBI on November 30, 1978, which was considered his official statement of the shooting of Congressman Ryan. However, the statement referred to by the FBI as: HQ 89-4286-1681 had pages deliberately deleted by the FBI and never made public. The reason(s) for the deletions are still unknown to this day.

The Death tape (labeled by the FBI as Q042) ran about 45 minutes in duration, but there were more than 20 times where the recording was stopped and restarted. The actual deaths likely took place over a five-hour time span. Dave Wise helped me clear up such things as where the P.A. was located in Jonestown; which Wise claimed, "In all the churches, Ukiah, San Francisco, and LA, and later in Jonestown there was a sound crew. They ran the microphones to people who were going to speak; they operated the sound controls on the Public Address System and operated a Teac reel to reel tape recorder which was turned on during sermons. Tapes were edited for the purpose of making playback sermons and filed away. So a reel to reel tape recorder was attached to the public address system even for recording the final act, the death tape, Q042."

Washington Post reporter, Charles Krause, also had his theories on what was going on in Jonestown, including one that it was a CIA was involved in some way with the November 18, 1978, happenings at Port Kaituma and in Jonestown. Krause, one of the reporters who accompanied Congressman Leo J. Ryan into Jonestown, wrote an article in the Washington Post in 1979, entitled *Guyana Exploits KGB Tie to Jonestown*. According to the artlcie Krause writes that "The best evidence of CIA involvement after the Nov. 18 incident has to do with a mysterious cable sent at 9:18 P.M.

the night Rep. Leo Ryan was killed. According to a reporter who saw the cable, it told of those who were killed and wounded at Port Kaituma, information the State Department did not have until late the next morning." The CIA opened up a secret file on the article in which they detailed the main charges of the article. Within the document reads, "Final two paragraphs insinuate CIA had knowledge of Jonestown events before State Department." The secret document was released to the public in May 2007.

The day after tape (Q875)

The details surrounding the deaths in Jonestown, as well as the reason for its existence in the first place, will likely be shrouded in mystery for the remainder of history. Of all the mysterious links and coincidences surrounding this story, perhaps the most mysterious piece of physical evidence is the tape labeled "Q875." This tape was found in Jonestown amidst hundreds of audio cassette tapes uncovered by the FBI. There was nothing special about the appearance or location of the tape that differentiated it from any other tap found. However, there was one distinctive characteristic that separated it from all other tapes that were discovered: it was recorded on November 19, 1878 (the day after the mass deaths took place).

It is generally accepted that the last of the deaths occurred around midnight of November 18, 1978. The material on the tape, however, consists of recordings of four new broadcasts, all pertaining to the deaths of Congressman Ryan and members of his party "last night" at the Port Kaituma airstrip in Guyana; two of the broadcasts are of American origin, and two are Guyanese, including an ABC broadcast. Throughout the duration of the tape an unknown number of people appear to be listening intently to the broadcasts. Doors can be heard opening and closing, chairs can be heard squeaking, and voices can be heard whispering and conversing. There appear to be four recognizable voices on the tape: three male and one female. All of them speak in English, and one appears to have a slight accent; one can assume of Guyanese origin.

Most of the conversations on the tape are unintelligible because of the poor quality of the recording and the fact that the people heard were undoubtedly not trying to be heard. Furthermore, the microphone on the recording device seems to have been placed very closely to the speaker(s) playing the news broadcasts, with the speaking persons some distance from it. However, there are a few instances where it is possible to speculate about what is being said. For example, when the ABC broadcast cuts to an interview with Congressman Ryan's mother, someone appears to quietly say, "*Oh boy.*" During the last broadcast on side one of the tape someone appears to say "*Shit*" after an announcement that autopsies will be done on the bodies at the airstrip. And the clearest voice heard was a man with what seemed like a Guyanese accent. During an exchange with another man in the room, just after a creaking wooden door slams, the man says, "*He was the, uh, executive of the, uh, settlement in Guyana, right. He's the bigwig.*" Some have speculated that the word "Guyana" was actually "Costa Rica," but it was clearly a three-syllable word uttered.

Speaking about the tape's origin, Dave Wise said it "was made after the suicides and in order for there to be a radio playing in the background it was likely made in the radio room on a cassette recorder by someone monitoring the unfolding media coverage and then accidentally left it there in haste." Wise also made a claim that the tape was made by the CIA: "the mystery tape is important *physical evidence* left by a medical team under the control of the CIA, whose role was to inject all of the bodies between the shoulder blades, a location preselected because it is the only place on the body that humans cannot inject themselves." It does not take much imagination to speculate that the CIA made and left behind this tape. However, the most credible sources on the subject somewhat oppose this notion.

It is widely accepted that tape Q875 was made on the day following the deaths. It is also widely accepted that last of the deaths occurred just before midnight of November 18th and that the Guyanese Defense Force (GDF) were the first to arrive on scene, at approximately dusk on the 19th. That leaves about a 20 hour window where Jonestown was completely empty of living soles. Perhaps the most telling part of the tape, in regard to the time it was made, is the statement by the first broadcaster (Guyanese Broadcast) announcing that "eight wounded people were flown out of Timehri airport *this afternoon*, following the ambush of Congressman Ryan and his party on Saturday afternoon. Jacky Spiers, Steve Sung, Anthony Capsaris,

Carolyn Boyd, Beverly Oliver, Ron Javers, and Vern Gosney were among the wounded flown out of Timehri airport on a U.S. C-141 military transport plane in the later afternoon, early evening.

Therefore, we must concluded that Q875 was made sometime in the late afternoon or early evening. This would mean that either the GDF had already arrived in Jonestown or some other party had made the tape and left the tape behind in haste. At the end of that same segment of the tape (Segment one), another newscast announced: "Meanwhile, unconfirmed reports reaching Georgetown say there have been mass suicides at the Jonestown settlement. A government spokesman said, they had received a report and have sent out an Army officer to clarify it, but he has not yet reported back." The fact that there were still three more segments of the tape to follow seems to prove that the group making the recording was not in a rush to leave after hearing that announcement. Finally, at the end of segment two, the newscaster reports, "Guyanese troops reportedly have arrived now in Jonestown. The Associated Press reports the troops have said nothing about reports of mass suicide in the commune."

From this it can be said almost with certainty that the tape was made by the GDF. Yet, this still does not explain the majority of voices that clearly had English accents. The GDF reported that when they arrived at Jonestown they noticed that it had been looted and ransacked. This has been attributed by many as the work of Amerindians and Guyanese living in the area. However, those on the Q875 are clearly American, aside from the one Guyanese accent that can be heard, and from the sounds of the tape they appeared to be rummaging around for something. It is conceivable to think that the CIA could have put together a team just after they themselves were the first to report the mass suicides in Jonestown, at approximately 0329 on November 19th (3:29 a.m.). However, this takes a bit more imagination; and worse, it conflicts with the timeline of the tape and the arrival of the GDF. It is also possible that the CIA was in cahoots with the GDF, and they were on scene with a medical team under the control of the CIA, as Dave Wise has asserted. Yet, this is speculation that to this day cannot and has not been confirmed in any way.

Still, questions remain as to why the tape was made in the first place, why it was left behind, what the people were doing while recording it, and where the tape was actually made. In response to where the tape may have been made, Dave Wise explained to me the workings of the audio systems in the Churches in the States as well as in Jonestown.

"In all the churches, Ukiah, San Francisco, and LA and later in Jonestown there was a sound crew. They ran the microphones to people who were going to speak; they operated the sound controls on the Public Address System and ...operated a Teac reel to reel tape recorder which was turned on during sermons. Tapes were edited for the purpose of making playback sermons and filed away. So a reel to reel tape recorder was attached to the public address system even for recording the final act, the death tape, Q042. However, Q875 was made after the suicides and in order for there to be a radio playing in the background it was likely made in the radio room on a cassette recorder by someone monitoring the unfolding media coverage and then accidentally left it there in the haste."

MILK/MASCONE & the Mysterious Aftermath

The fact is that Harvey Milk and San Francisco Mayor, George Moscone, both had an affiliation with Peoples Temple. Moreover, it is widely known that Jim Jones and his followers were instrumental in getting Moscone elected as Mayor of San Francisco. In return, the Mayor appointed Jones as the head of the San Francisco Housing Authority. Following the horror in Jonestown rumors emerged of a Peoples Temple hit squad that was poised to retaliate against Jones' enemies. The FBI investigated reports that Jones paid some $10 million to this hit squad – known as "Angels" – to kill certain people in case of his death. Specifically in response to this rumor, two armed guards were placed on duty at the reception area of the Mayor's office. These rumors had profound implications for many former Temple members. Former associate pastor of Peoples Temple church in Los Angeles, David Wise, told me that he went into hiding for 25 years out of fear that he was on Jones' alleged hit list. In addition, several other Temple members went underground or changed their names over fears of reprisal from Jones' loyalists or – in some cases – from Temple adversaries.

According to top Temple aide, Terri Buford, just after the Jonestown murders, Jim Jones paid $3 million to an unnamed group for death contracts on his enemies. Moreover, Buford also claimed there was a plan for followers at the San Francisco Temple "to stay alive at all costs and carry out the assassinations in the event of Jones' death." After the tragedy, Temple defectors, Wanda Johnson and Al Mills, confirmed that Jones used to brag about his Mafia connections. "He used to say that if anybody gave him trouble, he had that wonderful Mafia contact," Al Mills told investigators. Buford claimed that the total cash assets of the Temple were about $11 million, most of it in numbered bank accounts in Panama and Zurich, Switzerland. Other former elite Temple members had placed the total at approximately $10 million. Yet, Buford, being what many would call Jones' closest aide; she likely had a more accurate account of Temple finances. Before Buford fled Guyana, she said she signed over all but $2 million to an elderly White woman who died in Jonestown. Before escaping the San Francisco Temple on Nov. 27, 1978, Buford claimed to have signed documents transferring the remaining $2 million. She said she was able to leave

Jonestown only after convincing Jones that she could be of more help to the Temple in San Francisco, helping to prepare defenses against pending lawsuits. Buford claimed that at one point there was a physical hit list that she had seen, but claimed she was not aware if it was maintained over the years. Other Temple defectors scoffed at her story, claiming that Buford was "trying to cover herself," and that this was "just phase one of her plan to carry out Jones' orders." Al Mills claimed that Buford was "just as hateful of traitors as Jim Jones was."

In spite of such information, the FBI reported that they could find no evidence of a Peoples Temple hit squad. However, on November 27, 1978, just nine days after the Jonestown massacre, Mayor Moscone and City Supervisor Harvey Milk were murdered in their offices by former City Supervisor Dan White, who had avoided metal detectors by entering City Hall through the basement. Standing outside the building after the murders, Heather Cogswell reflected on the confusion when she said, "This is terrible what's happening around us. First it's the Peoples Temple crisis and then this." Her friend Holly added, "I feel frightened, as if something awful is going on all around me. There's no sense, there's mesmerization, irrationality, sickness, craziness, and it's all at random."

Dan White's attorney Doug Schmidt tried to link Jonestown to the murders during opening arguments. Although, the trial is more memorable for a defense psychiatrist's suggestion of what came to be known as the "Twinkie Defense," which was only raised briefly by psychiatrist, Martin Blinder; one of the five defense therapists called to the stand. According to Blinder, it was White's consumption of junk food that resulted in his depression (although it was actually HoHos and Ding Dongs that White ate, not Twinkies). White's main defense was "diminished capacity" that amounted to "a major mental illness," a strategy which ultimately succeeded.

On May 21, 1979, Dan White was convicted of "manslaughter by diminished capacity," the lightest sentence he could have been given for his crimes. Later that night crowds of angry people gathered around San Francisco's City Hall, finally erupting into violence, which has come to be known as the *White Night Riots*. White was paroled in 1984; and after a brief stay in Ireland, he returned to San Francisco. A little more than a year later, White committed suicide at his home, connecting a garden hose to the exhaust pipe of his car. Some say that White was one of the CIA's brainwashed assassins and that his death was programmed or outright perpetrated by the CIA. But there would be several other unexplained murders connected with Peoples Temple in the years following Jonestown and the Milk/Moscone shootings.

- In 1980, former Temple members and high-profile defectors Elmer and Deanna Mertle (who had changed their names to Jeannie and Al Mills), together with their 15-year-old daughter, Daphene, were found shot execution style in their Berkeley home. The Mertles had founded the Concerned Relatives organization that was responsible for getting Congressman Ryan to investigate Jonestown and they also founded the Human Freedom Center, which was used as a refuge for other Temple defectors. The crime was never solved.
- Concerned Relatives – likely the Mertles themselves – had hired a private detective, Joe Mazor, to investigate Jones. Mazor, a mysterious figure in his own right, later joined Jones' camp insofar as he provided the Temple's leader with information about his antagonists. Mazor was shot and killed – apparently during a domestic dispute with his wife – in 1985.
- In October 1983, Laurence Mann, Guyana's ambassador to the United States—whose relationship with Temple member Paula Adams began two years before Jonestown—shot and killed Paula and their young child in their suburban Washington apartment before turning the gun on himself.
- On March 14, 1980, Congressman Allard K. Lowenstein was shot dead by civil rights worker Dennis Sweeney, at Lowenstein's New York City law offices. Sweeny testified at his trial that the CIA (with Lowenstein's help) had implanted a chip in his head 15 years earlier, and he blamed the CIA for Moscone and Milk's deaths. Sweeney was found not guilty by reason of insanity and was released from an upstate New York mental hospital in 2000.
- Mike Prokes, the head of public relations at the Temple, called a press conference on March 13, 1979, in a Modesto,

California hotel room, with eight reporters in attendance. After reading a statement, Prokes excused himself, went into the bathroom, closed the door, turned on the faucet, and shot himself in the head with a Smith and Wesson .38 revolver. Prior to his involvement in the Temple, Prokes was a television reporter in Modesto. In September of 1972, Prokes read an article by Les Kinsolving questioning Jones' perceived benevolent nature. Prokes called Jones, believing that he could get a good story out of him. Days later Prokes claims he was contacted by a man claiming to work for the government, who offered him $200 a week to infiltrate the Temple as a staff member and file reports. Prokes quit his job and became a government informant working full-time for Peoples Temple in San Francisco. Allegedly, Jones eventually won Prokes over, and he quit his informing job and became a loyal follower of Jones.

There were only two convictions that came from this tragedy: Larry Layton and Charles Beikman. After over twenty years in prison, Larry Layton was released on parole in 2002. Charles Beikman was later arrested, pled guilty, and was sentenced in 1980, to five-years in a Guyana prison, for the attempted murder of nine-year-old Stephanie Jones—the adopted granddaughter of Jim Jones. Beikman was released from Guyana prison in 1982—at which time he moved to Indiana. Although her throat had been cut at the scene; fortunately, Stephanie survived the incident.

The closer we look at the story of Jonestown, the more bizarre it becomes. Several questions still remain, and unfortunately there have been a shortage of answers. Although the metaphoric smoking gun in this case may be lying somewhere in the relentless, unforgiving Guyanese jungle—or in the minds of leaders and officials long-gone by now—circumstantial evidence and total confusion over the tragic events still remains.

Bibliography

A. P. (1978, November 19). Coast Congressman Believed Shot Dead. *New York Times*, p. A1.

A.P. (1978, November 22). Cult Leader's Son Described Him As Ill Man, Frantic and Paranoid. *New York Times*, p. A4.

A. P (1978, November 20). Guyana Official Reports 300 Dead At Religious Sect's Jungle Temple. *New York Times*, p. A2.

A. P. (1978, November 21). Guyanese Report Finding 405 Bodies in Commune. *New York Times*.

A.P. (1978, November 22). U.S. Copters Reach Guyana to Aid in Jungle Hunt for Sect Survivors. *New York Times*, p. A4.

A Survivor Who Hid In a Treetop All Night Tells of the Shootings. *New York Times*, p. A4.

Alejandra, Patar. "Dan Mitrione, Un Maestro De La Tortura." 9 Feb. 2001. http://www.clarin.com/diario/2001/09/02/i-03101.htm.

Barnes, W. (1978, December 10). $3 million for hit list, says ex-Jones aide. *San Francisco Sunday Chronicle & Examiner*, front page.

Coleman, L. (2004). *The Copycat Effect How the Media and Popular Culture Trigger the Mayhem in Tomorrow's Headlines*. New York: Paraview Pocket Books.

Concerned Relatives. (1978, April 11). Accusation of Human Rights Violations by Rev. James Warren Jones Against Our Children and Relatives at the Peoples Temple Jungle Encampment in Guyana, South America. *Alternative Considerations of Jonestown & Peoples Temple*. Retrieved May 14, 2012, from http://jonestown.sdsu.edu/AboutJonestown/PrimarySources/concerned1.htm

Goodlett, C. (n.d.). Notes on Peoples Temple. *Alternative Considerations of Jonestown & Peoples Temple*. Retrieved March 3, 2011, from http://jonestown.sdsu.edu/AboutJonestown/PersonalReflections/goo dlett_notes.htm

Gribbin, P. (1979, May 16). Brazil and CIA. *namebase.org*. Retrieved August 14, 2013, from http://www.namebase.org/brazil.html

Hall, J. R. (1987). *Gone from the promised land: Jonestown in American cultural history* (Pbk. ed.). New Brunswick, U.S.A.: Transaction Publishers.

Hougan, J. (n.d.). Jim Jones and the Peoples Temple. *The Official Jim Hougan site*. Retrieved July 4, 2007, from http://jimhougan.com/JimJones.html

Jones lived well, kept to himself during mysterious Brazil stay. (1978, November 27). *San Jose Mercury News*, p. 17A.

Jonestown The Life and Death of Peoples Temple. Smith, M, and S Nelson. PBS. 25 Apr. 2006. Television.

Judge, J. (1985). The Black Hole of Guyana: The Untold Story of the Jonestown Massacre. *rat haus reality, ratical branch*. Retrieved February 25, 2007, from http://www.ratical.org/ratville/JFK/JohnJudge/Jonestown.html

Kilduff, M. (1978, June 15). Grim Report From Jungle. *San Francisco Chronicle*, p. 2.

King, R. (2008, November 18). Jonestown still haunts Hoosier couple who lost 20 family members in massacre. *Indy Star*. Retrieved December 12, 2008, from www.indystar.com/article/20081118/NEWS06/311180002/Jonestow n-still-haunts-Hoosier-couple-who-lost-20-family-members-massacre

Kinsolving, L. (1972, September 17). The Prophet Who Raises the Dead. *San Francisco Examiner*, p. 1.

Kinsolving, L. (1972, September). The People's Temple and Maxine Harpe. *Alternative Considerations of Jonestown & Peoples Temple*. Retrieved March 8, 2013, from http://jonestown.sdsu.edu/AboutJonestown/PrimarySources/Kinsolving5.htm

Langguth, A. J. (1979). *Hidden Terrors: The Truth About U.S. Police Operations in Latin America*. U.S.: Pantheon.

Langguth, A. J. (1979, June 11). Torture's Teachers. *The New York Times*, p. A19.

Lattin, D. (2003, November 18). JONESTOWN / 25 Years Later / How spiritual journey ended in destruction / Jim Jones led his flock to death in jungle. *SFGate: San Francisco Chronicle*. Retrieved July 11, 2007, from http://www.sfgate.com/news/article/JONESTOWN-25-Years-Later-How-spiritual-2548493.php

Layton, D. (1999). *Seductive poison: a Jonestown survivor's story of life and death in the Peoples Temple*. New York: Anchor Books.

Lewis, M. (2003, November 19). Jones disciple recovers from, recalls painful past. *Seattle Post-Intelligencer*, p. 7.

Lindsey, R. (1985, October 22). Dan White, Killer of San Francisco Mayor, A Suicide. *New York Times*.

McFadden, R. D. (1978, November 21). Leading Americans Backed Jones Sect: Guyana Cites Letters by Mondale, Mrs. Carter and Califano Vouching for the Group. *New York Times*, p. A3.

Mega Drought. (2007 - Episode 9, Season 2) [Television series episode]. In *Mega Disasters*. New York City: The History Channel.

Merrill, T. L., & Mitchell, W. B. (1993). *Guyana and Belzine: Country Studies*. Washington, D.C.: The Division.

Mills, J. (1979). *Six years with God: life inside Reverend Jim Jones's Peoples Temple*. New York: A & W Publishers.

Moore, R. (1985). *A sympathetic history of Jonestown: the Moore family involvement in Peoples Temple.* Lewiston, N.Y., USA: E. Mellen Press.

Moore, R. (2009). "Last Rights". *Alternative Considerations of Jonestown & Peoples Temple.* Retrieved May 13, 2012, from http://jonestown.sdsu.edu/?page_id=16585

Moore, R., McGehee III, F. M., Parker, E., & Wettendorff, R. (n.d.). *Alternative Considerations of Jonestown & Peoples Temple.* Retrieved March 5, 2007, from http://jonestown.sdsu.edu

Nordheimer, J. (1978, November 21). 400 Are Found Dead in Mass Suicide by Cult; Hundreds More Missing From Guyana Camp. *New York Times*, p. A3.

Nordheimer, J. (1978, November 24). Guyanese Patrols Search Jungle in Vain for Jonestown Suicide Survivors. *New York Times*, p. A16.

Parfrey, A. (1995, May). Militia Leader Talks Bo Gritz Interrogated by Adam Parfrey. *WHALE.* Retrieved June 15, 2007, from http://www.whale.to/b/gritz1.html

Peoples Temple Minister Receives National Award . (1976, April). *Peoples Forum: A Community News Service*, Vol. 1, No.1, http://jonestown.sdsu.edu/AboutJonestown/PrimarySources/PeoplesForum1.html

Pogash, C. (2003, November 23). Myth of the 'Twinkie defense' The verdict in the Dan White case wasn't based on his ingestion of junk food. *San Francisco Chronicle.* p. D-1.

Reiterman, T., & Jacobs, J. (2008). *Raven: the untold story of the Rev. Jim Jones and his people.* New York: J.P. Tarcher/Penguin.

Roberts, S. V. (1978, November 21). Wounded Aide to Ryan Worried And Wrote Her Will Before Trip. *New York Times*, p. A3.

Roller, E. (1975, July 16). Edith Roller Journals: Transcribed. *Alternative Considerations of Jonestown & Peoples Temple.* Retrieved June 9, 2010, from http://jonestown.sdsu.edu/AboutJonestown/JTResearch/eRollerJourn als/Trns/ER7507Jul.html

Rosenfelder, M. (1996, January 1). U.S. Interventions in Latin America. *Zompist.* Retrieved February 16, 2014, from http://www.zompist.com/latam.html

Sherman, J., & Wolochatiuk, T. (2007, January 15). *Jonestown: Paradise Lost* [Television broadcast]. Canada, France, South Africa: The History Channel.

Sims, H. (2003). Standing in the Shadows of Jonestown. *North Coast Journal, Inc.*

Stoen, T. O. (1972, February 6). Tim Stoen Affidavit on Paternity of John Victor Stoen. *Alternative Considerations of Jonestown & Peoples Temple.* Retrieved June 10, 2011, from http://jonestown.sdsu.edu/AboutJonestown/PrimarySources/TOSAffi davit_Text.html

Transcript Q050 (FBI Catalogue). (Summer, 1977). *Alternative Considerations of Jonestown & Peoples Temple.* Retrieved March 7, 2012, from http://jonestown.sdsu.edu/AboutJonestown/Tapes/Tapes/TapeTransc ripts/Q050.html

Tape Number Q134 (FBI Catalogue). (n.d.). *Alternative Considerations of Jonestown & Peoples Temple.* Retrieved January 12, 2008, from http://jonestown.sdsu.edu/AboutJonestown/Tapes/Tapes/TapeSumm aries/134.html

Tape Number Q579 (FBI Catalogue). (1977, Spring). *Alternative Considerations of Jonestown & Peoples Temple.* Retrieved January 12, 2011, from http://jonestown.sdsu.edu/AboutJonestown/Tapes/Tapes/TapeSumm aries/579.html

Transcript Q805 (FBI Catalogue). (Summer, 1977). *Alternative Considerations of Jonestown & Peoples Temple*. Retrieved March 7, 2012, from http://jonestown.sdsu.edu/AboutJonestown/Tapes/Tapes/TapeTransc ripts/Q805.html

The Rev. Jones 'Integrates' Hospital While a Patient. (1961, October 7). *Indianapolis Recorder*.

Tim Stoen vs. Peoples Temple. (2012, May 14). *Alternative Considerations of Jonestown & Peoples Temple*. Retrieved February 10, 2013, from http://jonestown.sdsu.edu/AboutJonestown/PrimarySources/StoenVs PT.html

Treaster, J. B. (1978, November 20). Ryan was a Friend of Disadvantaged. *New York Times*.

Turner, W. (1978, November 20). Deaths in Guyana Threaten Sect's California Church. *New York Times*, p. A1.

Turner, W. (1978, November 21). Little Attention Paid to Warnings by Sect's Leader. *New York Times*, p. A3.

VanDeCarr, P. (2003, November 25). He Lived to Tell. *The Advocate (The national gay & lesbian newsmagazine)*, *903*, 37-39.

Walliss, J. (2012, May 13). "Peoples Temple". *Alternative Considerations of Jonestown & Peoples Temple*. Retrieved September 19, 2012, fromhttp://jonestown.sdsu.edu/AboutJonestown/Articles/walliss.htm

Whittle, T. G., & Thorpe, J. (1997, August 1). Revisiting the Jonestown Tragedy: Newly released documents shed light on unsolved murders. *Freedom Magazine*, *1*, 1-17.

Yates, B. (2012, October 23). Eugene Chaikin: A Story from Jonestown. *Alternative Considerations of Jonestown & Peoples Temple*. Retrieved March 7, 2013, from http://jonestown.sdsu.edu/AboutJonestown/JonestownReport/Volume14/Yates1.htm

Zablocki, C. J. (*Chairman*) (1979, May 15). The Assassination of Representative Leo J. Ryan and the Jonestown, Guyana Tragedy . Report of a staff investigative group to the Committee on Foreign Affairs U.S. House of Representatives, Washington D.C.